THE VALLEY OF VISION

The author of this important contribution to the study of Blake was tragically drowned in a sailing accident when he had almost completed it in manuscript. His was a critical mind of singular erudition and power, as is abundantly evidenced in these chapters which Northrop Frye has prepared for publication. Fisher had made a careful study of Oriental philosophy and of Plato and the Neo-Platonists and this background especially enabled him to make an original and fruitful analysis of his central interest, Blake.

The book is not a study of Blake's sources but of his context. The author is trying to answer the question: given Blake's general point of view, why does he make the specific judgments he does make, judgments which so often seem merely glib or petulant or perverse. Blake himself, in explaining a painting, remarked: "It ought to be understood that the Persons, Moses & Abraham, are not here meant, but the States Signified by those Names." Fisher explains what Blake meant by "states," and shows that such names as Plato, Bacon or Newton, or such terms as "priest" or "deist" in Blake's writings, refer not to individuals but to cultural forces in Western civilization, the influence of which accounted for the social conditions that Blake attacked. The attack itself, Fisher shows, was based on a revolutionary dialectic, a sense of the underlying opposition between reactionaries committed to obscurantism and social injustice, the "Elect" as Blake calls them, and the prophets committed to a greater vision (the "Reprobate"), with the mass of the public (the "Redeemed") in between.

PETER F. FISHER was, at the time of his death, Head of the Department of English, Royal Military College, Kingston.

NORTHROP FRYE, author of a central study of Blake, *Fearful Symmetry,* is Principal of Victoria College in the University of Toronto.

THE VALLEY OF VISION

UNIVERSITY OF TORONTO DEPARTMENT OF ENGLISH

Studies and Texts, No. 9

THE VALLEY OF VISION

Blake as Prophet and Revolutionary

by

PETER F. FISHER

edited by

NORTHROP FRYE

Great is the cry of the Hounds of Nimrod
along the Valley
Of Vision, they scent the odor of War
in the Valley of Vision.

JERUSALEM 22: 8–9

University of Toronto Press

Reprinted in paperback 2017
ISBN 978-0-8020-5103-5 (cloth)
ISBN 978-1-4875-9856-3 (paper)

Publication of this book has been made possible by a grant from the Humanities Research Council out of funds provided by the Canada Council, and by a grant from the Publications Fund of the University of Toronto Press.

Editor's Preface

WHEN PETER FRANCIS FISHER was drowned in a sailing accident on September 2, 1958, at the age of forty, Canada lost one of its most brilliant and versatile scholars. A soldier with a fine military record, he had a keen interest in the theory of strategy, wrote papers on the campaigns of Alexander the Great, and was ready to discuss any aspect of military theory from Sun-Tzu Wu to Clausewitz. He took a doctor's degree in English literature, and his contributions to literary scholarship include articles on *Beowulf*, on *A Midsummer Night's Dream*, on *Heart of Midlothian*, and on Milton's logic and theodicy, besides two articles on Blake, "Blake and the Druids," and "Blake's Attacks on the Classical Tradition," and the present volume. But he was always more than anything else a philosopher, and while head of the English Department at the Royal Military College of Canada he expanded the curriculum there to include logic and the history of philosophy, in which he did most of his teaching. In philosophy too his interests showed the same breadth. Thoreau remarks that the adventurous student will always study the classics, in whatever languages they may be written, and in that sense I have never known a more adventurous student than Peter Fisher.

Blake had always been a central interest of his, and the year after his graduation he walked into my office and announced that he wanted to do an M.A. thesis on "Blake's method, in the Cartesian sense." He nearly walked out again when he discovered that I had not read the *Bhagavadgita* in Sanskrit, which he took for granted that any serious student of Blake would have done as a matter of course. Up to that time, misled by bad translations, I had been assuming that most Oriental philosophy represented an extreme form of the type of abstraction that Blake most abhorred. In that respect I learned far more than I taught, and our conversations thereafter took the form of a kind of symbolic shorthand in which terms from Blake and from Mahayana Buddhism were apt to be used interchangeably.

Fisher's careful self-teaching in Oriental philosophy focussed his attention on the philosophy-producing mechanism in the human mind that throws up one construct after another. Towards the constructs themselves he was detached and tolerant: he treated them all with respect, and none with servility. He had arrived by his own route at the strongly "existential" view, the sense of the priority of the philosopher to whatever philosophizing he does, that Blake himself had. His interest in Eastern thought he reinforced by a close study of Plato and the Neo-Platonists, in the course of which he developed a good deal of admiration for Thomas Taylor, often regarded as the main source of Blake's knowledge of this tradition, as an interpreter of Plato. Needless to say, he had an unusual sympathy with such mavericks in Western thought as Paracelsus, though he did not exaggerate their importance. In short, he was well equipped to be an interpreter of Blake, who was able to make equally selective use of Swedenborg and of Thomas Paine, of Cornelius Agrippa on magic and of Voltaire on history.

Fisher's book is not a study of Blake's sources but of his context. He is trying to answer the question: given Blake's general point of view, why does he make the specific judgments he does make, judgments which so often seem merely glib or petulant or perverse? Blake himself, in explaining a painting which included the figures of Moses and Abraham, remarked: "It ought to be understood that the Persons, Moses & Abraham, are not here meant, but the States Signified by those Names." Fisher explains what Blake meant by "States," and shows that such names as Plato, Bacon or Newton, or such terms as "priest" or "Deist" in Blake's writings refer not to individuals but to cultural forces in Western civilization, the influence of which accounted for the social conditions that Blake attacked. The attack itself, as Fisher shows, was based on a revolutionary dialectic, a sense of the underlying opposition between reactionaries committed to obscurantism and social injustice, the "Elect" as Blake calls them, and the prophets committed to a greater vision (the "Reprobate"), with the mass of the public (the "Redeemed") in between. It is only in a crisis that such opposition clearly reveals itself, but it is the duty of the "Reprobate" to keep provoking an intellectual and imaginative crisis.

The papers that came to me after Fisher's death indicate that he had planned a book in twelve chapters, the last three dealing respectively with Blake's three long poems, *The Four Zoas*, *Milton* and *Jerusalem*. Chapters II to X were in revised form, and I have been able to add a Preface, an opening chapter, and the beginning of an eleventh chapter from an unrevised manuscript. Thus his book is virtually complete except for the last chapter on *Jerusalem*, of which nothing remains except a note or two. It is clear that even the revised manuscript was due to be revised again, that the dry Aristotelian style was to be given more warmth and colour, that the sentences were to be tightened up and more examples given, and, perhaps, that less knowledge of Blake on the reader's part would be assumed. Even as it stands, however, *The Valley of Vision* is not simply a contribution to our understanding of Blake, but, as an interpretation of one of the great creative minds of Western culture by a critical mind of singular erudition and power, a lasting contribution to human intelligence.

N.F.

Author's Preface

THIS STUDY is an attempt to examine the works of William Blake within the historical perspective of the Age of Enlightenment. It will be primarily concerned with the written works, and an effort will be made to avoid the temptation to speak for the author when he did not speak for himself. This cannot always be avoided: in Blake's day, the critic was usually regarded as an antiquarian who gave insights into the outlook of less enlightened ages, and the radical opposition of Blake to this point of view made it difficult for him to assess the measure of his own isolation from current opinion. In this study attention is mainly focussed on Blake's effort to communicate by means of the written word a point of view not exclusively his own. It has been assumed that his writings fit the temper of Romanticism, and that they are a reaction against the preceding Age of Enlightenment. It has been assumed that he was a mystic incapable of expressing his intuitions except in a turgid and erratic way. A man of health and vigour, he has been associated with a type of aesthete that bears no relationship to him or to his ideas. Such assumptions, it is hoped, will be considerably modified by the following examination. British philosophy is traditionally less narrowly rational than that of the Continent, and more given to the toleration of contrary opinions. This is precisely Blake's heritage and the immediate condition of his thought.

Blake was not a utopian; he was on the contrary close to Swift without being enveloped by what has been called the "perverse agony" of that writer. His *Island in the Moon* is not unlike the third voyage of Gulliver in treatment and theme. His recognition that practicality is a fetish, and that the speculative theory based upon it is an escape, is a far-reaching indictment of all separations of theory from practice. In Blake's view, the attempt to solve a problem depends on the context in which it is seen. If that context is limited to conditions which are called natural, the solution will be trivial, for nature, logically enough, does not admit of solutions which supersede it, and the teleology of nature is death. If man has no other teleology on which to depend, his solutions to his problems in terms of "survival" are not only trivial but pathetic. They appear to become less so, however, when he accepts his natural conditions, and when that happens, the gift of self-deception becomes the measure of his superiority over other animals. Swiftian as this indictment may appear to be, it nevertheless is the first postulate of Blake's prophetic utterance. His claim that his own experience was rooted in a context which superseded that of nature can, of course, be interpreted as a more subtle form of self-deception. To those who so interpret it, neither he nor the present writer has anything to say.

One of the greatest difficulties confronting anyone who wishes to give an account of Blake's "system" is the difficulty of showing that it is not limited to any kind of philosophical system. He is not exclusively a dualist (and he certainly accepts none of the ascetic implications of the dualist position), but he gives expression to the polarity of a dualistic point of view when it suits his purpose. He also expresses the outlook of the monist, the idealist, the realist and the evolutionist. If the reality of which he speaks has in fact produced all these systems, why should not one who claims to be an inhabitant of Eden use them all in turn to describe an experience that transcends them? Blake is typically a prophet and seer in the priority that he gives to experience over all mental constructs derived from it.

To reconcile apparently contradictory theories, however, is not the same thing as obliterating all distinctions among them. Although it is Blake's conviction that it is high time for his contemporaries to outgrow the kind of "God" they are worshipping, he has no use for atheism and regards the agnostic as a menace. If the God who is, as he says, an "Allegory of Kings" can be profitably discarded, the "Nature" which is the allegory of the enlightened philosopher is no better. Neither theism nor naturalism provides man with an adequate description of his own possibilities: one gives him a false sense of security, and the other denies that his state is really insecure at all. The Enlightenment tried to destroy the religious allegory by an even stranger fiction: that man should become reconciled to nature. How, then, had he become unreconciled in the first place? The enlightened philosopher tried to put the blame on fantasy, as an unenlightened and irrational power. But for Blake fantasy is the sleeping eye of vision, and indicates that man possesses a power which resists his adjustment to nature. Blake calls this resistant "Imagination," and makes it the basis of his attack on both rationalistic naturalism and dogmatic theism. He also regards it as the clue to the riddle of man's possibilities.

P.F.F.

Contents

THE VALLEY OF VISION

1. The Prophetic Reprobate

WILLIAM BLAKE was born once in London in 1757. He was born again in the spirit of revolt. His inner revolt became a prophetic protest against the absolute law of either God or man when it pretended to establish the limits of human possibilities. His outer revolt became the revolutionary protest against arbitrary political power exercised in the name of this kind of law. He expressed in both his life and his thought what some might call the extreme limit of the Christian principle that neither doctrine nor ritual, nor even moral sanctity, constitutes any ultimate basis for individual justification. In fact, he went beyond the notion of justification to that of rebirth and regeneration—ideas which occupied the same place in his inner life that revolt did in his response to his social environment. Ethically, Blake gave no quarter to any moral prescription, political programme or rational theory, but relied solely on his experience of the essential source of human life and on the regeneration of the individual.

He was the professed opponent of the Greek spirit of compromise and adjustment between the state of nature and society. For he considered the rationalism of the philosophers a disguised attempt to discredit the inspired insight of the seer and provide instead some kind of external standard of knowledge and behaviour. Politically, he found in Greek rationalism the beginning of the utopian ideal of society which pretended to be a protection against the titanism of the despot and the tragic sin of *hybris*. But this kind of thinking seemed to him to lead to the theoretical rule of reason in the conduct of affairs and the tyrannical use of law as an absolute background to the very kind of political power which the theory was supposed to prevent. Here were the origins, in Blake's opinion, of the unholy union of priest and king—a union which threatened to destroy the roots of individual self-realization in human society and establish an organized deception to "save the appearances." It was this organized deception in morality and in the structure of society which Blake attacked in his dual role of prophet and revolutionary. Convinced that he had been born into the valley of the shadow of this death, the prophetic revolutionary strove to dispel the shadow and transform the death, and it was in this way that his valley became a valley of vision.

Both as revolutionary and prophet Blake stood apart from his contemporaries, but the isolation was accepted unwillingly, and he was without the mask of the eccentric. With astonishing perseverance he continued to address his remarks "To the Public" who paid no attention. They might have listened to him if he had told them how progress could be rendered inevitable and predictable, but it was precisely this which he did not tell them. In short, he was not a modern prophet, for the source of his prophecy was not the theory of the rationalist but the vision of the seer. The roots of the distinction lie embedded in the earliest chapters of the history of Western thought. The term "theory" itself originally meant "vision" and was associated with perception and contemplation rather than with conception and generalization.[1] The original theorist was a spectator rather than a speculator, a seer rather than a philosopher. It was perhaps due to the conceptualizing genius of the Greeks that the word lost its original connection with prophetic insight and came to mean rational speculation. Reason and nature took over from the vision of the ancient seer, and to the later Greek, prophecy was either speculative or oracular; that is, it was the pronouncement of either the philosopher or the priest. Blake rejected the Greeks and considered himself the heir of the Hebrew prophets, for he was obviously out of step with his contemporaries and their desire to understand man, society and the world in terms of reason and a system of nature which depended upon either revealed dogma or empirical investigation.

The rigorous delusion of theoretical prediction had already taken two forms in his day. The one was a confidence in the Newtonian universe of natural law. The other was derived from this confidence and was expressed in a belief in inevitable progress and in the natural philosopher's power of prediction. But prediction in terms of a necessary and predetermined pattern was no new fetish; it was, for

[1]In the translations of Plato and Aristotle which Blake is likely to have read, Taylor frequently translates θεωρία as "contemplation," and indeed that is the sense it usually bears. The highest form of intellectual activity is that of contemplative perception. "Hence, that which intellect appears to possess as divine, belongs more eminently to the first intellect than to ours: and his contemplation is the most delightful and the best" (*Metaphysics of Aristotle*, trans. Thos. Taylor, London, 1801, Book XII, chap. VII, p. 282).

Blake, as old as the race of false prophets who had pandered to man's desire to avoid the challenge of his own being and to be lifted clear of his mistakes and his problems by fate, destiny or some magical technique. A closed system—"closed" because it presupposed an outline of the entire structure of reality—was the panacea of the religious dogmatist, and it was now being used to support the reasonable theories of the natural philosophers. The positivists and economic determinists of a later age would not have surprised Blake.

Prophets, in the modern sense of the word, have never existed. Jonah was no prophet in the modern sense, for his prophecy of Nineveh failed. Every honest man is a Prophet; he utters his opinion both of private & public matters. Thus: If you go on So, the result is So. He never says, such a thing shall happen let you do what you will. A Prophet is a Seer, not an Arbitrary Dictator. It is man's fault if God is not able to do him good, for he gives to the just & to the unjust, but the unjust reject his gift.[2]

Whatever the "gift of God" might be, Blake obviously did not think of it as a closed system of either natural or revealed truth, for the "God" of any such system would surely turn out to be an "Arbitrary Dictator." The God of the seer was the Creator, and creative activity was the characteristic of the true prophet's existence.

Creative activity was the characteristic of any existence which was not merely the product of its conditions. The product of its conditions was a creature, and in order to achieve some kind of existence the creature became apparently the rival of its Creator. Blake spoke of Milton as a "true Poet and of the Devil's party without knowing it." The individual realized his existence not by a rational ordering of experience nor by a passive acceptance of his natural birthright, but by struggle and search (war and hunting, as Blake called it), involving a dialectical interplay of contraries.

Near the beginning of *Milton* Blake introduces the conception of three classes of men which explains his repeated reference to this interplay of contraries:

> . . . Three Classes of Men regulated by Los's Hammers and woven
> By Enitharmon's Looms & Spun beneath the Spindle of Tirzah.
> The first, The Elect from before the foundation of the World:
> The second, The Redeem'd: The Third, The Reprobate & form'd
> To destruction from the mother's womb.[3]

[2]*Annotations to Watson's "Apology for the Bible,"* p. 14.
[3]*Milton*, 6: 35; 7: 1–4. Cf. "The Voice of the Devil" in *The Marriage of Heaven and Hell.*

In both the traditional formal logic and in the Hegelian dialectic, contraries were expressed in positive and negative terms—thesis and antithesis—but in Blake, both contraries are given a positive or affirmative "quality," because both stand for "theses" or positive points of view. Logical error is reached by means of exclusion, but a point of view can never be error in this completely rational sense, although it can represent an individual in error. As he remarks in his *Vision of the Last Judgment:*

> There is not an Error but it has a Man for its Agent, that is, it is a Man. There is not a Truth but it has also a Man. Good & Evil are Qualities in Every Man, whether a Good or Evil Man. These are Enemies & destroy one another by every Means in their power, both of deceit & of open Violence. The deist & the Christian are but the Results of these Opposing Natures.

The "Opposing Natures" are both in man and outside him, and he tends to identify individuals with one or other of the "Qualities" in himself. But to Blake the individual is ultimately sacred, although he may be in a state of being which requires opposition.

To the rationalist, however, whose closed system requires a monolithic view of life, one of the contraries always possesses a negative quality, and one of them must always be false. It remains to contemn, subject or annihilate all opposition by establishing one system of doctrine. But any system of knowledge which claims to be exclusively true amounts to a conspiracy to destroy its own existence, for it denies its contrary, the force of the challenge to which its existence is the response. The point of view which tries to annihilate all opposition by declaring it utterly false, Blake calls the "Reasoning Negative," and the individual who adopts it is of the class of the "Elect." The term "Elect" is applied to those who want everything to be predictable and right, and it suggests the Calvinist cult of predestination. For them, free creative activity is senseless and even dangerous, and the prophetic "Reprobate" is an erratic absurdity in a world about to be ordered once and for all. Although the Reprobate is rejected by the Elect he is opposed by the "Redeemed" who lacks the prophet's vision but is still open to his influence. These three classes operate within man as well as outside him, and they provide the basis of whatever progress is possible.

Historically, the Redeemed formed the class of culture-bearers who received from the Reprobate and communicated to the solid mass of the Elect the formal expressions of myth and symbol which were to lead them through their own particular racial adventure. The three classes interacted to produce the movement of history, but their threefold significance is not limited to universal types; it also includes the inner life and growth of the individual.[4] A moment of revelation may bring out the buried Reprobate in the most confirmed and conventional of the Elect, and for a brief interval clothe him with the mantle of the prophet. As three qualities or powers operating within man, they correspond to imagination, emotion and the kind of reason most people use when they are faced with the new, the unusual and the unexpected. The interplay of any two of these places the third in the position of arbiter which either neutralizes the force of the conflict or completes and transforms it. Man can either rise or fall by means of the dialectic of struggle, but he ceases to exist without it. Blake's own works are the expression of himself as the field of prophet and sinner, God and Satan, within the context of Western thought and belief. His struggle effects a reception of the "gift of God" which is the ability to create through his art, and improve, as he calls it, "in the things of the Spirit."[5]

This progression by means of contraries has led to the assumption that the visionary dialectic of Blake anticipated the logical dialectic of Hegel.[6] The Hegelian "notion" led to its negative, since it was

[4]Blake does not give a definitive correlation with the threefold division of man into "Head & Heart & Reins" but he does suggest it (*Milton*, 5: 5–14).

[5]*Jerusalem*, 77. Paracelsus, to whom Blake refers in his *Marriage of Heaven and Hell*, emphasizes the creative power of the mind and its contact with superior states of being. "Thoughts are free and are encompassed by nothing (*a nullo coërcentur*). On thoughts the freedom of man is based, and they are above the light of nature . . . . This is also according to nature, that thoughts make a new Heaven, a new Firmament, new energy, from which new arts flow (*promanent*) . . . . When anyone is engaged in creating something, he makes for himself a new heaven from which the work which he has undertaken progresses (*ex quo procedit opus, quod facere instituit*)." *Astronomia Magna*, cap. VII, in *Opera Omnia* (Geneva, 1658), II, p. 573.

[6]J. Bronowski, *A Man without a Mask* (London, 1943), p. 93. Bronowski's claim that the *Marriage of Heaven and Hell* "shows that Blake made for himself, twenty years before Hegel, the dialectic of Hegel's formal thought" has some truth in it, but it fails to draw a distinction between the basis and application of Hegel's dialectic and those of Blake's. Hegel supposed that his dialectic *mirrored process* and could therefore be applied to it; Blake *saw process* as the interplay of the contraries. Bronowski does, however, accurately describe Blake's vision of progression as the strife of the Holy Ghost—a statement which he seems to limit to a revolutionary context. Blake was a prophet, and to see in him merely the social rebel is to omit ultimately the sustaining context of his visions. Cf. Martin K. Nurmi, "Blake's 'Marriage of Heaven and Hell' " in *Research Series III* (Kent, Ohio: Kent State University, 1957), p. 20. See also *Jerusalem*, 10: 7–16; 17: 33–9.

limited, and to that extent, untrue. The negation brought a new concept into existence and made a higher unity necessary, a unity in which both thesis and antithesis were confirmed and transformed, retained and yet finished (*aufgehoben*). This system of triads could be interpreted as a rational analogy of Blake's threefold division of classes, but still one which he would certainly have rejected as abstract and void of positive application. The "Reasoning Negative" could not unite the contraries in a higher synthesis; it could merely render them ineffective by reducing them to a conceptual conformity which negated their activity. In the first place, the universal negative proposition of traditional Western logic was not a true contrary at all.

> "Negations are not Contraries: Contraries mutually Exist;
> But Negations Exist Not."[7]

Hegel sought to understand all being as an analogy of ratiocinative thought which was made to interpret the whole of consciousness and was called "spirit" or "reason," but he himself recognized that some other kind of thinking which was not only hypothetical but active and positive was required for the realization of his own dialectical method. Blake's dialectic can more fittingly be compared with that of Heraclitus, the Hellenic philosopher-seer, for whom also existence was realized, and at the same time continually created by conflict.[8]

To Blake who regarded the Holy Ghost as "an Intellectual Fountain" and "Treasures in Heaven" as "Mental Studies and Performances" the pillar of the church and of society was as alien as the man of the world who despised humbug and was engaged in getting things done.[9] The former confused heaven with the roof of the church, and the latter

[7]*Jerusalem*, 17: 33–4. Cf. *Milton*, 46 [42]: 32–6:

> "There is a Negation, & there is a Contrary:
> The Negation must be destroy'd to redeem the Contraries.
> The Negation is the Spectre, the Reasoning Power in Man:
> This is a false Body, an Incrustation over my Immortal
> Spirit, a Selfhood which must be put off & annihilated alway."

[8]Blake's *Proverbs of Hell* are notably Heraclitean in spirit. The whole of the *Marriage of Heaven and Hell*, for that matter, is the Heraclitus in Blake answering the Aristotle in Swedenborg's *De Coelo et Inferno*. He might have summarized his position in the words of his predecessor: "They do not understand how that which is at variance also agrees with itself—harmonious tension like that of the bow and the lyre" (Frag. xlv).

[9]*Jerusalem*, 77.

reduced the expression of his existence to a consistent display of self-confidence. Blake disagreed with both at the root of their common desire to settle upon a final code of ends and means whereby each could consider himself one of the "Elect"—that is, one who could count on being right. The period was one in which individual morality and political theory had become divorced from supernatural religion and were increasingly associated with natural law; but the moral philosopher who thought in terms of generalizations instead of individual life could scarcely avoid a system as remote as the astronomical universe of Newton. Neither the ethics of moral feeling, nor the categorical imperative, nor the statistical calculus of the happiness of the greatest number, escaped Blake's charge of being at best substitutes for individual struggle and search. Any such system depended upon a reasonable hypothesis which was intended to explain the apparent effects of human conduct and be a basis for the external or imitative kind of justice—the pressure of respectability applied to the members of the community. Moral virtue was a way of speaking about enforced political justice as though it were primarily centred in the individual. But any system of moral virtue was merely an extended metaphor—a collection of typically good and evil actions lifted clear of individual behaviour and explained by a politically and socially necessary order. In the last analysis, the individual was judged, however sympathetically, by the reasonable taboos and moral allegories of his time.[10] Reason and reasoned observations could do no more than precipitate a closed system of psychological types or allegories, for it did not lie within the power of man, by any means of controlled observation alone, to understand, let alone judge, another.

Although man in his political state was unable to dispense entirely with moral virtue as the working hypothesis of the lawgiver, it was the duty of the prophet to combat any moral code or psychological system whatever, when it threatened to obscure his inner advance through and beyond his present state. Since man could not, in fact, judge, when he attempted to do so he succeeded only in accusing, and accusation not based on the real power to judge was essentially a lie.

[10]Cf. *Vision of the Last Judgment*, Keynes, p. 649: "Allegories are things that Relate to Moral Virtues. Moral Virtues do not Exist; they are Allegories & dissimulations." [Page references marked "Keynes" are to the fourth edition of *Poetry and Prose of William Blake*, ed. Keynes.—N.F.]

Blake associated the tendency to lie in this particular way with the father of lies. Satan, the Accuser, was the first of the Elect, and he had continued throughout human history to turn man away from the Tree of Life and turn him toward the Tree of the Knowledge of Good and Evil which had caused the fall of man from the state of innocence. In the *Songs of Innocence and Experience* (1789–94), this fundamental theme is developed. The *Songs of Innocence* make use of the imagery of children and animals, which suggests the life of impulse untutored in the school of moral virtue. Here also the dialectic of vision is expressed in the immediate conflict between parent and child within the family, in the social conflict between the will of the community and that of the individual, and in the natural relationship between man and his environment. Youthful rebellion becomes the expression of life and of the hope of a vital and promising future.

But the young rebel is converted into a reactionary or a criminal just when his energies should have begun to awaken him by the impact of experience on the spirit of growth which is innocence. In the *Songs of Experience* the life of impulse becomes conditioned by the savagery of nature and is oppressed by the sanctions and conventions of the social order. The "revolutionary" progress of the human spirit has been arrested. Blake indicates emphatically that he does not consider the mere life of impulse a solution to the dilemma of individual and communal activity. The moral sanction, however, perverts natural impulse in the attempt to surpass and control it, and places itself between the individual existence and the "gift of God" which is the expression of that existence. Unlike Rousseau, Blake does not think that man was born free, but that he was born with the possibility of freedom. His chains are "the cunning of weak and tame minds which have power to resist energy; according to the proverb, the weak in courage is strong in cunning."[11]

It is characteristic of the tame mind to confuse experience with disillusionment and to discard innocence as youthful illusion. Courage gives way to cunning, and energy becomes reasonable. Progress becomes why one lives, instead of how one lives. But experience isolated from innocence can teach nothing, for it is merely an assessment of past conduct "to save the appearances." Under these circumstances, self-justification can be endured by joining the conspiracy of

[11]*Marriage of Heaven and Hell*, Keynes, p. 187. See R. F. Gleckner, "Point of View and Context in Blake's Songs," *Bulletin of the New York Public Library*, LXI (Nov., 1957), 531–8.

dogmatic convention whereby the weak are justified and the cunning are protected. Because the spiritual reactionary regards tradition based firmly on the collective experience of the past as the code of truth and the revealed judgment of Providence, he is sardonically referred to by Blake as "The Elect from before the foundation of the World."[12] The phrase is derived indirectly from Calvin, and the inversion of Calvin's use of "Elect" and "Reprobate" is a prophetic assault on any particular cult of predestination. Any such cult projects self-justification into the inscrutable will of an omnipotent deity whose devotees can reflect on the effects of action—their own success or failure—as the providential sign of election or reprobation.[13] Abandoning the challenge and the responsibility of inner freedom of choice to reject or accept the "gift of God," the predestinarian also abandons the basis of inner growth. Blake is not concerned specifically with the Calvinists but with the closed attitude of mind which they represent. In his own day he was quick to notice a more restricted determinism among the most progressive contemporary thinkers whose naturalism was being applied to the spheres of political and ethical theory. He did not limit his attack to man's individual moral agency, nor to society and the state, nor even to the Newtonian world of nature; but he included each in its relationship to the others. The "Elect" are all those who passively submit to a closed code of conduct, government or system of nature.

In both the history of man's social and political acts and in the natural field of his environment, Blake sees the interplay of prophetic energy and conventional inertia. It becomes evident that the Elect is, in fact, not the real contrary but simply the negation of the creative activity of the Reprobate. The true contrary to the prophet is he who makes something of the originality of the prophetic word and is redeemed from the closed system of Satan and his Elect. It is characteristic of the "Redeemed" thinker to absorb and reconstruct prophetic inspiration into a new cultural form which finds expression in a development of the arts and sciences. Viewed in this way, history itself

[12] *Milton*, 7.

[13] Cf. Calvin, *Institute of the Christian Religion*, III: xxi, 7; xxiii, 2. See also Rom. ix: 15–24. As H. N. Frye points out (*Fearful Symmetry*, Princeton, 1947, p. 188), "though predestination was a doctrine Blake loathed, he does not attack it in Augustine or Calvin; he attacks a tendency to it in his master Swedenborg." Blake attributes the tendency to Swedenborg's attempt to make a rational pot of message out of his visionary experiences. See *Annotations to Swedenborg's "Divine Providence,"* p. 254: "What could Calvin Say more than is Said in this Number?"

is the field of this conflict of contraries, which, to the Elect, appear as the disturbing struggles of dreamers whose opinions may be brought down to earth by his own sound convictions. The Elect, however, is the destroyer of the very values he is supposed to be upholding, because he cannot, or will not, recognize their source. For both Reprobate and Redeemed the source of any progress in the individual or in history is not to be found within a ratio of five senses which place the barrier of a closed system of nature between man and his spiritual destiny, but in the totality of the perceiver's humanity, of which reason is only one faculty, and nature only one limited, immediate field of experience, to be constantly recreated by the impact of art. The Elect can be recognized by an inner resistance to this outlook, although he may profess any beliefs or adopt any opinions whatever. He is to be known by his inner disposition, for it is his being which places him in his particular class.[14] "Many are deists who would in certain Circumstances have been Christians in outward appearance. Voltaire was one of this number; he was as intolerant as an Inquisitor."[15] Blake regards this statement as a recognition of Voltaire's state of being and not as a final judgment of him as an individual; as an individual, he did not have to remain in his present state, although he was committed by an inner disposition to his class.

From another point of view the three classes of men are three aspects

[14]In the first book of *Milton*, Blake describes the apocalyptic vintage and harvest of the nations. Los, the Spirit of Prophecy, distinguishes the three classes of men (27: 32–9):

> The Reprobate who never cease to Believe, and the Redeem'd
> Who live in doubts & fears perpetually tormented by the Elect,
> These you shall bind in a twin-bundle for the Consummation:
> But the Elect must be saved from fires of Eternal Death,
> To be formed into the Churches of Beulah that they destroy not the Earth."

According to Swedenborg (*Arcana Coelestia*, nos. 4686, 4687, 5339, 7408, 10303), the use of the term "bundles" in the Bible (e.g. I Sam. xxv: 29; Matt. xiii: 30) meant the arrangement in series of a man's truths and falsities, and also the arrangement of men in whom were truths and falsities.

[15]*Vision of the Last Judgment*, Keynes, p. 649. It is characteristic of the "Elect" to interpret the work of inspiration in what Blake calls its "natural sense." According to Crabb Robinson's *Diary*, Blake spoke of Voltaire as one commissioned by God to expose the natural sense of the Bible. "I have had much intercourse with Voltaire, and he said to me, 'I blasphemed the Son of Man, and it shall be forgiven me; but they (the enemies of Voltaire) blasphemed the Holy Ghost in me, and it shall not be forgiven them.' " (*Diary, Reminiscences and Correspondence*, ed. T. Sadler, Boston, 1869, pp. 34–5.) The blasphemy against the Holy Ghost was "Imputing Sin & Righteousness to Individuals" (*Jerusalem*, 70: 17) and failing to distinguish between an individual and his state (*ibid.*, 25: 15–16).

of individual life. The individual may wish to change his way of life. The desire to change is represented by the active and open outlook of the Redeemed, but the inertia of acquired habits and the weight of resistance to the desired change are the passive and closed outlook of the Elect. These two aspects of life may produce a struggle which will continue without result, or one may completely overcome the other. That some change may take place, a third aspect must enter the conflict in the form of some new perspective, new revelation or new condition represented by the visionary Reprobate. In the prophetic books of Blake, these aspects of man's life form the basis of the action, and the *dramatis personae* are the human faculties. The Reprobate class is the individual's power of intellectual vision which redeems his reason. Reprobate and Redeemed are the two contraries of the visionary dialectic, and when the individual is active and constructive, the former predominates. He is either Elijah, the prophetic mentor of Israel, or Moses, the lawgiver and leader of the people. He has only to rest passively within the limits of the "Promised Land" to become the priest or the king—the arrested counterparts of the prophet and the leader —to consolidate the prejudice of the "Chosen People" and fall into the uncreative and destructive attitude of the Elect. The class of the Elect signifies the negative effect of reason,[16] listening only to accepted habits and opinions.

It is significant that Blake does not refer to the three classes of men as either universal qualities or natural forces, although he uses them in a way which sometimes suggests both of these terms. Least of all are they personifications of either qualities or forces. When a quality becomes a rational abstraction derived from individual existence, it also becomes a negation of the substance from which it is derived.[17]

[16]The three qualities of man's nature given by Blake may be compared with the three *gunas* of the *Bhagavadgita* which Blake had seen in the translation of Sir Charles Wilkins. "The *Satwa-Goon* prevaileth in felicity, the *Raja* in action, and the *Tama*, having possessed the soul, prevaileth in intoxication" (*The Bhagvat-Geeta, or Dialogues of Kreeshna and Arjoon*, London, 1785, p. 108). According to Paracelsus and the alchemical philosophers, the sensible world evolved from the *prima materia* interacting with the three basic principles—sulphur, the fiery or combustible force, mercury or mobility, and salt or the consolidating force. Blake conceives of a threefold interaction, not of forces but of agents, throughout nature (*Milton*, 27: 40–1):

"For in every Nation & every Family the Three Classes are born,
And in every species of Earth, Metal, Tree, Fish, Bird & Beast."

[17]*Jerusalem*, 10: 8–16. See also *On Homer's Poetry & On Virgil* and *Annotations to Berkeley's "Siris,"* 213.

When abstracted from substantial forms, qualities become negative in their effect by superseding individuals as categories or class-concepts to which the individual existence conforms. Intellectually, qualities are not self-constituted ideas but mere aspects of ideas, the real ideas being the images of vision. Ethically, Blake refuses to speak of absolute moral values for the same reason. He is therefore at odds with the kind of speculative formalism derived from Plato and Aristotle, whose followers tended to make qualities superior to individuals. He is just as opposed to the kind of naturalism inherited by the Baconians and Newtonians, who abstracted their descriptions of the relationship of observed effects into natural forces. If either universal qualities or natural forces have any reality apart from the intelligent agency which Blake calls "Human Existence," then they are ultimately superior to it, and they constitute it. Such is not the vision of the seer who sees the universal field of experience as a polarity of more or less conscious agencies operating according to the dialectic of the three classes. This dialectic is the informing principle of any scale of being, and without it, the speculative thinker loses all contact with the living forms of perception and makes up a rational analogy to explain them away. What can be seen is inescapably bound up with what one is as a perceiving subject. And a perceiving subject is one of the three classes which are Blake's "Two Contraries" (Reprobate and Redeemed) and "Reasoning Negative" (Elect).[18]

In still another sense, the two contraries represent the "Prolific" and the "Devouring"—the one providing from the depths of his own experience the ideas with which he enriches the object of thought or perception, and the other developing those very ideas in terms of a cult, a church or a system of thought. The "Devourer" is the consolidating factor in the process, and it is he who places the "ratio" or outer bound to the ideas of the "Prolific": "Thus one portion of being is the Prolific, the other is the Devouring: to the Devourer it seems as if the producer was in his chains; but it is not so, he only takes portions of existence and fancies that the whole."[19]

As priest the "Devourer" seeks to consolidate the prophetic message into the systematic form of dogma and church upon which a historical culture has generally been built, and thus gives an entirely different

[18]*Milton*, 5: 14; 46: 32–6.

[19]*Marriage of Heaven and Hell*, Keynes, pp. 187–8.

value to the work of the prophet. It is as if the immediate vision of the seer had been misconstrued and given a final validity he had not intended. This misconstruction placed on the prophetic creation by the priestly rationalist reduces the constantly active feud between them to a war of attrition in which the prophet is finally isolated and outlawed. The successor to the priest—although he may be the last to admit it—is the enlightened and liberal intellectual who, like Hume, Gibbon and Voltaire, has exchanged dogmatic superstition for reasonable naturalism, and who treats the prophet as an eccentric or a maniac instead of a heretic. He begins to appropriate the title itself and apply the term "prophet" to his own theoretical and oracular predictions. Blake refers to the actual prophet as the "Reprobate," hoping to indicate the position he holds in a society which has rejected him as unreasonable and as undisciplined. But the door which closes *against* the prophet also closes *in* his antagonists. The cave in which they have closed themselves is the state of nature, reason and commonsense.

Nevertheless, the Reprobate will make himself heard whether he is ostracized or not, and he does so in a variety of ways. He may express himself through the socially acceptable arts as Blake did, or through science and philosophy as Swedenborg did; or he may attach himself to the lunatic fringe as a so-called mystic as Saint-Martin did. Blake avoided the hinterland of mysticism, and he planted himself firmly in the midst of his contemporaries as engraver and artist with a wife to support and rent to pay. His reaction to the closed door was characteristic. Since the Elect had appropriated the term "Heaven" to describe those reasonable ideals which they thought right and proper and that reasonable system of nature which they considered obvious and true, he took the offensive and adopted "Hell" to describe the fire by means of which the damned visionary sees through this kind of "Heaven": "I have always found that Angels have the vanity to speak of themselves as the only wise; this they do with a confident insolence sprouting from systematic reasoning."[20] This "confident insolence" is the result of any closed system of assumptions concerning man and the world. Blake challenges the validity of such assumptions and their relationship to actual experience throughout his *Songs of Experience* and in *The Marriage of Heaven and Hell.* In such a context the term "systematic

[20]*Ibid.*, p. 190.

reasoning" is the reference of a point of view which is that of the closed system of natural law, the security of a moral order founded on nature and reason. This conception is the source of a confident insolence in the minds of those who are delighted to find themselves on the side of the "Angels."

The Marriage of Heaven and Hell is a manifesto against the passive acceptance of this outlook and its implied restriction of what is valuable to what has hitherto been natural and sensible. Value is the individual's approach to fact, and since fact alone does not determine the approach made to it, there can never be any values derived from facts. A sense of values is what Blake calls "Spiritual Sensation," or simply "Vision." A man's vision of anything determines its value for him, and what he values indicates his "Humanity." The creation of any system of values is an effort—repeated by each succeeding civilization—to establish the rules for the constant conflict between art and nature, between value and fact. The Elect is always the child of nature who eliminates the values which are not already facts for him, and who refuses to see that the extension of values is the basis of a specifically human life. As an artist, Blake noticed the multiplication of facts at the expense of values in his own day—a situation he attributed to the unchallenged supremacy of the Elect. "Without Contraries is no progression," he says, and "progression" means creation, the response of art to the challenge of nature, and the constant recognition that this is a process, an end to be continually realized. "What is the Life of Man but Art & Science? is it Meat & Drink? is not the Body more than Raiment? . . . expel from among you those who pretend to despise the labours of Art & Science, which alone are the labours of the Gospel."[21]

But Blake did not call art what was usually called art in the eighteenth century. Faced with the decorative and representational art of his contemporaries, he reasserted the reality of genius and the possibility of inspiration. Commenting in a marginal note on the third of Reynolds's *Discourses*, he quotes a passage from Milton: "A work of Genius is a Work 'Not to be obtain'd by the Invocation of Memory & her Syren Daughters, but by Devout prayer to that Eternal Spirit, who can enrich with all utterance & knowledge & sends out his Seraphim with the hallowed fire of his Altar to touch & purify the lips of whom he

[21]*Jerusalem*, 77.

pleases.' "[22] He then proceeds to relieve himself of a few words of prophetic invective at Reynolds's expense: "The following Discourse is particularly Interesting to Block heads, as it endeavours to prove That there is No such thing as Inspiration & that any man of a plain Understanding may by Thieving from Others become a Mich. Angelo." The "plain Understanding" is natural fact unchallenged by art which is the gift of the Divine Muse.

The intellectual activity of the prophet is to be identified with inspiration only when the ordinary rational theory derived from memory is subjected to—and indeed replaced by—the prophetic "theoria" of the Divine Vision. Having seen his vision, he is privileged to communicate it to others, and since he can only do this by means of words or symbols, what he has seen becomes the "Word of God" in him. This experience is apparently characteristic of any prophetic writings, and, in a sense, the sermon itself is analogous to the experience of the prophet. First, there is the "Divine Vision" in the form of the revealed Word of God open to all men. This is followed by an examination of the text which corresponds to the prophet's individual message; finally, the text is given an application which is comparable to his consciousness of the time, place and kind of audience he is addressing.

According to tradition, the seer had not been limited to the spoken or written word, but he had frequently been associated with the beginnings of culture and of society in all its aspects. As such, he is the familiar culture-hero who is imaginatively viewed in retrospect by a people as the source of their arts and sciences. The Celtic bard and the Nordic *scald*[23] are his representatives and heirs whose re-creation of the past in epic form reminds their hearers of the existence of the gods

[22] *Annotations to Reynolds's "Discourses,"* p. 50. Cf. Milton, *Reason of Church Government*, Book II, Preface.

[23] In the second edition of his *Reliques*, Thomas Percy rewrote the passages which referred to the ancient minstrels and asserted that they were originally the custodians of the arts and sciences. "The origin of their art was attributed to Odin or Woden, the father of their Gods; and the professors of it were held in the highest estimation. Their skill was considered as something divine; their persons were deemed sacred; their attendance was solicited by kings; and they were every where loaded with honours and awards." *Reliques of Ancient English Poetry* (London, 1767), p. xx. He corrected the former impression of confusion which the close association between *scald* and bard had evidently created in the minds of some antiquarians, notably Samuel Pegge (*Archaeologia*, London, 1773, II, p. 101), who later acknowledged that the explanation had been satisfactory (*ibid.*, III, p. 310). Bard and *scald* still represented two parallel examples of a similar line of development within the outlook of Blake.

and of a point of view which "Measur'd this transient World, the Race of time."[24] Blake draws a distinction, however, between these successors of the pagan seers and the Hebrew prophets. Because they idealize the past in their memories, the seers in the pagan tradition reduce their creative activity to a temporal level and re-create the accidental and the transitory, rather than the substantial and the eternal. In short, they turn history into myth and worship the prophets instead of the source of prophecy.[25] They also abstract the deities of man's inner life—which are the "Zoas" of Blake's prophetic books, the faculties of imagination, intellect, affection and instinct—and exalt them into a pantheon of gods.[26] According to Blake, however, the Hebrew prophets remained consistently aware of the inner source of prophecy which he calls the "Poetic Genius," and they rebuked Israel for every relapse from this point of view.[27]

The Poetic Genius is defined as the first principle of perception, and Blake invariably identifies it with imagination. In an age when imagination has come to be regarded as an accessory to perception, he uses the word to describe perception as the common root of sensation which unites sense-data and, at the same time, re-creates the material of sensation into the perspective of individual life. It is, in fact, the individual when he is most conscious of himself and his ultimate aims, and its operation determines the extent to which he can be said to exist. As a reflection of this genius, man's natural existence is derivative

[24]Milton, *Paradise Lost*, XII, 554.

[25]A similar confusion between the prophet and the source of prophecy was the measure of the Jews' failure to understand Christ's assertion that he was the "Son of God." They therefore accused him of blasphemy (John, x: 30–7). Blake considers this to be the perennial fate of the prophet and of the class of the Reprobate of which Christ was the archetype: "He died as a Reprobate; he was Punish'd as a Transgressor" (*Milton*, 14: 27).

[26]Cf. *Marriage of Heaven and Hell*, Keynes, p. 185: "The ancient Poets animated all sensible objects with Gods or Geniuses, calling them by the names and adorning them with the properties of woods, rivers, mountains, lakes, cities, nations, and whatever their enlarged & numerous senses could percieve . . . . Till a system was formed, which some took advantage of, & enslav'd the vulgar by attempting to realize or abstract the mental deities from their objects: thus began Priesthood; Choosing forms of worship from poetic tales. And at length they pronounc'd that the Gods had order'd such things. Thus men forgot that All deities reside in the human breast." See also *The Four Zoas*, I, 19.

[27]The prophet Jeremiah rebuked the exiles of Judah who lived in Pathros in Egypt for sacrificing to the Queen of Heaven (Jer. xliv: 15–19). In Blake's opinion, one of the final stages in the degeneration of religion takes the form of an external worship of the "Powers Of this World, Goddess Nature, Who first spoil & then destroy Imaginative Art" (*The Laocoön Group*).

and dependent; as the full participation in its operation, his human existence is original and independent. The God of Israel described himself to Moses not as a rational unity, the One of the philosophers, nor as the goal of aspiration and desire, nor yet as the omnipotent God of power, but as He Who Is.[28] Blake's Poetic Genius likewise unites the other faculties of man in the final source of perception and existence, and imagination is the common factor between temporal and eternal existence. To know this kind of God it is necessary to be like him, and the only way to reject his gift is passively to accept and reflect the natural limitations of perception. As the term "Poetic Genius" implies, perception, which characterizes existence, is inseparable from creative activity. It is therefore impossible to remain unimaginative in this sense without being destructive or negatively hostile to the source of creation. The prophet's duty is to teach man to use his powers of perception and to warn him against the worship of the lesser deities of his own momentary aims.

Read in this way, the Hebrew and Christian scriptures which Blake calls "an original derivation from the Poetic Genius"[29] provide two main examples of prophetic activity. First, there is the figure of Moses who typifies divine law. As the inspired leader and liberator of Israel, he received the law which was to be worn on the head and on the left arm during prayer, signifying that it was the means and the guide for the faithful in the moment of aspiration and devotion, as well as during the course of life. The conception of Israel as a whole people engaged in the common enterprise of creating a new communal existence had a great appeal for Blake. The legal code of the Ten Commandments did not appeal to him, but he used it to illustrate the reduction of the prophetic word to a system of moral virtue and legal sanctions.[30] The second figure, that of Elijah, represents the

[28]Cf. Exod. iii: 14. In his *Vision of the Last Judgment* (Keynes, p. 643), Blake calls an "Aged Figure with Wings" the "Angel of the Divine Presence" who acts as the Recording Angel "taking account of the numbers who arise." He is the pillar of cloud and fire which guides the Israelites through the wilderness, according to Blake's reference (Exod. xiv: 19), and is identified with Jehovah Elohim, the "I am" or Eternal Existence which the soul asleep in Generation seeks to discover, and hence, become.

[29]*All Religions are One.*

[30]Retributive and prohibitive legal sanctions were manifestly degenerate aspects of the law which Blake, along with the testimony of Christ in the Gospels, utterly rejected. The criminal code of eighteenth-century England was an example of negative and destructive legal sanctions, Cf. *The Everlasting Gospel, passim*; Luke xi: 45 ff.

prophet in a truly archetypal sense.[31] In the class of the Reprobate he remains a constant witness to spiritual integrity apart from the priest and the king, delivering his message fearlessly and effectively. Blake criticizes Byron for being an Elijah who doubted the word he had been given and for forgetting the duty of the prophet to his society.[32]

To forget this duty is not only a failure to fulfil an obligation, but it is also a failure to realize the prophetic vision itself, or what amounts to the same thing, to falsify it. For the prophet who abandons the world through doubt or forgetfulness revolts like Byron's Cain from the tilling of the soil as an intolerable burden imposed on him for the fault of another. From the wilderness of his own sense of injured merit, he sees the false vision of a capricious and self-sufficient Omnipotence—God without mankind. In Blake's opinion, God cannot be perceived as separated from mankind without becoming Satan, the accuser of man. It is not the part of the prophet to accuse or judge but to utter the word of God which judges him who rejects it. The Hebrew prophets kept alive the spirit of the law whose letter had been taken over by the priest and the king in Israel until the coming of Christ. Christ was the fulfilment of the spirit of the law and of the word of the prophets; he was the judge of man in the true sense, just as Satan was the accuser and judge of man in the false sense. The Satanic judgment took the form of accusation according to natural reason and natural morality which was an abstract ethical code based on a blur of generalizations. It is Blake's contention that Christ did not judge in this way, and the contention may be supported by various quotations from the Christian scripture. One will serve as an example.

> And if any man hear my words, and believe not, I judge him not: for I came not to judge the world, but to save the world. He that rejecteth me, and receiveth not my words, hath one that judgeth him: the word that I have spoken, the same shall judge him in the last day.[33]

The vision of God continually expressed through the medium of the prophetic word judges the world, for those who reject it are judged already in so far as they continue to reject it. Continual rejection is the mark of Satan and his Elect.

[31] In his *Vision of the Last Judgment*, Blake depicts Elijah as the one who comprehends "all the Prophetic Characters" (Keynes, p. 645).

[32] *The Ghost of Abel* ("To Lord Byron in the Wilderness").

[33] John xii: 47–8.

Redemption is thus a continuous process within the realm of nature, and there is the constant danger of man shutting out the vision by surrounding himself, either individually or in a group, with a closed system of doctrine. Once this is done, he tends to become passive, to abandon the struggle and search which are the sources of life and accept mystery and authority which are the sources of death. This attitude in the work of Blake had its counterpart in the anti-clericalism of the *philosophes*. His anti-clerical views had a very different basis, but both his dislike of organized religion and his republican fervour were in the temper and mood of the American and French revolutions. Revolution is the social aspect of redemption, as it resists the tendency to make the citizen the mirror of social authority. Any form of absolute government in church or state leaves the prophet only two choices short of becoming a martyr: he can either become the prophet of the central authority and surrender his birthright, or he can leave the country and his duty to society. With the exception of one incident in the course of his career, Blake was too completely ignored as a political entity ever to be faced with the decision, and it certainly never entered anyone's head to consider him a threat to the Established Church.

Although he gained no public fame, he was nevertheless known and recognized by a fairly extensive group of people. It was probably at the house of Aders that he met Coleridge whose conception of the imagination was related to his own.

> The IMAGINATION then, I consider either as primary, or secondary. The primary IMAGINATION I hold to be the living Power and prime Agent of all human Perception, and as a repetition in the finite mind of the eternal act of creation in the infinite I AM. The secondary Imagination I consider as an echo of the former, co-existing with the conscious will, yet still as identical with the primary in the *kind* of its agency, and differing only in *degree*, and in the *mode* of its operation.[34]

Coleridge's outline of the secondary imagination differed little in content, but much in context, from Blake's visionary imagination. Coleridge began with a primary imagination which was the reflection of the original creative act, and which was therefore the dependent

[34]S. T. Coleridge, *Biographia Literaria*, ed. J. Shawcross (Oxford, 1907), I, chap. XIII, p. 202. It was at Aders' home also that Götzenberger, the German painter, met Blake. After returning to Germany he declared: "I saw in England many men of talent, but only 3 men of genius—Coleridge, Flaxman and Blake, and of these Blake was the greatest." Alexander Gilchrist, *Life of William Blake* (Everyman ed., London, 1942), chap. XXXVI, p. 332.

perception of the natural creation in the finite mind. He derived the secondary imagination from the original creative act through its repetition in the finite mind. Blake evidently considered his visionary imagination to be a direct participation in the "living Power and prime Agent of all human Perception" which was his Poetic Genius; there was no mention of an "echo" or a "repetition," and he found the finite and derivative perception of an outward creation a "hindrance & not Action."[35] Fancy, however, as Coleridge pointed out, is not to be considered the same as imagination, for it is a mode of memory. The introduction of fancy into imaginative creation produces a representational imagery which depends largely on natural perception and an assortment of mnemonic associations which Blake noted in the poetry of Wordsworth. The use of fancy is arbitrary, and its confusion with imagination results in a subjective dilettantism in which Blake had no part. On the contrary, Blake's imagery or symbolism was surprisingly unequivocal, and its internal scheme of reference was distinct and clear to the "eye" of imagination.

This internal scheme of reference does not differ in kind, but rather in depth and emphasis, from any other work of the imagination. The unity of any such work depends on the creation of a coherent world by metaphor and simile, so that the author's relationships between one image and another may be established. The process involves the outline of a verbal universe which will show the author's vision of his subject to the "eye" of his reader's imagination. Usually, communication is made easier by the author's initial reliance on an external scheme of reference which includes typical characters, events and places familiar to the reader. Inescapably, the writer will speak eventually from his own point of view, but this has been accommodated to a more or less usual form of presentation, prevailing opinion and at least some of the current ideas of his audience. Dante wrote for readers who were aware of the political, philosophical and religious implications of his words. The "Elizabethan world-picture" was available to those who watched Shakespeare's plays. Milton could rely on his reader's knowledge of the Bible and on his interest in political and religious controversy. Swift's satire was couched in the familiar form of the travel story. The internal significance was left to the reader's insight, if he chose to make the effort to try to understand the author's point of view. Blake gave his reader

[35] *Vision of the Last Judgment*, Keynes, p. 652.

no such accommodating comfort, but, in the prophecies especially, confronted him at once with the starkly individual point of view of his own prophetic vision. Referring to one or both of his later epics, he reminded the reader that he must look to the internal scheme of reference for an understanding of the author's meaning in a poem with "the Persons & Machinery intirely new to the Inhabitants of Earth."[36]

It would therefore be misleading to approach Blake through any external scheme of reference without constantly bearing in mind this originality of subject-matter and treatment. His mental life was rich, and it would be just as misleading to suggest that he did not make considerable use of the Neo-Platonic tradition, the lore of the Cabbalists and alchemists and the more usual patterns of Western thought. He even indicated that he knew something of Indian philosophy, but whatever he "borrowed" became an intrinsic part of his own vision. The main approach to his imagery, therefore, must be through his own internal scheme of reference.

The images which are perceived in the moment of vision and which are derived from the Poetic Genius are associated through imaginative activity for the purpose of interpreting the insight of the seer. They are consequently symbols, and the basis of this kind of symbol is rooted in the effort to interpret and communicate what is otherwise incommunicable. If the significant meaning of any symbol can be expressed in any other way, the symbol *qua* symbol is eliminated, or becomes the representation of the meaning as otherwise expressed. An image which is associated intrinsically, because of resemblance, with a thought, emotion or sensation is not a translation of vision but merely a paraphrase of fancy. Such a symbol will be based on the process of association which Blake considers an act of memory concerned with the accidental volitions and passions of the natural man. Wordsworth, in his description of the poet, attributes to him "a disposition to be affected more than other men by absent things as if they were present."[37] Images which are thus related through resemblance in the memory of the poet acquire an indefinite and equivocal significance as symbols, because they are associated somehow or other with the common experience of men within the range of the poet's experience. These are representational symbols and are the products of an art which attempts

[36]Letter to Thomas Butts, April 25, 1803.

[37]*Lyrical Ballads* (2nd ed., London, 1800), Preface.

to imitate nature over which is thrown a "certain colouring of imagination, whereby ordinary things should be presented to the mind in an unusual aspect." The symbolism of Blake is not representational, and the images are related to one another in the act of interpreting the prophetic vision which is already a unity in the moment of its perception. He emphatically rejects memory from the prophetic, and hence, from the poetic creation. The language of prophecy and of poetry should be concerned entirely with the expression of what he calls the "Divine Vision" and not with an imitation of the world of nature.

With this view he considers poetic inspiration and prophetic vision to be the same thing, and he deplores the distinction made between the Hebrew prophets and later poets such as Milton. Hebrew prophecy is simply poetry of the highest order.[38] The vision of these ancient poets has been seized in the interests of the vulgar. The language of prophecy was originally the universal language of men, before they accepted the limitations of the natural senses and fell from the vision of nature into the world of nature. Blake sees the biblical Eden and the Hellenic Golden Age as visions of man's original spiritual condition, and this reading of pagan myth and sacred legend implies a consistent historical process beginning with prophetic vision and ending with its formulation in religious cults. In the process, symbolism ceases to be a living language and becomes fixed in the liturgy and iconography of an ecclesiastical institution. From having been the living tongue of prophecy, it becomes the dead language of professors of prophecy who assume the sacerdotal role of priests. The prophet is succeeded by the priest who is the representative of sacred law, but he survives in the inspired poet who is the original representative of the arts and sciences.

It is in the arts particularly that the language of prophecy finds its expression within the context of a civilized society. By reason of man's natural condition and through the medium of his organs of perception, this universal, symbolic language is translated into the particular

[38]*Annotations to Watson's "Apology for the Bible,"* pp. 8–9, 10–11, 15–16. The literal meaning of the Greek word προφήτης is "forth-teller," referring to one who speaks forth a message derived from some kind of divine inspiration. Among the Greeks, it acquired the meaning of "interpreter of oracles." But in biblical usage and in the sense in which Blake uses the word, it connotes inspired insight and the concomitant power to communicate, or the gift of the "word." In one passage of the New Testament (Titus i: 12), the term "prophet" is apparently applied to a Greek poet as if poetry were a form of inspired writing.

"dialect" of a society.[39] The auditory symbolism of words and speech becomes the song and story of the poet, and at the beginning of a civilization's development, the poet is indistinguishable from the prophet. The inspired poet gives way to the literary artist, the orator and the philosopher, for Blake is convinced that there is more inspiration in literature than in the liturgy of any organized religion. Visual symbolism in the original, prophetic sense is the act of seeing visions, but in its social manifestation it becomes the end-product of this act—the art of painting which is at first related to the representation of speech.

The hieroglyphic script, as the name implies, is the pictorial representation of living speech exalted into a sacred mystery by the priestly colleges of Egypt. Related to this development of the written word is the symbolism of gesture and dance which survives in the folk-festival concerned primarily with the rites of fertility. From the phallic processions and the orgies of Dionysus came the dramatic genres of comedy and tragedy, and according to Olympiodorus' commentary on Plato's *Phaedo*, both comedy and tragedy were assigned to Dionysus and associated with the Eleusinian and Bacchic rites.[40] In its sacrificial and mystical aspects, the dramatic ritual was absorbed into the Hellenic worship of the gods, but in its representational aspect, it tended more and more towards the imitation of social manners. Another expression of the symbolic language of prophecy lies in the development of the plastic symbolism of sculpture and architecture which reflects the desire to make the prophetic vision of the eternal city a reality in the natural world. This desire is itself the basis of the arts and sciences, and can be productive of error only when the prophetic vision is rejected or despised, and man seeks to live merely in the light of nature.

Blake is alert to condemn any religious doctrine which teaches that salvation cannot be won outside it. His dislike of systematic theology is founded on the belief that the theologian is trying to protect himself from the prophet by means of a rational system of dogma. This attitude of defence resists the notion of immediate and constant revelation. In the history of the Christian church, Blake sees the original

[39]*All Religions are One*: "The Religions of all Nations are derived from each Nation's different reception of the Poetic Genius, which is every where call'd the Spirit of Prophecy."

[40]Thomas Taylor, *The Eleusinian and Bacchic Mysteries*, ed. Alexander Wilder (4th ed., New York, 1891), sec. II, pp. 192–4.

word of prophecy incarnate in Jesus become the cult of Christ in the Pauline epistles, and true to his conviction that the only rule of conduct which Jesus taught was the forgiveness of sins,[41] he regards the apostle Paul, in his attempt to define a system of doctrine and a code of conduct, as the actual founder of ecclesiastical Christianity. Once the foundations of the temporal church were laid, the Christian community was obliged to defend itself against a society which was in the process of disintegration, and the machinery of defence was gradually developed in the form of a definitive system of theology. This was a purely temporal measure, and for Blake it represents the entrance of the church militant into the political arena; henceforth, he treats the church as a political entity. Plato reacted against the murder of Socrates by what he considered an irrational democracy, and moved in the direction of a rationally ordered society which would prove to be a defence against unreason. Blake decides that such a society would defend itself against another Socrates, and that it was the closed system of Judaic law which condemned the prophet Jesus.

As a way of explaining his views at greater length by an examination of his written works, it will be necessary to outline the historical background in which he lived with special reference to the history of thought as he saw it. Blake's judgments of his age were not due to ignorance or prejudice. They were the expression of a point of view which has already received some attention in a few of its more important aspects. These are: that the true creative artist or poet must also be an inspired prophet; that the social order, by its very nature, tends to restrict, and even destroy, the freedom of expression—both in life and thought—necessary for him; that this restriction takes the form of a bondage to reasonable rules of thought and conduct, ostensibly for the preservation of the civilized arts and sciences from unregulated self-interest, but actually for the defence of established authority in church and state; that such an attitude of defence produces the very disintegration it is supposed to prevent.

It remains to be seen how this outlook was affected by the traditions of European speculative thought and political practice as seen by Blake; but first it will be necessary to begin the outline of his historical perspective and describe his attitude toward the older traditions to which he fell heir. To Carlyle, history was divine truth expressed as

[41] *The Everlasting Gospel*, Preface.

both epic and scripture, as both the re-creation of the past in the bard and the revelation of its meaning in the prophet. To Blake, however, both bard and prophet were united in those "honest Men" who formed the "Conscience" of human history—and he counted himself one of their number—whose works were the "Word of God Universal."[42] The canon of this inspired scripture was the full extent of the human mind, and it was also the expression of an author's attempt to be, as Plato put it, the spectator of all time and all existence.

[41]*Annotations to Watson's "Apology for the Bible,"* pp. 7–9.

2. The Circle of Destiny

BLAKE'S VISION of his own field of experience finds expression in the form of an epic which makes use of the events of history as material for a parable of the human predicament. The events of his own life and the traditions of his race are treated as the materials of the artist, and they provide the content of experience which finds expression, finally, in *The Four Zoas*, *Milton* and *Jerusalem*; but what gives this content its particular form? One element in the form is a distinction between the imaginative and the rational attitudes towards the material of experience. Logically, an ordered pattern or picture of the world is produced by classification and definition. Definition places particular objects of experience in a class of objects with specific qualities, attributes and properties in common. But the metaphor and analogy of the imagination relate the existence of anything to other existences in terms of a common life. It is logically possible to define any object of experience by enclosing it in a classification which can be extended to include the entire world of objects, and this is the rational form which the field of experience takes. But this rational panorama represents to Blake only the static world of objects without subjects, of spatial extension without the subjective condition of temporal experience. Human history is, however, about subjects as well as objects, and man's condition cannot adequately be represented apart from a form of expression which includes the objective world within the observation and experience of a universal subject. Blake represents this universal subject as a Giant Man (Albion) who is the final environment of particular men within the field of history.

Universal history becomes the analogy of individual biography, and goes through the same phases until, at last, the metaphorical likeness between the two is recognized as identical, and the separate experiences which form the events of history become one common human experience in the vision of the Giant Albion. Complete knowledge means the identity of the knower and the object of knowledge, and man can know neither history nor the world of objects except as one act of observation on the part of one observer. The epic form of history is still only the mythical representation of the dream of universal humanity expressed as a "Divine Analogy,"[1] because it can only be reproduced in an image or likeness until the awakening into the realization of a final unity actually takes place. An analogy depends on a likeness between a part and the whole, or between one part and another; it derives its validity from the assumption that the field of experience ultimately makes up one whole. In this sense, definition is always approaching metaphor by attempting to classify by means of like qualities, properties and attributes, although it goes against metaphor by abstracting these qualities from the objects themselves. Metaphor, however, is the imaginative basis of analogy, and, when used, suggests that no pattern of experience is utterly discrete, but rather that it is like some other. These patterns of experience, or what Blake calls states of existence, form the visionary geography of both individual life and universal history. They form the body of a common experience.

Common experience, however, implies common belief. But the relationship of common belief to the eternal, unchanging source of experience in the human existence itself is not a constant one. Just as the earth passes through the seasons, and the individual through the stages of life, so also history passes through the changes of belief which Blake calls "Churches." As long as man remains a separated part of an unrealized unity, his common experience remains limited to a cycle of recurrent possibilities—an "Eternal Circle" stretching from Adam to Luther.

> And where Luther ends Adam begins again in Eternal Circle
> To awake the Prisoners of Death, to bring Albion again
> With Luvah into light eternal in his eternal day.[2]

But if Albion is the unconscious life of human existence, and Luvah the faculty of devotion and belief, what has separated mankind into the "Prisoners of Death" and caused the affections to turn aside from "eternal day"? The answer to this question implies a paradoxical identity between humanity and the human being, so that Albion may

[1] *Jerusalem*, 85: 7.
[2] *Ibid.*, 75: 24–6.

be seen as asleep or awake according to the condition of any one individual observer. If asleep in the circle of time which is the state of Generation, the observer remains a part of Albion's dream; if awake, he becomes a human existence in his own right, after the model of his original in the Giant Man. The total resolution of life in the moment of awakened vision also brings about the resolution of the entire human experience of which the life of the visionary has been only a fragment. But the visionary perspective makes the events of time simultaneous, and the course of history is united to the field of the natural environment and the biography of the observer.[3]

Blake's vision of history takes the final form of a myth which describes the state of Generation as a cycle of temporal stages corresponding to the individual course of life of everyone in it. Everyone derives his existence from his essential humanity, the eternal existence of which he is a particular expression. Every acorn is part of an oak, yet also a potential oak itself by virtue of its origin and inherited form.[4] The part and the whole may be included in one vision, if the history of the acorn can be seen as falling away from, and returning to, the "Existent Image" of the original oak. This is the form of Blake's historical cycle, and history begins with the dismemberment of an original ordering of existence—like the fall of an acorn from the parent oak—in which unity and diversity were reciprocal aspects of one being. The fall from this essential unity into an enforced diversity is represented by the dismemberment of the Titan Albion and the creation of the natural world out of his body. As the original breadth and scope of what Blake calls "Human Existence," he falls into the circle of time, and his fall is a falling asleep. In sleep he moves in the direction of eternal death and the decline of his powers from their original vigour and excellence. In other words, he enters "Chaos," and falls away from unity of being into the disorganized state of the dreamer. Inertia, automatism, weakness, lack of purpose and delusion come over him, and yet the fall is no consignment to oblivion, but to the enforced movement of the state of nature. The fall is arrested by the established conditions of his sleep in the form of the natural order.

[3]As a prelude to the final awakening of Albion, and as a description of the perspective from which he is writing the work, Blake says: (*ibid.*, 15: 8–9):

> I see the Past, Present & Future existing all at once
> Before me.

[4]Cf. *Vision of the Last Judgment*, pp. 68–9 (Keynes, p. 638).

Blake is impressed with the compulsion underlying the natural order and the clock-work which the deists made of it, but he is also aware that this very compulsion is what keeps fallen man from dissolving into chaos and disappearing into non-entity. Human experience, that is, history, is contained and supported by the order of nature which is "the Body of Divine Analogy."[5] Temporal succession and spatial extension become the Mundane Egg, the form of man's fallen perception, the analogy of an original unity in the field of observation. The immediate effect of the fall is the loss of power suggested by the myth of the creation of Adam from the dust of the ground and the gradual degeneration of the patriarchs in the first chapters of Genesis. Subsequent effects include conflicting affections, slowness of understanding and, most important, disorganization of the visionary faculty into fantasy. With this disorganization comes the loss of original understanding based on a common insight into a shared experience which united the particular life of the individual to his universal human existence. The biblical account of the confusion of tongues represents this decline from community of experience to community of interest held together by circumstance and necessity.

History moves through the same circular course as the individual in it; although accidental events may vary, the substantial pattern continues to revolve in an "Eternal Circle" from creation and birth to judgment and death. Fallen man is bound like Ixion to the wheel of time, unless he can break loose from it and turn from death and judgment to the "Last Judgment" and the awakening into eternal life. Death and judgment form the enforced return to the original starting point in every moment of life—a return which may destroy or transform, depending on the condition of the race or the individual. As

[5]*Jerusalem*, 49: 53–8:

> "Jehovah is before, behind, above, beneath, around.
> He has builded the arches of Albion's Tomb, binding the Stars
> In merciful Order, bending the Laws of Cruelty to Peace.
> He hath placed Og & Anak, the Giants of Albion, for their Guards,
> Building the Body of Moses in the Valley of Peor, the Body
> Of Divine Analogy;"

Moses suggests Jehovah's covenant with Israel, and his body the natural covenant or the order of nature. The giant kings who build the structure of this order in the valley of Peor (Num. xxv: 8) where some of the children of Israel worshipped Baal are used elsewhere (*Milton*, 22: 31–40; 41: 47–50) to represent the regents of Chaos, so that Chaos is bent to the service of an enforced order in the natural world. See also *The Four Zoas*, II, 474–5.

the observer is, such is the field of his observation. The relationship between observer and field constitutes an individual's "state" which limits and prescribes his beliefs or his "church," and even forms the goal of his aspirations or his "heaven." Blake's cyclical pattern includes "Twenty-seven Heavens" and their respective "Churches" which bear the names of patriarchs and leaders throughout the three periods of history. The course of history, like the life of man, is divided into "the Three Regions immense / Of Childhood, Manhood & Old Age."[6] Each period corresponds to a fundamental balance between the self and the world, expressed through a sexual symbolism which emphasized the implied psychic relationship.

The first of these periods is the age of the giants and is called "Hermaphroditic," implying that man and the elemental powers of his world are in some sort of equilibrium or communion. This age corresponds to that of "Childhood," and in his *Vision of the Last Judgment* Blake represents it by the figure of Seth. It begins with Adam who is a son of God and ends with Lamech who is a descendant of Cain, showing it in its beginning and in its final decline.

> Above the Head of Noah is Seth; this State call'd Seth is Male & Female in a higher state of Happiness & wisdom than Noah, being nearer the State of Innocence; beneath the feet of Seth two figures represent the two Seasons of Spring & Autumn, while beneath the feet of Noah four Seasons represent the Changed State made by the flood.[7]

The first age declines from the "State call'd Seth" and is finally swept away by the flood. The next one begins with Noah and ends with Terah, the father of Abraham. This age is called that of the "Female-Males" in which the created world has established its precedence over man. This age ends with the astrology of the Chaldeans, the oracular priestcraft of the Egyptians and the sacrificial rites of the Druids—the worship of sun, moon and stars and the observance of times and seasons. The lore of the Druids is deeply rooted in traditions coming from the first age, but its remains show it in decline. "Adam was a

[6] *Jerusalem*, 98: 32–3; 14: 25. See also Karl Kiralis, "The Theme and Structure of William Blake's *Jerusalem*," *ELH* (1956), 129–32. Throughout his *Arcana Coelestia*, Swedenborg also refers to three great "Churches." The first is the Most Ancient church which he says (nos. 1121–4) is described in the early chapters of Genesis. After the flood, there exist various churches which are called the Ancient church (nos. 1125–7). In the Most Ancient church there is direct revelation from heaven; the Ancient church enjoys revelation by a system of correspondences, the church of Israel by an audible voice, and the Christian church by the Word (no. 10355).

[7] *Vision of the Last Judgment*, pp. 82–4 (Keynes, p. 645).

Druid, and Noah; also Abraham was called to succeed the Druidical age, which began to turn allegoric and mental signification into corporeal command, whereby human sacrifice would have depopulated the earth."[8] The "Druidical age" evidently includes the whole of antiquity up to Abraham and the beginning of the Hebrew dispensation. In fact, Blake speaks of Greek rationalism as a "remnant of Druidism" and connects it with the deists of his own day.[9] The remnants of each age persist and show the resistance of man's fallen nature to every new revelation.

Since the fallen nature of man is the result of self-will, or what Blake calls the "Selfhood," each age ends with the triumph of the Selfhood over man's original "Human Existence." Consequently, the last "church" of each era represents the final perversion of self-sacrifice into the sacrifice of others in the "Druidical" rite of atonement. Sacrificial atonement becomes the great negation which organized religion substitutes for the actual contrary of creative activity—the sacrifice of self-will. The mutual existence of these two contraries—creative activity and self-sacrifice—is the basis of real religion in Blake's opinion, and he shows Abraham fleeing from Chaldea "shaking his goary locks."[10] The historical cycle has reached the stage of "Old Age," that of the "Male-Females," beginning with the heirs of the promise and ending with Luther and the wars of religion. In the first part of this last period, the prophetic succession is exemplified in the antiquities of the Jews. The three great figures which symbolize the early history of Israel—Abraham, Moses and Solomon—also repeat the process of decline which has taken place in the preceding ages, for Abraham is led by a direct providential inspiration, Moses establishes the rites and observances of a priesthood, and Solomon builds the Temple at Jerusalem. Religion is finally contained by the form and aim of the state—"Religion hid in war."[11] After Solomon the guidance

[8] *A Descriptive Catalogue &c.* (no. V: The Ancient Britons), Keynes, pp. 608–9. In his reference to the Greek philosophers, Clement of Alexandria classed the Druids with the Egyptians, Chaldeans, Persian Magi and the Indian gymnosophists (*Stromata*, I, xv, 131).

[9] *Jerusalem*, 52, Preface.

[10] *Ibid.*, 15: 28.

[11] *Ibid.*, 75: 20. Cf. *Vision of the Last Judgment*, pp. 76–7 (Keynes, p. 640): "It ought to be understood that the Persons, Moses & Abraham, are not here meant, but the States Signified by those Names, the Individuals being representatives or Visions of those States as they were reveal'd to Mortal Man in the Series of Divine Revelations as they are written in the Bible; these various States I have seen in my Imagination; when distant they appear as One Man, but as you approach they appear Multitudes of Nations."

of the prophets is rejected, and the mission of Israel becomes, like those of the surrounding nations, an expression of self-interest and political necessity.

By his constant use of biblical tradition, Blake does not intend to restrict the prophetic vision of history to the Hebrew scriptures. "The antiquities of every Nation under Heaven, is no less sacred than that of the Jews. They are the same thing, as Jacob Bryant and all antiquaries have proved."[12] But the persistent strength of the prophetic tradition in Israel had made the original break with Druidism more definite, and had clarified the subsequent course of history into the perversion and rejection of vision. The name "Druidism" comes to symbolize the perverse substitution of an oracular formalism for the active life of the prophetic mentor and the arrogant reduction of the inner sacrifice of man's natural self to the imitative rite of human sacrifice. With the rise of abstract speculation, notably among the Greeks, the whole idea of sacrifice became an urbane genuflexion to the head of the state, and the philosopher rejected prophetic vision in favour of natural virtue and an acceptable scepticism.

Although the Druids of Britain exhibited in their decline an idolatrous husk of ritual debased by ignorant imitation into the orgiastic expression of energy, Blake's account of them in his *Descriptive Catalogue* shows an enthusiasm for what he considers their "ancient glory."

> The Britons (say historians) were naked civilized men, learned, studious, abstruse in thought and contemplation; naked, simple, plain in their acts and manners; wiser than after-ages.... The British Antiquities are now in the Artist's hands; all his visionary contemplations, relating to his own country and its ancient glory, when it was, as it again shall be, the source of learning and inspiration.[13]

The "Welch Triades" to which he refers offer the antiquarian and the merely curious a wealth of traditional dogma mingled with later additions, but still presenting a coherent system of doctrine. Within this system Blake finds the remnant of a conception of "genius" (*awen*) involved with the framework of a bardic institution which later degenerated, in his opinion, into the worship of nature.[14] Inspiration

[12] *A Descriptive Catalogue &c.* (No. 5, The Ancient Britons), Keynes, pp. 609–10.

[13] *Ibid.*, Keynes, p. 608.

[14] *Ibid.*, Keynes, p. 589. Cf. Edward Williams, *Poems, Lyric and Pastoral* (London, 1794), II, p. 194: "The Patriarchal Religion of Ancient Britain, called Druidism, but by the Welsh most

became dogma, and dogma became estranged from its source by an inverted reliance on the natural limitations which the light of genius originally transformed. Patriarchal in its beginnings and prophetic in its derivation, the bardic doctrine is understood to be a supernal revelation, and it attempts to describe the circle of man's ultimate destiny as a memorable journey through every kind of existence.

"Druidism" weighs heavily upon Blake's early attempts at expressing his complete system. The insistent appeal of a rationally satisfactory formulation of experience is resisted throughout *The Four Zoas.* Ahania, the wisdom of experience restricted to memory, cries aloud to Enion, the spirit of earthly growth in the "Caverns of the Grave,"[15] and despairs of ever redeeming mortality, but Enion's reply turns from the cave of the confined intellect to the field of vegetative and instinctive life. As the seed experiences the death which is also growth into fruition,

> " 'So Man looks out in tree & herb & fish & bird & beast
> Collecting up the scatter'd portions of his immortal body
> Into the Elemental forms of every thing that grows.' "[16]

Nature as the state of Generation and the field of growth is the womb of man's ultimate "Humanity" and the basis of the Circle of Inchoätion (*Abred*) from which the Druids traced the progress of animated beings through the three states of existence.

All animated Beings are subject to three Necessities: a beginning in the Great Deep (lowest point of existence), Progression in the Circle of Inchoätion, and Plenitude in

---

commonly *Barddas* (Bardism), though they also term it *Derwyddoniaeth* (Druidism), is no more inimical to Christianity than the religion of Noah, Job or Abraham:—it has never, as some imagine, been quite extinct in Britain; the Welsh Bards have through all ages, down to the present, kept it alive: there is in my possession a manuscript synopsis of it by Llewelyn Sion, a Bard, written about the year 1560; its truth and accuracy are corroborated by innumerable notices, and allusions in our Bardic manuscripts of every age up to Taliesin in the sixth century, whose poems exhibit a complete system of Druidism, by these (undoubtedly authentic) writings it will appear that the Ancient British Christianity was strongly tinctured with Druidism." Williams admits no degeneration in the maintenance of these religious institutes and claims (p. 199) that "Bardism always refers its origin to Divine communication, and never talked of, I know not what, Religion of Nature." The aphoristical form of the "triad" is most commonly used by the bards in the preservation and communication of their traditional doctrines (p. 225).

[15] *The Four Zoas*, VIII, 480, 521.

[16] *Ibid.*, 549–51. The final regeneration from generative mortality takes place when the mortal disappears in "improved knowledge" and passes on to other "States of Existence" (*ibid.*, 537–42).

Heaven, or the Circle of Felicity; without these things nothing can possibly exist but God. Three things are necessary in the Circle of Inchoätion: the least of all animation, and thence the beginning; the materials of all things, and thence increase, which cannot take place in any other state; the Formation of all things out of the dead mass, hence discriminate individuality.[17]

"Discriminate individuality" has its beginning in the Great Deep (*Annwn*), its progression in *Abred* and its fruition in the Circle of Felicity (*Gwynfyd*), but it is contained by the Circle of Infinity (*Ceugant*), the void beyond the bounds of the created universe into which none but the Deity can penetrate.[18]

The outline of this doctrine forms the background of cyclical transmigration which obsesses the Zoa of intellect, Urizen, throughout the nine nights of *The Four Zoas*, as he moves with the course of the drama from fall to judgment and from creation to redemption. The search for a final void which may contain the cycles of Generation degenerates into a desperate and frustrated aggression, and the lament of Enion, preceding the beginning of the ninth night or "Last Judgment," becomes a concluding *pietà* on the breaking of eternal life on the wheel of fate or circle of destiny—the prototype of gestation, and constructed as the form of creation at the beginning of the first night. As such, the form of creation is the causal aspect of historical effects, the essential form which conditions the accidents of history and defines the limits of the possible. By the time Blake has fought his way clear of the tragic vision of *The Four Zoas* and has attained the perspective of *Milton* and *Jerusalem*, the "Circle of Destiny" has become a "Divine Analogy" and "Druidism" has taken on the symbolism of inverted vision rooted in the failure to distinguish the analogy of eternal reality, which includes created nature, from the natural world of the five senses from which the imagery of the analogy is drawn. The failure is not limited to a conceptual blunder merely,

[17]Williams, "Triades of Bardism, or Theological Triades" in *Poems, Lyric and Pastoral*, II, pp. 241–2.

[18]*Ibid.*, pp. 234 n., 241. The Druidic Circle of Infinity (or Vacuity) is obviously closer to the intellectual *tour de force* of the "Abstract Void," according to Blake, than to his own conception of "Eternity," but the starting point of both concepts must have been much the same originally. The Druidic traditional account, however, speaks of the eternal condition as insupportable to finite beings (*ibid.*, p. 202), while Blake calls creation "an act of Mercy" (*Vision of the Last Judgment*, Keynes, p. 648). See also *Milton*, 26: 72–3:

> Time is the mercy of Eternity; without Time's swiftness,
> Which is the swiftest of all things, all were eternal torment.

but includes a decline of conscious perception and a gradual hardening of the arteries of vision,

> As the Senses of Men shrink together under the Knife of flint
> In the hands of Albion's Daughters among the Druid Temples,
> By those who drink their blood & the blood of their Covenant.[19]

From fire-mist to Stonehenge, man and the field of his experience have consolidated into the corporeal degeneration of the fallen senses and into the apparently opaque matter of the world which the senses disclose. What is weak, dependent, ignorant and passive is also prone to a cyclical form of activity distinguished by endless repetition and pointless automatism. The automatic and cyclical repetition observed throughout nature is the pale reflection of creative activity *sub specie aeternitatis*, and the circle of destiny is no more than a "Divine Analogy."

Blake's figure of Generation is the circle, and for him it becomes the symbol of that nature-worship which forms the residuum of the original patriarchal religion. The circular temples of Stonehenge and Abury finally give him one symbolic image into which he concentrates the effective results of man's utter reduction to the state of nature in which his field of experience is spatially limited to three dimensions and temporarily limited to fading mnemonic impressions. Memory becomes the measure of knowledge, and retributive justice the rule of conduct, so that the possible becomes the necessary through a complete deprivation of contact with the eternal and original roots of being and life. Prophetic vision which alone gives man the possibility of avoiding what is otherwise necessary in the circle of destiny is represented in the character of Los as calling for liberation from crime and punishment, in order that these may be made to

> "Appear only in the Outward Spheres of Visionary Space and Time,
> In the Shadows of Possibility, by Mutual Forgiveness for evermore,
> And in the Vision & in the Prophecy, that we may Foresee & Avoid
> The terrors of Creation & Redemption & Judgment: Beholding them . . .
> Where the Druids rear'd their Rocky Circles to make permanent Remembrance
> Of Sin, & the Tree of Good & Evil sprang from the Rocky Circle & Snake
> Of the Druid, along the Valley of Rephaim from Camberwell to Golgotha,
> And framed the Mundane Shell Cavernous in Length, Bredth & Highth."[20]

[19]*Jerusalem*, 66: 83–4; 67: 1.

[20]*Ibid.*, 92: 17–20, 24–7. Cf. *Illustrations of the Book of Job*, ed. S. Foster Damon (New York, 1950), plate 20; S. Foster Damon, *William Blake: His Philosophy and Symbols* (Boston and New

"Visionary Space and Time" are space and time seen as phenomena of Eternity rather than as categorical conditions of natural perception limited to the three dimensions of the "Mundane Shell"—the cave of the fallen senses. As the imagery suggests the stern troop of Druids winding their circular way through the labyrinth of rocky groves, at least part of the terror which the spectacle of man's earthly fate provokes in Blake is communicated to his reader. The threefold submission of the natural creature to being born, being redeemed and being judged is set over against the subjection to a fixed environment of threefold extent. The emphasis, however, is placed on the basic opposition between freedom and necessity, between the world as the shadow of possibility and the world as the cave of necessity. But with the period of Druidism comes the complete identification of man with his natural state of existence and with its accidental effects requiring that balancing of accounts which so easily develops into the concept of retributive justice and the "permanent Remembrance of Sin."

Cyclical transmigration became an obsession of the Druidic age under the influence of a conception of experience conditioned by the memory of error and its necessary expiation. Sacrificial justice is the means of satisfying the natural man's inability to liberate himself from the memory of past experiences or even from the identification with present activities and the pressing uneasiness of future effects. The ethics and cosmology of Druidism are the imitative remnants of an inspired genius, which has remained as a *tour de force* perverting both emotion and instinct in the ritualistic expression of misunderstood tradition and dogma. Blake does not apparently doubt that a prophetic inspiration has perennially revealed the free ethic of Christ—"the most Ancient, the Eternal & the Everlasting Gospel."[21] But each age inverts its inspired wisdom and turns what has been the symbolic representation of inner significance into the dogmatic mockery of outward imitation. The dead weight of memory and habit makes a circle of necessity out of the panorama of natural effects, and reduces

York, 1924), pp. 235–6; Northrop Frye, *Fearful Symmetry* (Princeton, 1947), p. 434. The Job engraving illustrates the meaning of the text by showing the unfallen condition in which the environment consists of possibilities which are the necessary and unavoidable contingencies of fallen existence.

[21]*Jerusalem*, 27. Cf. *A Descriptive Catalogue &c.*, Keynes, p. 610: "All had originally one language, and one religion: this was the religion of Jesus, the Everlasting Gospel. Antiquity preaches the Gospel of Jesus."

the intellectual grasp of experience to the compulsion for keeping a record of what might otherwise be forgotten because it has never been understood. Urizen, as the type of the fallen reason, keeps this kind of enforced record of his transmigrations during the sixth night of *The Four Zoas*, and in so doing lays the basis for the subsequent sacrifice of man's energies, in the person of Orc, on the "tree of Mystery."[22] Sacrificial expiation is inseparable from submission to fate or destiny as the rule of life, and the belief that a criminal or heretic is somehow redeemed by being punished results in the worship of ritualistic torture as both the symbol and the actual means of reformation and salvation.[23] Suffering inevitably degenerates into a fetish for curing the effects of individual and collective guilt, and sacrifice becomes an exaggerated reprisal for the sins of the community. Blake does not deny the unavoidable necessity for some kind of suffering, any more than he denies the pain involved in setting a broken arm; but he resists the natural urge to punish the individual for breaking the arm, and insists that the concept of vengeance for sin, far from being a liberating corrective, encloses man more surely within his natural circle of destiny.

Sacrificial atonement, as the later characteristic of the Druidic religion, is the degenerate relic of the former discipline in the service of the seer's development and use of genius (*awen*); it is the moral excuse for the evident decline in the actual prophetic powers of the Druids. The perverse imitation of real inner discipline takes the form of the masochistic self-torture of the flagellant or the sadistic victimization of some sacrificial scapegoat. Blake traces the obsession with atonement to the preoccupation with the effects of action in relation

[22]*The Four Zoas*, VI, 156–72; VII(a), 157–71.

[23]Cf. Williams, *Poems, Lyric and Pastoral*, II, p. 199: "Man, having been guilty of crimes that are punishable by Death, must be so punished; and by giving himself up a voluntary victim to Death, being conscious of deserving it, does all that lies in his power to compensate for his crimes. . . ." The Druidic penances of the Gauls were placed under an interdict by Augustus, as noted by Suetonius (*De vita Caesarum* (Divus Claudius), lib. v, cap. 25), and Tacitus also remarked on the studied cruelty of their treatment of prisoners (*Annales*, lib. xiv, cap. 30), "for they considered it lawful to offer the blood of captives on their altars, and to consult the Gods by means of the nerves of men (*hominum fibris consulere deos*)." According to a later apologist (J. Williams ab Ithel, *Barddas*, Welsh MSS Society, Llandovery (London, 1862), I, p. lxix), the practices to which Tacitus alluded were the expression of the doctrine of *eneidvaddeu* which taught that it was both just and merciful to punish the transgressor in this way, because he would be immediately reincarnated in another body, cleansed of the crime for which he had been made to suffer. Cf. *Jerusalem*, 39.

to the conventional sanctions of a group. The only conventions which can ultimately be condoned are those which make organized social life completely predictable, and are therefore demonstrable and recurrent patterns like the revolutions of the stars and the return of the seasons. But men become no better than the field of their waning perceptions. "They become like what they behold!"[24] And what they behold is the cyclical round of nature which they come to associate with the measure and extent of the world, suggesting an underlying order which can be hypostatized as natural justice. The tyranny of this conception applied to the arbitrary sanctions of society indicates man's propensity for thinking of his own conventions as based on the natural order which forms the field of his observations. It does not matter to Blake that later Druidism claimed supernatural authority for its sacrificial rites; this is merely an example of priestly deceit and of the inversion of original prophetic inspiration into its opposite—natural religion and natural morality.[25] Druidism had finally become the symbol of man's identification with the cycle of nature, represented by the circular groves of Stonehenge with which Blake associates the enemies of the new dispensation of Israel.[26]

The cycle of history had run well over half of its course by the close of the Druidic age, and had seen the eventual triumph of mother nature over *homunculus* who is gestated, supported and contained by her womb—"A Male within a Female hid as in an Ark & Curtains."[27] First, there was the balance of the knower and the field of experience; then, the subversion of the knower by the field; and finally, the effort of the subdued creature of nature to conquer and encompass the order of which he has become an aspect—the epicycle of the "Male-Females" extending from Abraham to Luther. The Church of Abraham succeeds the Druidic age, and by a reduction of sacrificial atonement to the rite of animal sacrifice opens the way, through the Mosaic Covenant, for the intervention of a constant succession of prophetic mentors.[28]

[24]*Jerusalem*, 65: 79. Cf. *ibid.*, 49: 21–2:

"The visions of Eternity, by reason of narrowed perceptions,
Are become weak Visions of Time & Space, fix'd in furrows of death."

[25]*Ibid.*, 52 *passim*.

[26]*Ibid.*, 92: 23.

[27]*Ibid.*, 75: 15.

[28]Indicated by the statement of Moses to Joshua (Num. xi: 29), quoted by Blake in his Preface to *Milton*: "Would to God that all the Lord's people were Prophets."

The original direction of Israel is established by the initial guidance of Abraham, and the modification of sacrifice is illustrated by his change of heart before sacrificing his son, Isaac. But the movement from the church of Abraham to that of Moses is a decline from the prophetic altar to the priestly tabernacle, from visionary faith to a sense of racial destiny, and ultimately, to the "State Religion" of Solomon and the Temple at Jerusalem. With each of his "Churches," Blake clearly associates a "Heaven" which is the spiritual form or divine body of the particular church. Such a church is either assimilated to its Heaven through prophetic vision, or separated from it by the exclusive conceptions of the natural man. When separated from it, the church becomes the mere reflection, the "feminine" aspect of state policy, or "State Religion"—"Religion hid in War."[29] State religion may be absolute in the Druidic sense of a totalitarian community controlled by enforced belief and the sacrifice of heretics. It may also be relative in the deistic sense of a secular community controlled by public opinion and the exclusion of individuals. Deism is the secular and rational remnant of Druidism—the sceptical reaction against the Druids' delusion. Blake identifies the outlook of the contemporary deist with the outlook of the Greek sophist, but he goes even farther than this. He attributes to Greek speculation as a whole a preoccupation with natural means and ends, so that the natural creature limited to reason and the senses becomes the sum total of what is humanly possible.

The error of naturalism—as Blake sees it manifested in the immediate heirs of Druidism, the Greek thinkers—arises out of the world of Homer and the poets. The foundation of the Homeric world is the central experience of man in conflict with the powers which sustain nature. Both gods and demons form a somewhat capricious background to nature, and this background finally trails off into the limbo of non-entity. Reality is to be found in the natural foreground, the stage of human achievement. To illustrate the requirements for success on this stage, Homer made use of his race of heroes in whom heroic virtue is the power to succeed in the struggle with fate. What Blake calls "the Selfish Virtues of the Natural Heart,"[30] provide the

[29]*Jerusalem*, 75: 20. In his *Annotations to Watson's "Apology for the Bible"* (pp. 7–8), Blake asserts that "the Jews conversed with their own State Religion which they call'd God & so were liars as Christ says. That the Jews assumed a right Exclusively to the benefits of God will be a lasting witness against them & the same will it be against the Christians."

[30]*Jerusalem*, 52. In his description of Dante's universe, Blake does more than suggest that the

hero with his score of successes. Such is the criterion for judging whether he has been right or not, and whether he has understood what is morally valuable. The Homeric perspective is a view of experience already accommodated to the natural man's acceptance of the world as a battle between wit and necessity. The knowledge of the hero is displayed by his skill in wresting the fullest success from fate; this is the measure of his virtue (ἀρετή). The successful hero is apparently the one who acquires the most trophies from fortune by means of a superior prowess—or, in Blake's eyes, by an effective display of force.[31] Morally, the hero is self-justified by his own success, but technically, he is guided by his more or less enlightened grasp of the possibilities. This grasp of what is possible forms the whole of his religious belief. Such a religion is, in essence, the hero's rationalization of his score, and it is entirely limited to success followed by acquisition and to failure followed by retribution. Blake sees this picture of the world as a rational calculus, derived from the Druidic rule of destiny, and later developed by the Greek philosophers as the reasonable man's answer to the human quest for self-knowledge.

But this kind of salvation establishes an obstacle to real enlightenment by restricting man's notion of well-doing to the primary stage of his development—that is, to his natural birth as a Selfhood.[32] As a Selfhood, man is merely a "natural organ subject to sense," a factor within the processes of nature. Everything which is negative, deadening and false in man, his selfishness, his vices and his inability to see beyond his present state are the characteristics of the Selfhood. The dead and oppressive weight of habit, both in thought and act, keeps this natural creature within the circle of its necessary destiny. Such is the "Spectre" or natural man, according to Blake, and such is his recurrent and

---

Ptolemaic system has become an excuse for giving the central position to the natural field of experience glorified by Homer. "Round Purgatory is Paradise, & round Paradise is Vacuum or Limbo, so that Homer is the Centre of All—" (*Notes on the Illustrations to Dante*, design no. 7). Ulysses congratulates Achilles in Hades on his *earthly glory*, and refers sympathetically to his consolation prize of rule over the shades, but Achilles is not impressed. "In order that I might live on earth, I should choose to serve as the servant of another . . . rather than rule over all the dead who have perished." *Odyssey*, XI, 489–91.

[31]Cf. *The Laocoön Group*, Keynes, p. 581: "Satan's Wife, The Goddess Nature, is War & Misery, & Heroism a Miser."

[32]The term "Selfhood" is derived from Swedenborg (*The True Christian Religion*), no. 658 who opposes it to the process of regeneration and rebirth.

automatic fate. Man, however, is not utterly limited to this natural condition. He can exist apart from circumstance or fate, and he must do so, if he is to exist at all, for natural existence is that of a "Vegetated Spectre," completely passive to the effects of its environment and its conditioning. There is a "Humanity" which is the eternal seed of his future possibilities, but the Selfhood usurps the role of this humanity and remains the slave of fate like the heroes of Homer. The brooding Selfhood of Achilles causes him to retire to his tent and lament the loss of his rightful prize. His moral virtue or his good name and fortune have suffered, and the only recourse is to assert his virtue in the face of an unkind fate. Unfortunately, this self-righteous assertion of "rights" is no more than the attempt to express the Selfhood. The result can only be to intensify and exaggerate the conditions of man's slavery. The only real hope is to counteract the Selfhood, not with a view to rendering its activity perfect and effective—the Greek conception of virtue, in Blake's opinion—but rather to subject its activity to the humanity.

Blake sees the whole of Greek philosophy as an attempt to reconcile man to his natural state and, more particularly, to establish the propensities of the Selfhood as socially acceptable. The creature of nature was to be made reasonable and to be taught the natural morality of mutual conformity and social adjustment. If this view of Hellenism makes it the successor of the hierarchical despotisms of Egypt and Babylon—which Blake includes in the term "Druidism"—that is exactly what he has in mind. Hellenism was a superb rationalization of man's plight as a natural creature, and it glorified his cross by making it appear not only bearable but honourable. The virtue of the Selfhood is to keep one's eye on the odds and one's bets for the main chance. In this respect, Blake's view consistently contradicts the ideal of the citizen as understood by his contemporaries with their "Greek" conception of enlightened self-interest.

He never can be a Friend to the Human Race who is the Preacher of Natural Morality or Natural Religion; he is a flatterer who means to betray, to perpetuate Tyrant Pride & the Laws of that Babylon which he foresees shall shortly be destroyed with the Spiritual and not the Natural Sword .... Man is born a Spectre or Satan & is altogether an Evil, & requires a New Selfhood continually, & must continually be changed into his direct Contrary. But your Greek Philosophy (which is a remnant of Druidism) teaches that Man is Righteous in his Vegetated Spectre: an Opinion of fatal & accursed consequence, to Man . . . .[33]

The essence of Blake's manifesto against the sources of that tradition which his contemporaries had taken over is put starkly but unmistakably. Man's struggle is not to be interpreted as an effort to withstand and remake fate by an assured confidence which finally becomes that desperate aggression called *hybris* by the Greek tragedians. Nor does his way lie in the direction of a heroic indifference. On the contrary, his real struggle ought to be an incessant re-creation of himself and the field of his experience, for the two are inseparably connected, and their relationship constitutes the "state" in which the individual finds himself.

The whole of temporal life takes the form of the circle of destiny which is a series of states so constituted that they provide a "Divine Analogy" of eternal existence, and are, in fact, an aspect of Eternity. Each state has its own privations or evils to which the individual is subject while he is in it. As a creature or "Spectre," man is born a very limited organ subject to sense, and to the best of his ability he should oppose this Selfhood with a "New Selfhood" or the image of that humanity which is his eternal origin.[34] However, he can only escape the evils of any state by superseding or passing out of it, not by attempting to get rid of the evils themselves. In order to eliminate the privations of his state, an individual would have to reduce his activity until it approaches complete inactivity, and this is a negation of any kind of development. Blake is convinced that the ethical doctrines of the Greek philosophers who follow the poets have this negative and stultifying effect. The rational concept of moral virtue becomes the attempt to approximate a general standard of excellence, and finally degenerates into a code of prohibitions. This kind of virtue is the result of the opinion that man can be "Righteous in his Vegetated

[33]*Jerusalem*, 52. Edward Davies (*Celtic Researches* (London, 1804), p. 184) refers the origin of the philosophy of Greece to the Celtae, and the Pythagoreans also related their own doctrines to those of the Druids (Iamblichus, *De Pythagorica vita*, xix, xxviii, xxxii, xxxvi).

[34]Swedenborg does not make this specific use of the term "Selfhood," but the biblical distinction between the new and the old Adam (Rom. v: 14; I Cor. xv: 45) would be familiar to Blake. The dialectic of this conflict which leads to self-realization is also mentioned in the *Bhagavadgita:* "Self is the friend of self; and, in like manner, self is its own enemy. Self is the friend of him by whom the spirit is subdued with the spirit; so self, like a foe, delighteth in the enmity of him who hath no soul (*anatmanah*)." *The Bhagvat-Geeta, or Dialogues of Kreeshna and Arjoon*, trans. Sir Charles Wilkins (London, 1785), vi, 5–6, pp. 62–3.

Spectre," that he can be complete while still being incomplete and produce perfection out of imperfection.

Blake's treatment of Greek philosophy is, of course, never systematic, and his point of view is often expressed in an epigram. But the basis of his charge against the effects of Greek thought turns on the use made of rational generalization. As the successors to Homer and the poets, the philosophers apparently sought a reasonable means of establishing civilized freedom. Traditionally, their earlier attempts concentrated on the natural environment, and reached a point of consolidation in the atomism of Democritus and Leucippus. The combination of the atoms in the void of space gives the human observer a fixed relationship to the machinery of nature, but he also becomes a fixed relationship within a scheme of efficient causes within which it is difficult to see how he can either move or act as a free agent. Dissatisfied with this absence of moral agency, Socrates connected the origin of man and the world with a designing intelligence, so that man might participate in the agency of the creative mind which is the basis of nature and its effects. This very doctrine, however, when it is applied to ordinary thinking and the conduct of affairs, gives man the prospect of developing a theory of ethical perfection apart from his powers of attainment. He can think about action without acting, and establish a righteousness for himself without really altering his actual condition in any way. Recognizing the limitations of his natural estate, he can pretend to a theoretical freedom which is illusory.[35] In this way the earlier ceremonial law of what Blake calls Druidism was replaced for the Greek citizen by the code of conventional ideals of right conduct. The Greek thinkers were still a long way from the situation in which Blake found his contemporaries, but they had made a beginning.[36] By treating knowledge as abstracted from the state of the knower, they had founded speculative science and given the lie to knowing as an act of perception. Using rational argument, the philosopher could now know without understanding and talk without doing, since he had been provided with an admirable technique for this purpose.

[35]Cf. *Vision of the Last Judgment*, pp. 92–5 (Keynes, pp. 650–2).

[36]Cf. *Annotations to Watson's "Apology for the Bible,"* pp. 6–7: "That mankind are in a less distinguished Situation with regard to mind than they were in the time of Homer, Socrates, Phidias, Glycon, Aristotle, etc., let all their works witness."

The ceremonial rites which were originally the expression of prophetic vision had been given a fixed and tyrannical form in the "Druidic" cultures of Egypt and Babylon. Rational speculation was at first an attempt to liberate man from this kind of tyranny, but it showed itself a "remnant of Druidism" in the end by being merely another kind of magical technique, another kind of distraction to escape from the challenge of actual, inner growth. Aristotle could define moral virtue as the production of custom, and still admit that nothing which subsists according to nature can develop an activity different from its natural tendency. Even if natural tendency and an acquired disposition unite to fulfil the intention of the lawgiver, the individual gains nothing but a comfortable and acceptable self-righteousness. His character which Blake regards as the imprint of an "eternal Principle" in him has been supposedly corrected to suit the aims of the state. The supposed correction of character—which is actually a denial of it—is the Selfhood's way of rationalizing the subjection of man's larger possibilities to its own immediate ends. The Selfhood is the vehicle of error, and by attributing goodness and badness to character, it reduces the essential form of man's positive and active possibilities to the point of reacting passively to the ephemeral conditions of circumstance and environment.[37] Goodness and badness are the acquired habits, tastes and ideals of the Selfhood, and they can only be opposed and transformed by character—the "New Selfhood" of which Blake speaks. The sophistry of the Greek moralists attempted to subject man's innate and inherent possbilities to rational generalizations of conduct abstracted from actual life.

In *The Song of Los*, Blake describes the kind of inherited knowledge which moved from Egypt to Greece as "abstract Law." Such was the form which the hierarchical wisdom of the Egyptians finally took, and for the Greek world, it was eventually embalmed in the books ascribed to Hermes Trismegistus. Through the culture-bearer, Palamabron, a type of the Redeemed, Greece is represented as having received this "remnant of Druidism."

[37]Aristotle, *Ethics*, II, ii, 1103a–b. Blake's references to "character" indicate that he regards it as the "imaginative form" or what Aristotle would call the *entelechy* of individual existence. Cf. *A Descriptive Catalogue &c.*, no. iii. See also *On Homer's Poetry & on Virgil* (Keynes, pp. 582–3): "Aristotle says Characters are either Good or Bad; now Goodness or Badness has nothing to do with Character: an Apple tree, a Pear tree, a Horse, a Lion are Characters, but a Good Apple tree or a Bad is an Apple tree still; a Horse is not more a Lion for being a Bad Horse; that is its Character: its Goodness or Badness is another consideration."

> To Trismegistus, Palamabron gave an abstract Law:
> To Pythagoras, Socrates & Plato.[38]

Pythagoras may be said to have founded within the tradition of Greek thought the kind of abstract speculation which Blake distrusts. Philosophy soon became the intellectual luggage of the sophists who succeeded in establishing cultivated taste at the expense of applied understanding. The Pythagorean communities defended themselves against this misapplication of doctrine, but the main defect in Blake's eyes is the preference given to an abstract symbolism as a means of communication and the apparent preoccupation with general rules in the conduct of life. For it is easy to appear to conform to such rules, but the kind of knowledge which can be learned apart from actual application and an immediate understanding can deceive as well as enlighten. The wisdom of the prophetic seer is concrete and immediate in its application, and cannot be restricted to reason and memory. Druid and Egyptian had succeeded in abstracting man's immediate understanding of life into a definitive system of ceremonial law interpreted by professional authority. The Greek philosophers inherited this procedure and established the cult of the professional intellectual.

Professionally, Socrates was no ordinary intellectual, and Blake does not make use of him as a type of that kind of authority. Instead, he takes the Socratic method of a life examined according to moral virtue, and pronounces upon its effect rather than upon its original intention. The effect is a life lived according to an ideal of moral perfection in the eyes of gods and men, and he sees this as essentially a process of adjustment rather than as a continuous act of inner transformation. Self-examination leads only too easily to self-righteousness and the attainment of the good man who is good in his own eyes or in the eyes of others or in the eyes of the gods; and there he remains, caught in the net of his own best interests. In his Preface to the fourth book of *Jerusalem*, entitled "To the Christians," Blake notes a further refinement of this method when it is misapplied to the Christian doctrine of repentance. He aptly describes the result as "the tortures of self-reproach" and as "the intanglement with incoherent roots." This form of flagellation may have been unknown to the Greeks themselves but, as far as Blake is concerned, it is involved with the

[38]*Song of Los*, 18–19. Blake's references to Pythagoras are limited to this passage and to the satirical portrait of the Pythagorean in *An Island in the Moon*. Thomas Taylor's translation of Iamblichus' *Life of Pythagoras* and other Pythagorean fragments were not published until 1818.

whole scheme of moral virtue. "If Morality was Christianity, Socrates was the Saviour."[39] Over against the ethic of Socrates, he places what he considers to be the main ethical principle of Christ: the forgiveness of sins, which provides the possibility of transformation by eliminating the search for, and the imitation of correct moral values. Only the mind which is free from such conditioning can be a creative mind, and only the creative mind can remain open to the redeeming force of what he calls inspiration.

Plato, however, is Blake's supreme professor of Greek wisdom, and in the symbolism of the prophetic books, he comes to represent the ultimate effect of rational authority. By making the best of man's lack of visionary perception, Plato makes the most of his need for moral discipline and the supremacy of reason over instinct and desire. To act well is to live according to an established ethical rule, and to understand correctly is to know according to the rational process of the dialectic. His rejection of Homer and the poets may seem to agree with Blake's view that they left inspired vision or stole from earlier works and fell below the status of prophets. But Plato appears to be rejecting them solely because they do not follow his rational procedure: "Plato has made Socrates say that Poets & Prophets do not know or Understand what they write or Utter; this is a most Pernicious Falshood. If they do not, pray is an inferior kind to be call'd knowing? Plato confutes himself."[40]

The aim of Plato is also the aim of Blake: the vision of what eternally exists; but the means are different. Plato reduces imagination to the lowest level of fantasy which perceives through the senses the shadows

[39] *The Laocoön Group*; *Vision of the Last Judgment*, pp. 91–2 (Keynes, p. 648).

[40] *Vision of the Last Judgment*, p. 68 (Keynes, p. 638). In his translation of the *Republic*, Thomas Taylor (*The Works of Plato*, 5 vols., London, 1804, I, p. 447) quotes Proclus (*In Platonis Rem Publicam Commentarii*, 406) on the reasons for Plato's rejection of Homer and the poets. "Proclus concludes his apology for Homer with observing as follows: 'The reason', says he, 'as it appears to me, that impelled Plato to write with such severity against Homer, and the imitative species of poetry, was the corruption of the times in which he lived: for philosophy was then despised, being accused by some as useless, and by others entirely condemned. On the contrary, poetry was then held in immoderate admiration; its imitative power was the subject of emulation; it was considered as adequate alone to disciplinative purposes; and poets, because they imitated every thing, persuaded themselves that they knew all things, as is evident from what Socrates says in this dialogue. . . . But he considers Homer as deserving a similar reprehension, because he is the leader of this species of poetry, and affords to tragedians the seeds of imitation'." Through the medium of the commentaries of Proclus, Taylor repeated Blake's main charge against the Greek poets: that they had "Stolen and Perverted" works of original vision.

on the wall of his cave. Further use of such a debased faculty is eliminated in the ascent to intellectual vision. From Blake's standpoint, one may just as well pluck out the eyes because they fail to reveal Eternity, as destroy the last vestige of imagination which fantasy represents.[41] Plato gives every indication of having rejected perception through the senses as a hindrance to vision, and his follower is evidently supposed to move from the shadow-world of appearances through the gloom of opinion into true intellectual light. Blake sees this ascending passage barred by the "Abstract Horror"[42] within the dark cave in which man's fallen reason is both prisoner and jailer. By rejecting perception through the senses as insufficient and misleading, Plato gives the impression that the ideas can be known by other means than that of direct vision. His emphasis on the study of mathematics suggests that the universals can be approached by a process of generalization; this, at least, is the heritage which he has passed on to the new science of Blake's contemporaries.

The subsequent effect, as Blake sees it, of Plato's description of the dialectic is to confuse intellectual vision with reasoned argument and to suppose that the ideas can be understood by logic and inference and especially by means of mathematical abstractions. Platonism can too easily degenerate into vain speculation, abstruse calculation and intellectual sterility. The dialectic seems to move from sensation to generalizations corrected by reflection and ultimately to the "Abstract Void" of unreality. At this rate, Blake can hardly be blamed for remarking that the Greek gods are "Mathematical Diagrams" and that Plato's philosophy blinds the "Eye of Imagination, the Real Man."[43] Plato's method leads to the assumption that the concept can lead to the eternal idea, but Blake, like the empiricists, denies that conception derived

[41]In the most ascetic of works within the Platonic tradition, Porphyry (*De Abstinentia*) frequently expresses a point of view which is the direct contrary of that of Blake. In one passage, he seems to praise those who "have not spared even their eyes, through a desire of not being divulsed from the inward contemplation [of reality]" (*Select Works of Porphyry*, trans. Taylor, London, 1823, i, 36). Blake regards the improvement rather than the denial of sensation the means to visionary perception which will "come to pass by an improvement of sensual enjoyment" (*Marriage of Heaven and Hell*).

[42]*Milton*, 3: 9.

[43]*The Laocoön Group*; *Annotations to Berkeley's "Siris,"* p. 241. In his translation of Plato's works (I, p. xxvii), Thomas Taylor quotes the "Hymn to Jupiter" of Pherecydes Syrus:

"Jove is a circle, triangle and square,
Centre and line, and *all things before all.*"

from reflection is any more than the abstraction of qualities from things perceived. He does, however, maintain that the "Existent Images" of Eternity can be reached, not by an education in rational abstractions but by the use of the imagination which does not violate the basic integrity of perception. Imagination keeps a direct contact with the thoughts, affections and instincts of human experience while rational abstractions give the thinker a false sense of detachment or objectivity with respect to them. Plato's use of the dialectic is also in line with his use of myth, or what Blake calls "Allegoric Fable," for the myth is used as an extended metaphor for representing the philosophic abstraction and not primarily for expressing the immediate vision of the seer. This particular use of myth provides a likely account of the appearances and accommodates the imagery of metaphor to the illustration of a rational system. Blake insists on drawing a distinction between such "Allegory" and his own kind of "Vision" for the "Sake of Eternal Life."[44] Although he finds fault with the Platonic method, he is in agreement with what he is convinced Plato is actually talking about: the forms or ideas of eternal existence.

The Greek philosophers had misrepresented the problem of human destiny by deriving man's existence from nature, as the cosmologists had done, or by deducing his existence from some archetypal essence in a universal rational order which, whether transcendental, as in Plato, or teleological, as in Aristotle, still left him a natural organ subject to sense. This whole-hearted reliance on rational *scientia* reveals a dilemma to which there is no practical solution, and it also accounts for the subsequent oscillation between materialism and idealism in classical thought. Rational speculation forces a decision in favour of a logical explanation of human nature and identifies this with the actual realization of human existence. The failure of Platonic idealism and the metaphysics of Aristotle to reach the crux of man's actual predicament can be traced, in Blake's opinion, to their emphasis on logical method. Such abstract speculation creates a gap between

[44]*Vision of the Last Judgment*, p. 68 (Keynes, p. 638). In one of his comments (no. 9) on his illustrations of Milton's *Il Penseroso*, Blake describes the spirit of Plato unfolding "his Worlds to Milton in Contemplation." His conviction that allegoric fable is distinct from prophetic vision does not prevent him from stating that "Fable or Allegory is seldom without some Vision." He obviously does not deny that the Platonic myths contain "some vision," and he even associates this allegorical use of myth with his own work in a letter to Thomas Butts (July 6, 1803).

man's mental life and his perception of natural objects and suggests a reliance on the latter as a more fundamental basis for understanding experience. Using the atomism of Democritus, Epicurus accepts the picture of an autonomous world of nature,

> Calling the Rocks Atomic Origins of Existence, denying Eternity
> By the Atheistical Epicurean Philosophy . . .[45]

The content of man's mental life is limited to a reflection of his natural state, and he is under no other influences than those which that state produces. Mind and imagination cannot go beyond nature, and to suppose that they can is the result of mere enthusiasm. Mere enthusiasm, however, is what Blake considers the original condition of all activity, and Epicurus had reduced experience to the atomic structure of nature. Activity without an inspired enthusiasm is unconscious, mechanical activity, and the Epicurean aim of imperturbability is best achieved by the "Rocks" which are the "Atomic Origins of Existence." Neither the dialectic of Plato nor the logic of Aristotle had saved Greek rationalism from becoming the servant of a naturalism which subordinated the formal identity of anything to an enumeration of its constituent parts. This kind of reasoning points directly to the experimental method of Bacon who is "only Epicurus over again."[46]

In Blake's imagination, rational analysis is closely associated with the ritual murder of the victim in Druidism, and he refers to the fall of man as the dismembering of one universal life in the form of a Giant to see if that life can be realized by putting together its separated parts.[47] The mechanical model suggests that the sum of the parts is the same as the unity of the whole, and that in this sum lies the answer to life itself. Analysis precedes synthesis, and the universe, including man, has been brought together out of a primeval chaos. Along with

[45]*Jerusalem*, 67: 12–13. Cf. *Annotations to Reynolds's "Discourses,"* p. 198: "The Artifice of the Epicurean Philosophers is to Call all other Opinions Unsolid & Unsubstantial than those which are derived from Earth." The Newtonian outlook is associated with the Epicurean (*Annotations to Reynolds's "Discourses,"* p. 204) which considers "Mind & Imagination not to be above the Mortal & Perishing Nature." See also *Miscellaneous Poems and Fragments*:

> The Atoms of Democritus
> And Newton's Particles of light
> Are sands upon the Red sea shore,
> Where Israel's tents do shine so bright.

[46]*Annotations to Reynolds's "Discourses,"* p. 35.

[47]*Jerusalem*, 31: 2–12; 66: 1–15.

the Platonists, Blake rejects this notion that life has come from the lifeless, that consciousness has come from unconsciousness or that life is simply an effect of its conditions. In his opinion, formal reality (that is, Eternity) precedes the created universe which is merely an aspect of it. Consciousness is not the product of temporal process, but the productions of time are the effect of conscious activity which remain prior to them and contain them.

> Many suppose that before the Creation All was Solitude & Chaos. This is the most pernicious Idea that can enter the Mind, as it takes away all sublimity from the Bible & Limits All Existence to Creation & to Chaos, To the Time & Space fixed by the Corporeal Vegetative Eye, & leaves the Man who entertains such an Idea the habitation of Unbelieving demons. Eternity Exists, and All things in Eternity, Independent of Creation which was an act of Mercy.[48]

Unlike the atomists and their Baconian successors, he also rejects the evolution of cultivated life from primitive savagery, and he declares that cultivated life existed first, meaning that it existed before the fall of man into the state of nature. Nature itself was also originally perfect, according to its created form, but its order has been perverted by the fallen beholder, and this perverted vision cut off from its source has become the basis for man's rational conception of reality.[49]

Classical *scientia* had completed the withdrawal from inspired vision. Just as Druidism was hypocrisy in religion, "Greek Philosophy" was sophistry in thought, or worse still, it was simply naturalism—a conviction that there was nothing but the universe of the fallen senses, limiting "All Existence to Creation & to Chaos, To the Time & Space fixed by the Corporeal Vegetative Eye." In the biblical tradition, however, Blake finds enough to convince him that the Hebrews had taken what was still alive in Druidism before that tradition had died. The lyric which opens the second chapter of *Jerusalem* expresses the belief that the real basis of human life is a community of conscious understanding and not one of moral law. The Preface states that this understanding is itself based on a conscious life which contained the form of the world before creation. The philosophy of the Greeks lost sight of this vision and substituted the inferences of

[48] *Vision of the Last Judgment*, pp. 91–92 (Keynes, p. 648). Cf. Ovid, *Metamorphoses*, I, 5–9.

[49] *Annotations to Watson's "Apology for the Bible,"* p. 6. *Annotations to Reynolds's "Discourses,"* p. i.

theoretical speculation for it. The prophetic tradition of Israel retained and expressed it through an understanding of eternal types and symbols related to natural things and events—an understanding which Swedenborg calls the science of correspondences.[50] Swedenborg's "science," however, is more akin to what Blake calls "Allegoric Fable" than to "Vision," for it emphasizes Swedenborg's own vision of types and makes it appear that this is the only way biblical symbolism should be interpreted. To make any prophet's vision absolutely valid exclusive of individual insight or conscience is to move in the direction of "Druidism" once again. Even the Mosaic ceremonial becomes an imposture when it ceases to be an expression of an inner realization and is identified with a religious doctrine of which it is the allegory and with a political authority of which it is the divine sanction.[51]

The withdrawal from vision is a cyclical repetition of the fall, and it occurs continuously throughout the circle of destiny. The apocalyptic counterpart of this withdrawal is the recurrent act of revelation in the form of each of the Seven Eyes of God—an act which reaches its culmination in the Incarnation of Jesus Christ. In this last revelation the "Word of God Universal" is not only given through a prophet but embodied in the prophet himself. In this sense, Blake considers it unique; in no sense does he consider it exclusive. The exclusive attitude of the Jews betrayed the prophetic tradition. Greek philosophy helped to prevent the development of such a tradition by failing to recognize its source, while the Jews attempted to appropriate its benefits. Christianity, although it possessed the greatest of revelations, combined the failings of both Greeks and Jews, for it moved farther from the source of prophecy than the Greeks and made an even greater attempt to appropriate the "benefits of God" than the Jews. This epiphany of error accompanies the greatest visionary revelation, and the error is the attempt to realize one's human existence, or what

[50]Swedenborg, *Divine Providence*, no. 220. Cf. *Vision of the Last Judgment*, pp. 68–9 (Keynes, p. 638). *Annotations to Swedenborg's "Divine Love and Wisdom,"* p. 295.

[51]*Annotations to Watson's "Apology for the Bible,"* pp. 4–5, 8–9. According to Jewish tradition itself, the efficacy of the ceremonial rites declined, and the Second Temple was not like that of Solomon. In five things the first sanctuary differed from the second: the ark, the cherubim, the sacred fire, the *shechinah* and the *urim* and *thummim* (*Babylonian Talmud*, ed. Isidore Epstein (London, 1935–48), Seder Mo'ed V, Yoma 21b, p. 94).

Blake calls Albion, by the exclusive means of self-will and hatred. This produces the "Polypus" or "Albion's Tree" which stems from Druidism and all it signifies. On the other hand, "Vision" is the effort to realize one's human existence by the inclusive means of self-sacrifice and love.

> As the Mistletoe grows on the Oak, so Albion's Tree on Eternity. Lo!
> He who will not comingle in Love must be adjoined by Hate.[52]

The mistletoe or *vis naturae* is the by-product of the oak in the same sense as the falling away from the eternal vision is the by-product of Eternity and the motive force of the circle of destiny.

Within the cycle of history as Blake represents it, the falling away from vision had two polar constants which took the form of the "Eyes of God" and the "Churches of Beulah." The "Eyes of God" were the recurrent revelations of the prophetic Reprobate, accepted or rejected by the Redeemed who created cultivated life. The "Churches" and their "Heavens" were what could sustain and re-create the belief of the Elect. As long as some of the Elect were informed by the everlasting gospel of the prophetic revelation they remained the positive basis of what Blake calls the "Religion of Generation," but when this ceased to be true, the "Religion of Generation" became "Natural Religion" or "Druidism" till "the Great Polypus of Generation covered the Earth." There is an inevitable movement away from inner life to outer death in every historical tradition throughout the circle of destiny, and this very movement makes it necessary to regard each tradition from two contrary points of view. Both Jews and Greeks have two sides to their respective traditions, but the Greeks lost contact with the visionary side through sophisticated unbelief and a preoccupation with rational argument, while the Jews took over the outer expression of prophetic vision as a national heritage and as a divine promise of future political supremacy. In Christianity there is an inner vision which never completely gives way to the outer allegory of the church. It is to this visionary Christianity which survives the religious and political struggles that

[52]*Jerusalem*, 66: 55–6. *Annotations to Watson's "Apology for the Bible,"* pp. 6–8. Cf. *The Four Zoas*, IX, 627–42.

[53]*Jerusalem*, 7: 62–4; 67: 34. Cf. *Milton*, 5: 11–12:

> For the Elect cannot be Redeem'd but Created continually
> By Offering & Atonement in the Cruelties of Moral Law.

Blake gives his allegiance. Its expression is to be found in the poets rather than the philosophers, in the "art" of the alchemist rather than in the experiments of the natural philosopher, in Chaucer and Milton rather than in Bacon and Descartes, in Paracelsus and Boehme rather than in Locke and Newton.

3. The Allegory of the Church

THE EARLY CHRISTIANS who fished in the troubled waters of the Mediterranean world caught stranger fish than one would suppose the apostle found in the Galilean lake. The various communal churches were not only defending themselves from a hostile society, but were also in frequent danger of disintegrating inwardly from the storm of every wind of doctrine. Since it has already been suggested that Blake repudiated the definitive theology which was gradually being developed to combat this uncertain state of the early church, it might be assumed that he approved of one or other of the prevailing heresies. Gnosticism with its collection of sects and its arcane teaching concerning the spiritual nature of man might appear to have much in common with his own interpretation of the fall, the tyranny of created nature and the doctrine of the plurality of celestial worlds. Some of the Gnostics also divided all men into three classes: the material, the psychic and the spiritual. Cabbalism, particularly, as the secret tradition of the Hebrews, might seem to be a source with such strikingly Blakean doctrines as that of the cosmic Adam Kadmon, spectre and emanation, progression through the dialectic of the contraries and the interlocking of the Cabbalistic spheres. Blake was certainly aware of these systems, but the traditional secrecy with which some of them were guarded did not reflect his insistent desire to communicate without rite or ceremony through the medium of his art.[1] It would be misleading to associate him with any specific occult tradition, when he gave no indication in his written works of being in harmony with the notion of a secret society or a secret teaching. Even if, like the apostle Paul, he had ever "heard unspeakable words, which it is not lawful for a man to utter,"[2]

[1]*The Laocoön Group*: "The Whole Business of Man Is The Arts, & All Things Common. No Secresy in Art." This statement should be compared with the no less definite remark in his letter to Trusler (Aug. 23, 1799): "The wisest of the Ancients consider'd what is not too Explicit as the fittest for Instruction, because it rouzes the faculties to act."

[2]II Cor. xii: 4.

he did not leave any record of it. His visions were not dissociated as ecstatic revelations from the labours of the artist in the natural world.

There is no need to go to the remains of the Gnostic heresies or to the works attributed to Hermes Trismegistus to find the duality of man's nature emphasized. The apostle Paul's letters, within the canon of the Christian scriptures, provide ample evidence that this conception was widely held. As the ancient world tottered to its fall, the sense of man's unworthiness—the result of that guilt which follows failure—became more apparent and oppressive. The separation between the spiritual and the natural man became more definite, and along with this dichotomy in man's nature arose a renewed emphasis on his inability to apprehend the mysteries of God. "But we speak the wisdom of God in a mystery, even the hidden wisdom, which God ordained before the world unto our glory."[3] A double standard of truth emerged from such statements, which could be read either as injunctions to mortify the flesh and glory only in its infirmities until, by the grace of God, the believer was initiated into the "hidden wisdom," or as mysteries to be accepted outright by the layman through the medium of the sacraments while he went about his business. The first reading evidently proved acceptable to the primitive church, for it was under no obligation to guide and instruct the state. When it became necessary to do so, what had been a mystery to be realized by the devotee, according to the grace given him, became a mystery to be accepted on the authority of a priesthood whose desire to bring the church into recognition by the temporal power was made a reality by the Emperor Constantine.

Constantine did more for the Western church than establish its ascendancy in the political sphere. He solved the problem of the double standard of truth by giving the criterion of temporal success to an organization which had in its beginnings looked for no earthly reward. Henceforth, the priesthood took over the "hidden wisdom" in its external manifestations of doctrine and sacrament and applied the methods of civil jurisprudence in the form of ecclesiastical councils to the solution of theological problems which had been hitherto a matter of controversy, and before that, of illumination by divine grace. What had been outside the reach of man's natural faculties

[3]I Cor. ii: 8.

became easily accessible to the minds of ecclesiastics who sat in council, and what had been a matter of visionary perception by the ecstatic or the seer became formulated as doctrine to be accepted and as rites to be observed. The corporate character of the church forbade the existence in it of any other standard of truth than that of revealed scripture and conciliar interpretation of it. Under these circumstances, it was increasingly difficult to distinguish between the spiritual and the temporal sword. If there was any truth in the story told by Eusebius, Constantine had united them, and by taking as his motto *In Hoc Vince*, had given the church a vested interest in its own temporal success and an infallible criterion for judging whether a dogma was of divine origin or not. Supernatural agency which was in the best interests of the established church was to be accorded the stamp of approval by conciliar or papal authority.

In this way the mysteries of divine truth became subject to the test of temporal expediency by an organization which was politically effective. Paul had heard "unspeakable words," but although they were unspeakable, he had seen fit to record the vision. The various followers of the Gnosis had likewise admitted two standards of truth—one esoteric and the other exoteric. In the language of Paul, the mysteries of the faith still remained open to all through the gift of the Spirit, but among the later Gnostics, the actual rites of initiation provided a necessary aid to the understanding of esoteric truth. The latter view reflected not only the beginning of that degenerate reliance on outward ceremony rather than inner attainment, but also an increasing sense of the unworthiness of man.

The gradual development by the primitive Western church of a liturgy and a ritual marked the growth of a pessimism which affected not only Christianity but every other cult of the Empire. From the third century, when Plotinus took over the Platonic school, until the beginning of the next, his disciples followed the same course from individual experience to a preoccupation with sacred rites. Iamblichus, the Syrian, transformed the Plotinian goal of "unification" by means of thought and devotion into a system of ritualistic theurgy based on the *Chaldean Oracles*.[4] After Porphyry the Platonists appear to have

[4]Cf. Iamblichus, *De Mysteriis*, lib. ii, cap. 11. In his version (London, 1821, p. 109), Thomas Taylor gives the following translation: "For a conception of the mind does not conjoin theurgists with the Gods; since, if this were the case, what would hinder those who philosophize theo-

held two different opinions on the method of achieving salvation—one group emphasizing the philosophic approach, and the other that of the priestly art.[5] This development in the history of the greatest rival of the Christian church provided a pattern which was not unlike the one outlined by Catholic Christianity from Paul to Constantine. The original "hidden wisdom" of Paul which was the living utterance of his own experience became, for others, a scriptural tradition expressed through the moral code and the rites of a priesthood. The Donation of Constantine gave that moral code and those rites a temporal justification in the active life of a society.

As far as Blake was concerned, this amounted to the repudiation by the church of the individual's perception of the inner truth of scripture in favour of promulgated dogma and outer ceremony. He thought of a man's religion in terms of direct revelation, an individual transformation, which it was his duty to express through the arts of communication and the active life. This attraction for direct revelation and constant expression made him repudiate the corporate ceremonial of orthodox Christian tradition which he symbolized by the names "Paul, Constantine, Charlemaine, Luther."[6] It will be necessary to explain exactly what meaning this tradition had for him without constant reference to the text of his works, in an effort to present the development of Christian doctrine in the West as a progressive reduction of the prophetic language of scripture to a sacerdotal system which culminated during the Reformation in the "word" of the preacher.

Side by side with this development in systematic religion was the development in the arts. Dante illustrated the attempt on the part of a poet to present a creative synthesis of theology, the arts and the sciences in harmony with the teachings of the Roman Catholic church. He

---

retically from having a theurgic union with the Gods? Now, however, in reality, this is not the case. For the perfect efficacy of ineffable works, which are divinely performed in a way surpassing all intelligence, and the power of inexplicable symbols, which are known only to the Gods, impart theurgic union." Iamblichus is here speaking against an empty intellectualism but, from Blake's point of view, he is speaking in favour of what became an empty ritualism. Cf. *Annotations to Swedenborg's "Divine Love and Divine Wisdom,"* p. 181: "The Whole of the New Church is in the Active Life & not in Ceremonies at all."

[5]Olympiodorus made a statement to this effect (*In Platonis Phaedonem Commentaria*, ed. Norvin, ii, 170) by observing that "some gave first place to philosophy, such as Porphyry, Plotinus and many other philosophers, others, the priestly art, such as Iamblichus, Syrianus, Proclus and all who were of the priestly school (οἱ ἱερατικοὶ πάντες)."

[6]*Milton*, 41: 40–3; *Jerusalem*, 75: 16–20.

created a vast allegory of church and empire and placed his creative imagination at the disposal of a political and religious ideal and the moral and judicial laws which supported it. In this respect he was the perfect example of a prophet who surrendered to the vested interest of a closed society ruled by the priest and the king. Such a politico-religious system which translated prophetic vision into allegoric revelation and then into corporeal command was repeating the degeneration of Druidism, and Blake regarded the *Commedia* as an imaginative work which had been made to conform to a context dictated by priestly interest and political policy.[7]

Dante adopted the fourfold interpretation of scripture which had already been developed by his time and which will serve to represent the four stages through which the Christian tradition passed. The inner sense of scripture was applied externally, as it were, to the task of instituting a universal church upon which to found the closed society of Christendom with its moral taboos and its magical rites.[8] With Milton, whose influence on Blake was very great, the fourfold synthesis gave way to the vision of the poet as expressed through the literal word uncomplicated by any other sense than that of the vision itself.

Considering the Christian tradition from this point of view, the

[7]Blake regarded Dante as a prophet who had been inspired both by "Satan" and by the Holy Ghost or "Poetic Genius." In one of his conversations with Crabb Robinson, he is reported to have said: "Dante saw devils where I see none." In another conversation he remarked: "But Dante and Wordsworth, in spite of their Atheism [nature-worship], were inspired by the Holy Ghost." H. Crabb Robinson, *Diary, Reminiscences and Correspondence*, ed. T. Sadler (Boston, 1869), II, chap. II, p. 27, and chap. III, p. 39.

[8]The terms "open society" and "closed society" have been derived from Henri Bergson (*Les Deux Sources de la morale et de la religion* (Paris, 1932), chaps. I and IV *passim*) who used them to establish a distinction between the social mechanics of an ant-hill and the mystical humanism of a society which, in principle, embraced the whole of humanity. Bergson, however, described the closed society as the primitive and natural beginning of the social order, while Blake obviously believed that society had begun "open" under its original prophetic mentors and had degenerated into the "closed" order of naturalism. The "closed society" was categorically that from which the prophet was effectively excluded, and his exclusion followed upon the denial of the source of prophecy and the introduction of some absolute principle of authority as the sole arbiter of truth. K. R. Popper (*The Open Society and Its Enemies*, London, 1945, II, p. 178), on the other hand, regarded Bergson's "open society" as "the product of a mystical intuition." "My terms indicate, as it were, an *intellectualist distinction*; the closed society is characterized by the belief in magical taboos, while the open society is one in which men have learned to be to some extent critical of taboos, and to base decisions on the authority of their own intelligence."

reader of Blake's prophetic books should interpret the names which mark the stages in the development of this tradition as symbols. He ought not to reduce them to representations but interpret them in harmony with the context in which they occur, and to which reference has already been made. The names are Paul, Constantine, Charlemaine and Luther, and they occur at the end of the third chapter of *Jerusalem* in the context of the cyclical vision of the unit of historical time—six thousand years. During the period immediately following the flood, man's active attitude towards the natural environment, or his imaginative control of it, becomes hidden within the "female" which symbolizes the fallen life of the five senses passively receptive to natural phenomena. In the next period the attempt is made on the part of the natural man to dominate by means of the will the "hidden mystery" of the natural environment symbolized by "The Female hid within a Male."[9] The only active response which remains under these conditions is what has come to be called the *will to power* and what Blake calls the "female will." Beginning with Abraham, it is this will which characterizes the Hebrew dispensation, and not until the coming of Christ is the veil of the temple of Jewish religion, with its secret place of mystery, rent in twain by the voice of prophecy. Under Paul, however, who is the successor of Abraham, Moses and Solomon, the mystery of the faith in the Christian dispensation is reconstituted.

The way in which Paul describes his vision exalts the mystery of grace beyond the sphere of terrestrial nature, but his respect for the inner meaning of scripture shows his desire to retain the connection with the letter of the Hebraic tradition. The double standard of truth which has for him a living significance becomes a technique applied to the reading of sacred literature, and this inner sense in which scripture can be understood acquires the epithet *anagogic*, since it is supposed to elevate the mind of the reader to the apprehension of divine truth

[9]*Jerusalem*, 75: 9–18. Los, the prophetic spirit of time, is represented as the shuttle which moves through the extended form of six thousand years to consolidate both law and history (*ibid.*, 75: 7–9):

> For Los in Six Thousand Years walks up & down continually
> That not one Moment of Time be lost, & every revolution
> Of Space he makes permanent in Bowlahoola & Cathedron.

"Bowlahoola" is the ability to assimilate or "digest" the possibilities—the "stomach" of Albion—while "Cathedron" is the organic form or body which is produced—history as the mean between nature and vision.

beyond the letter of the text.[10] A scripture with an anagogic meaning provides the basis for a cult and also a priesthood to interpret the written revelation and impart it to the layman through the medium of the sermon, the liturgy and the commemorative rites. Once the mystery of salvation has been enshrined in the church, the religion of Christ becomes a historical phenomenon subject to the "female will."[11] The link with the Hebraic tradition's deep sense of history is complete, and Christianity commences its successful career.

The religion which Constantine ostensibly chose from among the others which flourished throughout his Empire was in the very act of his choosing it justified in the moral sense as well as in the political. The political recognition came as a divine gift ratifying the conviction of the Western church that it had a moral mission in the temporal world. Hitherto, Christian morality had been the discipline of a cult; it now became the ethical code of a church under the authority of the Emperor. Scripture could be interpreted confidently in a third sense which came to be known as the *tropological* or moral. The "trope" which turned an event into a lesson of moral significance had been a favourite exercise of the rabbins and was to be the favourite exercise of the Catholic church as the mentor of Western society. The moral strength which the church possessed as an organization with authority under imperial patronage outlived its patron and carried it forward in its duty to humanity as a whole.

Whether Pope Leo III had or had not the right officially to crown Charlemagne Emperor of the Romans has been a matter of dispute. The event, however, bridged the gap between the northern society and the Roman church of the West. The sacramental character of the act and the stage it represented in the development of the church were to be closely connected with the interpretation of Blake's use of the name "Charlemaine." He was either ignorant of the Byzantine Patriarchate or indifferent to it, but the Empire of Charlemagne evidently suggested a stage midway between Constantine and the

[10]E.g., Gal. iv: 22–6. Here the term "allegory" evidently means "*to speak otherwise.*" The sense in which the passage is interpreted by the apostle is in accord with the so-called "anagogic" meaning which concerns "eternal truth."

[11]Cf. *Jerusalem*, 56: 41–2. Los, the spirit of prophecy, utters the following words:

> "Look back into the Church Paul! Look! Three Women around
> The Cross! O Albion, why didst thou a Female Will Create?"

Subjection to the "three Fates" of historical destiny is a condition adopted by the church militant.

Reformation, when the Western church adopted a historical field for its labours and became committed to the task of moulding the culture known as Christendom. This Christian culture which had reached its peak by the time of Dante had become a vast allegory of Catholic doctrine and reflected the projection into the field of history of the earlier method of interpreting scripture. The particular kind of interpretation was called *allegorical*, and it related the narrative of man's redemption to every other part of scripture and to the life of humanity as a whole, with special reference to Christ as the ruler of mankind.

The third inner sense of the revealed "word" was, therefore, the manifestation in the active life of the story of Christ's passion and its final consummation in the redemption of humanity. An emphasis on the pre-eminence of this conception in the rule of society distinguished the genius of the Roman Catholic church in its guidance of a race new to civilization. Blake shared with the Romantics an admiration for mediaeval culture. It should be clear by now that he did not do so for the usual reasons. His was not a primitivistic sympathy for an earlier period that had been less sophisticated and more natural, nor was it a sympathy derived from a nostalgic love of the remote, the vague and the mysterious. But he admired the vitality of the Gothic cathedral and was attracted by the conviction it gave of the inspired quality of mediaeval symbolism.[12] The church itself represented the human body with the transepts for arms and the chancel for the head where the mental act of communion was signified by the outward ceremony of the mass. Woven into its structure were the sanctified images of grace, the demonic gargoyles and the arched and buttressed forests of the natural world. The Gothic nave and the flanking aisles were

[12]Cf. H. Flanders Dunbar, *Symbolism in Mediaeval Thought and Its Consummation in the Divine Comedy* (New Haven, 1929), p. 399: "Modern culture is full of dead symbols, for the most part ignored or treated as curiosities; but a cathedral is with difficulty ignored, and its symbolism carries conviction of persistent vitality. Perhaps, then, it is little wonder that those whose interest is in the static arts have led all groups of modern symbolists in the understanding of mediaeval thought." The same author (p. 399 n.) mentions a rather amusing incident which illustrates the attitude of the Enlightenment to the art of the Gothic cathedral. Apparently "at the coronation of Louis XVI, eighteenth-century screens were employed to conceal the cathedral of Rheims, the 'crudeness' of Gothic decorations." Over the eastern part of Notre Dame de Paris can still be seen an interesting grouping of the twelve apostles descending to earth for the final consummation. They are preceded by the four "living creatures" of the *Apocalypse*—Blake's "Zoas." It is not difficult to understand why Blake regarded the unknown builders of the Gothic cathedrals as fellow visionaries.

the dead groves of Stonehenge come to life; the "Druid Rocks" had been given "Living Form" by the Gothic builders, but they had been rendered "reasonable" and regular by the Classical architects of Greece and Rome. It was not surprising that Blake turned away from the Palladian architecture, popular in the eighteenth century, as a "mathematical" form of art: "Grecian is Mathematic Form: Gothic is Living Form."[13] Nevertheless, within this "Living Form" was enshrined a sacramental mystery relying on the temporal sword of authority with which Blake did not agree.

He was in fundamental disagreement with the conception of the Holy Roman Empire which Dante held. The Empire itself was a successor to the Augustan ideal of *romanitas* founded on the Classical belief in the sufficiency of the natural reason to provide the necessary uniformity of outlook and conduct for the creation of a world made safe for civilization—a belief which he found led ultimately to perpetual war and the destruction of the arts and sciences.[14] The papacy, by placing itself on the side of the imperial power in the time of Constantine, had succumbed to the influence of statecraft and policy, and after Charlemagne, to political ambition. This result, however, was not due to the personal ambition of any pope, as Dante suggested, nor to the usurpation by the papacy of the role of the Empire in the divine plan. It was due to the misinterpretation of the mental significance of the revealed "word" of scripture in terms of corporeal command.[15] Blake regarded the process which has been outlined in brief as the reduction of the inspired writings to a code of political

[13]*On Homer's Poetry & on Virgil* (*circa* 1820). Cf. note engraved under the design *Joseph of Arimathea among the Rocks of Albion:* "This is One of the Gothic Artists who Built the Cathedrals in what we call the Dark Ages Wandering about in sheep skins & goat skins of Whom the World was not worthy." "Gothic" was that "Art" which embalmed the Body of Christ which Joseph was said to have begged of Pilate (John xix: 38).

[14]In the utopia of rationalism a planned unity inescapably became uniformity, and moral virtue became rational generalizations on individual conduct. "Unity & Morality are secondary considerations, & belong to Philosophy & not to Poetry, to Exception & not to Rule, to Accident & not to Substance; the Ancients call'd it eating of the tree of good & evil. The Classics! it is the Classics & not Goths nor Monks, that Desolate Europe with Wars" (*On Homer's Poetry & on Virgil*).

[15]Cf. *A Descriptive Catalogue &c.*, Keynes, p. 609. A decline into some kind of "Druidism" was the ultimate earthly destiny of every revelation in turn. Cf. *Jerusalem*, 79: 65–7:

" . . . I walk & count the bones of my beloveds
Along the Valley of Destruction, among these Druid Temples
Which overspread all the Earth in patriarchal pomp & cruel pride."

and moral sanctions applied to the rule of society. Poets such as Homer, Virgil and Ovid had brought the literal language of prophecy into the service of political ambition, and he noticed that Virgil had openly supported the empire of Augustus. Instead of rendering unto Caesar the things that were Caesar's, the Roman poet had rendered those things which were at least supposed to be God's. With this point of view, Blake could hardly be expected to agree to Dante's grandiose conception of the role of the Empire in the plan of redemption.

Dante and mediaeval tradition regarded the *pax Augusta* as the divinely ordained condition of authority for the birth of Christ and the successful completion of his task. The Divine Son had desired to be a part of that particular political régime during the period of his incarnation. Dante made the traditional claim that the Empire not only possessed penal jurisdiction over the whole human race by right of conquest but also by divine right, for if Christ had not been judged by one who was so qualified, he could not have atoned lawfully for the sin of Adam.[16] The union of Roman authority and the Hebraic law of sacrificial atonement completed the concept of retributive justice in both its political and moral aspects. Christ's crucifixion was, therefore, the vicarious atonement of a divine scapegoat, but its actual significance for Blake lay in the conclusion of a conflict between the outer imposture of the ceremonial law supported by judicial authority and the inner discipline of self-sacrifice actively realized by the greatest prophet.[17] The original Law of the Covenant had been debased into the judicial law of political prosperity, and what had been instituted

[16]Dante, *De Monarchia*, lib. ii, cap. 13: "Et si Romanum imperium de iure non fuit, peccatum Adae in Christo non fuit punitum: hoc autem est falsum; ergo contradictoriam eius ex quo sequitur est verum. . . ." This was the culmination of an outlook which went back to Eusebius' union of Church and Empire as a direct act of Providence (*Praeparatio Evangelica*, i, 4; *Demonstratio Evangelica*, iii, 2). Dante's mentor, Virgil, had prepared the ground in the sixth book of his *Aeneid* (779 ff., 841–53—a passage often referred to by Blake).

[17]Cf. *The Everlasting Gospel*, *passim*; *The Gates of Paradise*, Prologue:

Against the Accuser's chief desire,
Who walk'd among the Stones of Fire,
Jehovah's Finger Wrote the Law:
Then Wept! then rose in Zeal & Awe,
And the Dead Corpse from Sinai's heat
Buried beneath his Mercy Seat.
O Christians, Christians! tell me Why
You rear it on your Altars high.

Swedenborg (*True Christian Religion*, chap. II, no. 126) also separated the passion on the cross

as a disciplinary corrective had become the mask for personal ambition and the excuse for tribal conceit. The death on the cross could not be exalted into a divine ordinance without revealing the bloody culmination of the ritual sacrifices prescribed by the "Druidism" of Jewish law. Such was the inevitable end of every system of belief which found the main feature of justice in the sacrificial rule of retribution. "Every Religion that Preaches Vengeance for Sin is the Religion of the Enemy & Avenger and not of the Forgiver of Sin, and their God is Satan, Named by the Divine Name."[18] "Vengeance for Sin" was inseparable from the civil code of retributive justice, and to see that code as the work of divine Providence was to reduce the status of Providence to the realm of the natural world and fallen humanity. When Dante spoke of the vengeance of God on the Jews through Titus for the death of Christ, which had itself been the "vengeance" for the sin of Adam, he vitiated the vision of his *Commedia.*[19]

This might seem to be a very facile judgment of Dante's work, but to understand the nature of Blake's charge, it is necessary to recall his conception of the relation between creative activity and society. The prophetic artist should be the mentor of the social group and not the servant of the state. Once he becomes involved in supporting political authority, he exchanges his freedom of mental activity for the necessity of justifying his existence in the political structure. He has to be of use to the state or exalt himself above it. The early church endeavoured to take both courses by the institution of the papacy and the lay clergy who worked assiduously at the task of making the spiritual sword at least as effective as the temporal. Dante fought against the supremacy of the papacy in temporal matters, but he did not alter his conception of retributive justice which Blake regards as the basis of ecclesiastical ambition.

---

from the divine act of redemption. "The passion on the cross was the last temptation which the Lord endured as the greatest prophet; and it was the means of the glorification of His humanity, that is, of union with the divinity of His Father, but it was not redemption. . . . But although redemption and the passion on the cross are two distinct things, yet with reference to salvation they make one; since the Lord, by union with His Father which was completed by the passion on the cross, became the Redeemer for ever." Cf. *Annotations to Watson's "Apology for the Bible,"* p. 4: "Why did Christ come? Was it not to abolish the Jewish Imposture?"

[18] *Jerusalem*, 52.

[19] *Paradiso*, vi, 82–93. The story of the triumph of the "eagle" as the symbol of Roman authority and political power is given a similar treatment in his other works (*Convivio*, iv, 4–5; *De Monarchia*, lib. ii, cap. 3–5).

It seems as if Dante's supreme Good was something Superior to the Father or Jesus; for if he gives his rain to the evil & the Good, & his Sun to the Just & the Unjust, He could never have Built Dante's Hell, nor the Hell of the Bible neither, in the way our Parsons explain it—It must have been originally Formed by the devil Himself; & So I understand it to have been.[20]

This is Blake's answer to Dante's closely articulated argument which leaned heavily on the apparatus of Thomistic logic in favour of the conception of imperial authority as the instrument of divine justice.[21] The symbol of the *Sol Invictus* around which Dante's vision revolved was creative only when related to the soul's mystic progress towards vision and became destructive when exalted into an object of worship by the natural man. Long before the time of Blake, the symbol had become the centre of that broken fragment of Christendom—the nation—and the survival of both the metaphor and the reality at the court of the *Roi Soleil* might have surprised Dante as much as it repelled Blake.

The vision of the *Commedia* was distinguished by a faith in the rational faculty as a means of arriving at a suprarational truth. In this respect, Dante was a convinced rationalist. The ideal representations of truth were derived from revealed scripture, and the cosmos took the form of these "ideas." Under the guidance of Virgil, the type of natural reason in the service of a universal state, he saw the immutability of natural law and was oppressed by the severity of its outline. The gospel of rational conduct in the regulation of human affairs was constantly present to his mind. The gloom of the *Inferno* was inescapably connected with man's inability to order his life according to the dictates of reason because of the fall, and the reader is impressed by the ordered and rational way in which he disposed of the disordered and irrational in the bowels of the earth.[22] Dante, following the Thomistic lead, made his way through the inferno of the irrational by the light of the natural reason and proceeded still farther by means of right reason illumined by grace, until he found the rational transcended in the suprarational vision. To Blake, however, the *ratio* was what gave

[20]*Notes on the Illustrations to Dante*, no. 101 (a diagram of the Circles of Hell).

[21]Cf. *Ibid.*, no. 7 (the classical conception of the Universe): "Every thing in Dante's Comedia shews That for Tyrannical Purposes he has made This World the Foundation of All, & the Goddess Nature Mistress; Nature is his Inspirer & not . . . the Holy Ghost."

[22]Dante was warned by Virgil at the very entrance to Hell (*Inferno*, iii, 18) that he was about to explore the realm of those who had lost "il ben de l'intelletto."

form to one's vision of reality, but to think in terms of a *supraratio* was inadmissible, for it abstracted form from content. To think of a good man was as far as one could safely go, but to think of the "Good" placed the thinker under the tyranny of a ratio abstracted from the living content experienced by perception. This procedure tended to reduce the symbol, through the deprivation of the affective in favour of the rational, to a mathematical diagram. It was not without significance that the essence of Dante's final vision took the form of this very problem—the relationship between the symbolic image and the mathematical circle.

> Veder voleva come si convenne
> L'imago al cerchio, e come vi s'indova.[23]

Just as it was impossible to express the circumference of a circle in terms of the radius, so also the relationship between the temporal and the eternal was demonstrated to be incommensurable. Dante found, however, that although the relationship was incommensurable, it could be realized by the power of love which ultimately disclosed the image of a human face—the human nature of Christ—within the threefold circular representation of absolute divinity. The final solution was the same as that of Blake with this notable difference: the apocalyptic vision of the Divine Humanity at the close of *Jerusalem* did not attempt to include the supraratational "something Superior to the Father or Jesus."[24]

Although Dante did not suggest that his final vision could be reached either by reason or the senses, his image of the Divine Sun indicated to Blake that he had accepted external nature as the ultimate analogy of the Divine Vision. The solar orb was a natural symbol, and by seeing the ineffable ring of light as the representation of his vision united to the human image of Christ, Dante was in fact worshipping the *supraratio*, mysterious and tremendous, towards which a sacerdotal system always tended. Following in the footsteps of Thomas Aquinas, he had taken the revealed word of scripture and had related it to the world of nature in harmony with the practice of organized religion. To Blake, therefore, the *Commedia* was partly visionary in its use of human symbolism, but also a religious "fable" in its use of natural analogy and

[23]*Paradiso*, xxxiii, 137–8. Cf. *Annotations to Reynolds's "Discourses,"* p. 201: "God forbid that Truth should be Confined to Mathematical Demonstration!"

[24]*Notes on the Illustrations to Dante*, no. 101. Dante, *Paradiso*, xxxiii, 131–2.

geometric representation. By using the natural sun as a central image, Dante had made a concession to the process which has been briefly outlined. This process of externalizing the inspired word of scripture had begun with the exaltation of it into the revealed word of a supernal mystery and had culminated in the mediaeval church with its ordering of the accidental realm of human action in the fixed ceremonial and judicial codes. Once these codes had been established as forms to be observed and as laws to be obeyed, the natural world itself came to be considered as the projection of a Supreme Deity into the field of accident, and scripture was read in the light of a reasonable comprehension of the nature of the creature and of the created environment. Thomas Aquinas stated that God was to be known through the scripture which testified of his existence, but also by the rational conception of a universal cause:

> Therefore we must inquire how we know God, Who cannot be grasped by the mind or the senses. Would it be true to say that we do not know Him according to His nature? For this is unknown and beyond the reach of reason and intuition. Yet by means of the ordering of all things, which has been as it were projected out of Him and which bears certain images and likenesses of its divine patterning, we ascend in ordered degrees so far as we are able, to that which is above all things, by the ways of negation and transcendence and the conception of a universal cause.[25]

This was the conception of a universal cause which provided Dante with his solar symbolism, and in his work the inspired poet and philosopher met.

It was clear that Dante regarded his *magnum opus* as a derivation from what Blake called the Poetic Genius, that is, as a scripture, and the work was therefore to be read according to the fourfold method of interpretation.[26] In his letter to Can Grande, he referred to the *Commedia* and expounded the various senses in which it was to be interpreted. Apart from the literal, there were three allegorical or mystical senses: the anagogic which has already been connected with the mysteries of the faith, the tropological or moral and the allegorical or temporal which dealt with the salvation of man as an individual and

[25]*De Divinis Nominibus*, vii, 4, in *Selected Writings*, ed. M. C. D'Arcy (*Everyman*, no. 953), p. 186.

[26]Dante, *Epistola X*, 15: "Sed omissa subtili investigatione, dicendum est breviter quod finis totius est et partis est, removere viventes in hac vita de statu miseriae, et perducere ad statum felicitatis."

as a member of the Christian community.[27] These four senses have been examined and related to the development of the church up to the time of Dante. The process has been described as one of realizing the word of scripture in terms of a universal church. It might also be called a prolonged effort to incarnate the message of the Divine Logos in the institutions of a society. Dante's work translated this achievement into the form of the *Commedia*. As a poet, he sat at the feet of Gamaliel and learned from the theologian and the philosopher the ceremonial and the judicial law. Living in a world of mystic correspondences which were partly predetermined by the outline of Christian doctrine and partly by his own insight and experience, he combined formal allegory with imaginative symbolism. The balance between the allegoric fable and the symbolic vision was tenuous, for although the work was regarded as an inspired scripture by its author, the literal sense did not possess the authority or the validity of revealed scripture. Milton, however, chose a theme which possessed both the literal truth of scripture and the symbolic truth of revelation and inspiration. For him the allegoric fable had been eliminated before he began to write his *Paradise Lost.*

Milton did not reject allegoric fable—where the literal sense was fictitious—for reasons of poetic theory, since the poet Spenser whom he admired and the whole of the Renaissance tradition supported the device, besides the influence of his religious convictions and perhaps the example of the Protestant orator in the pulpit. Both Milton and the preacher regarded themselves as inspired, and it is doubtful if Milton drew any sharp distinction between the inspired orator and poet. In fact, he frequently associated the art of the preacher with that of the poet when he had occasion to speak of inspiration and the freedom from the ceremonial law and from the stylistic devices such as "the troublesom and modern bondage of Rimeing."[28] Milton's

[27]*Ibid.*, 7: "Ad evidentiam itaque dicendorum, sciendum est quod istius operis non est simplex sensus, immo dici potest *polysemos*, hoc est plurium sensuum; nam promus sensus est qui habetur per literam, alius est qui habetur per significata per literam. Et primus dicitur literalis, secundus vero allegoricus, sive moralis, sive anagogicus." See also *Convivio*, ii, 1. Although the work of Dante has been interpreted in terms of Blake's disgruntled and fragmentary comments, the anagogic sense of the Catholic poet bears a striking resemblance to the "Poetic Genius" or "Imagination" which liberates the individual from the corporeal and fallen "ratio." For a full treatment of Blake's view of Dante, see Albert S. Roe, *Blake's Illustrations to the Divine Comedy* (Princeton, 1953).

[28]*Paradise Lost*, "The Verse."

conception of inspiration was associated with freedom from the outward accretions of religious and poetic conventions, so that a return to the literal word informed by the gift of God might be made. This was not a rejection of the best standards of composition which, along with the divine argument or prophetic vision, were the evidence of inspiration in poet or orator.

These abilities, wheresoever they be found, are the inspired gift of God, rarely bestowed, but yet to some (though most abuse) in every nation; and are of power, beside the office of a pulpit, to imbreed and cherish in a great people the seeds of virtue and public civility, to allay the perturbations of the mind, and set the affections in right tune; to celebrate in glorious and lofty hymns the throne and equipage of God's almightiness, and what he works, and what he suffers to be wrought with high providence in his church; to sing the victorious agonies of martyrs and saints, the deeds and triumphs of just and pious nations, doing valiantly through faith against the enemies of Christ; to deplore the general relapses of kingdoms and states from justice and God's true worship.[29]

God's true worship was civil and ecclesiastical freedom in the literal sense of the word.

To Blake, therefore, Milton was one who restored the primacy of the literal truth of inspiration in the work of the poet. When the symbolism of a poet was in its literal or immediate sense considered untrue, and true only in an inner sense, the symbolism became representational, and vision was concealed in allegoric fable. Allegoric fable might be accommodated to judicial and ceremonial law, and as already illustrated, was intimately involved with the origin of these laws. The three allegorical senses of scripture were projected into the ceremonies of the church. Before the abrogation of the ceremonial and judicial codes by Luther, mystic symbolism and poetic imagery had already tended to become dissociated from the thought and feeling of the writer—mere figures of speech. Poetic diction or the stylistic devices of oratory might bear a certain relationship to the vision of the poet or the word of the orator but they were not that vision nor that word. Luther himself discredited the value of allegory even when it was used by the apostle in that passage in the Epistle to the Galatians to which reference has been made.[30] For he separated the argument or

[29]Milton, *Reason of Church Government*, Book II, Preface.

[30]Gal. iv: 22–6. On the subject of allegory, Luther wrote: "Allegories do not strongly persuade in divinity, but as certain pictures they beautify and set out the matter. For if Paul had not

truth of the passage from the allegory which adorned it in the manner of a rhetorical device. But Blake put first the recognition of its validity as an act of direct insight; no argument could make a man really understand any scriptural truth, although it might gain his rational assent for one reason or another. Recognition, without any need for argument which concealed some kind of appeal to self-interest, was the real basis for an understanding of the literal sense of scripture, and recognition required an insight for which reason was no substitute. Otherwise, the literal sense had its dangers, and when associated with a system of belief or an organized cult, such as the Lutheran and other Protestant sects, it might become confused with demonstrations of natural law. Read literally, the Bible presented a series of "visions" to the reader; but when read naturally, it became a false textbook on anthropology, geology or any other empirical science. The confusion of the literal sense of scripture with natural fact culminated in the discarding of everything but natural fact in the realm of religion—in "Deism." The Reformation was the last stage in Blake's cyclical vision of the development of the Christian cultus before it dissolved utterly into deism or the worship of nature based on the observations of the senses and rational inference.[31]

Milton himself was far from untouched by deistical tendencies. In choosing the theme for his *magnum opus*, he abandoned the Arthurian cycle, partly because he believed that the subject of poetry should be divine truth. If he meant that the story of Arthur was untrue for him and that, as an artist, he could not verify his experience by expressing it in the form of an epic, he was rejecting representational symbolism

---

proved the righteousness of faith against the righteousness of works by strong and pithy arguments, he should have little prevailed by this allegory. But because he had fortified his cause before with invincible arguments, taken of experience, of the example of Abraham, the testimonies of the Scripture, and similitudes: now in the end of his disputations he addeth an allegory, to give beauty to all the rest." *A Commentary on St. Paul's Epistle to the Galatians*, ed. Erasmus Middleton (London, 1810), p. 420. The notion that one could somehow "prove" scriptural truth by means of argument was nonsense to Blake. "He who does not Know Truth at Sight is unworthy of Her Notice." *Annotations to Reynolds's "Discourses,"* p. 201.

[31]The insight which was an elevation of the understanding beyond the natural perspective was not self-derived and the product of "Enthusiasm & Madness" according to Blake. He did, however, ask: "is it not plain that self-derived intelligence [rational inference] is worldly demonstration?" *Annotations to Swedenborg's "Divine Love & Wisdom,"* p. 233. "Demonstration is only by bodily Senses." *Ibid.*, p. 33.

or allegory. If, however, he meant that the legend could not be correlated with natural fact, he was subjecting his art, in this respect, to the critical judgment of naturalism. The same may be said of his rejection of the Graeco-Roman mythology. It is evident that Milton did not reject the authenticity of the Arthurian legend nor the existence of the pagan gods, but he distrusted the authority upon which their records rested. Discrepancies in the accounts of the English historians who were human and fallible, and the conviction that the pagan myths were ultimately the work of the father of lies made him turn to the certainty of inspired scripture. This pursuit of temporal and factual certainty disclosed a predilection, shared by his Puritan contemporaries, for emphasizing the natural and temporal authenticity of the sacred narrative, an authenticity which, of course, it did not, in fact, possess.

Although Milton only partially came under the influence of Puritanism, he reflected both aspects of this typical product of the Reformation. The Puritan's desire to remove the covering of Catholic allegory—including both the inner ceremony which bound the individual to the ecclesiastical hierarchy for his spiritual sustenance and the outer ceremony which subjected him to the power of an organization—impelled him to return to the letter of the scripture which enshrined the spirit. It was perhaps inevitable that he should come to regard the "letter" as the spirit itself. The book or sacred code which Blake called an original derivation from the Poetic Genius continued to be the only derivation from it; and hence, the secondary word of God—to the Catholic a ceremony, and to the Protestant a book—maintained its precedence over the primary word of God: the prophetic vision. It was for this reason that Blake did not associate Luther and the Reformation with a complete casting out of the allegory of the church, but simply with the consolidation of the literal sense of scripture into a series of historical cults. The "letter" of scripture was for him the outward form or rationale of vision; but when this outward form became dissociated from vision, it was interpreted as natural fact. Milton struggled with this aspect of his religious heritage in his *De Doctrina Christiana*—that tortuous rationale of the imaginative vision of *Paradise Lost*. The other aspect of Puritanism which influenced Milton and distinguished the Reformation as a whole was the emphasis suddenly concentrated on the sermon, the tract and the pamphlet.

The insistent voice of the preacher and the persuasive rhetoric of the pamphleteer transferred attention from the priest at the altar to the individual orator in the pulpit. The consolidation of the sacred office into the performance of ceremonial acts had been redeemed for the moment in the creative activity of the sermon. In fact, scripture as expounded by the preacher, or the word along with the sacraments, was considered by Luther and certain other reformers the means of grace.[32] However, because of the sacramental character which the "word" retained, it was not the free utterance of the prophet on which Blake insisted. Freedom of utterance was only possible when the preacher re-created the literal sense of scripture by means of his spiritual vision or "conscience" and did not force his discourse to conform to a sacred code independent of conscience: "The Bible or Peculiar Word of God, Exclusive of Conscience or the Word of God Universal, is that Abomination, which, like the Jewish ceremonies, is forever removed & henceforth every man may converse with God & be a King & Priest in his own house."[33] It would be doing the reformers an injustice to assume that they considered the word of the preacher to be merely an exposition of scripture. Luther explicitly condemned both Zwingli and Oecolampadius for maintaining that it was only an external symbol or sign and not a direct vehicle of the Spirit. He seemed at times to exalt the spoken word of the preacher above the written word of the scriptures, to suggest that revealed scripture received its sanction from the sacramental act of preaching. The sermon which Catholic Christianity had regarded as a devotional act was fast becoming the central sacrament of the Reformed church. Luther and Calvin bound the human word of the preacher so in-

[32]Cf. Martin Luther, *Colloquia Mensalia*, trans. Capt. Henry Bell (2nd ed., London, 1791, chap. 1, p. 14: "But [said Luther] I say, teach and acknowledge that the Preacher's words, his absolutions, and the sacraments, are not his words nor works, but they are God's words, works, cleansing, absolving, binding, &c.; we are but only the instruments, fellow-workers, or God's assistants, through whom God worketh and finisheth his work." Calvin's statement on the same subject illustrates a similar emphasis. "Wee have set for signes to discerne the church by, the preaching of the word and the observing of the Sacraments. For those can bee no where but they must bring forth fruit, and be prospered with the blessing of God. I doe not say, that wheresoever the word is preached, there by and by springeth up fruit: but I say that no where it is received and hath a stayed seate, but that it bringeth forth the effectualnesse thereof." John Calvin, *The Institute of Christian Religion*, trans. Thomas Norton (London, 1634), Book IV, chap. 1, sec. 10, pp. 501–2 (see also sec. 5 *passim*).

[33]*Annotations to Watson's "Apology for the Bible,"* pp. 8–9. Cf. *All Religions are One:* "The Jewish & Christian Testaments are An Original derivation from the Poetic Genius . . . ."

tegrally to the sacramental word of God, both written and unwritten,[34] that the preacher was in danger of becoming the passive oracle of the mysterious workings of divine Providence.

Blake chose to see in Milton not the oracular prophet who considered himself merely a vehicle for the source of his inspiration, but a literal prophet in whose "Conscience" the "Word of God Universal" was liberated by the imaginative activity of re-creating the literal sense of scripture in his epic verse.[35] He did not think of Milton as a theologian lost in the maze of disputation, quoting authorities and proving points of doctrine, but as a prophet for whom the prayer of the devotee, the word of the preacher, the inspiration of the poet and the free speech of the citizen were the gifts of the spirit of God liberated from outward ceremony.

> In vain, therefore, do they pretend to want utterance in prayer, who can find utterance to preach. And if prayer be the gift of the Spirit, why do they admit those to the ministry who want a main gift of their function, and prescribe gifted men to use that which is the remedy of another man's want; setting them their tasks to read, whom the Spirit of God stands ready to assist in his ordinance with the gift of free conceptions?[36]

It was precisely in the gift of free conceptions, or what Blake called the Poetic Genius and imagination, that Milton found his freedom which contained the sum and essence of the moral, ceremonial and judicial laws. He did not abrogate the law as Luther claimed to have done, any more than Blake himself abrogated the "reason" which was the ratio or outer bound of aspiration and desire, but he found direct access to the spirit within the letter of the law in his conception of Christian liberty.

[34]Both in the written and the spoken Gospel, it was the Holy Spirit who spoke, and the voice of the preacher was also the voice of God. "I am sure and certain [said Luther] when I go up to the pulpit, or to the cathedral to preach or read, that it is not my word which I speak, but my tongue is the pen of a ready writer, as the Psalmist saith: The holy men of God spake as they were moved by the Holy Ghost. Therefore we must not separate nor part God and man according to our natural reason and understanding. In like manner, every hearer must conclude and say, I hear not St. Paul, St. Peter, or a man speak; but I hear God himself speak, baptize, absolve, excommunicate, and administer the holy sacraments of the Lord's supper." Luther, *Colloquia Mensalia*, trans. Bell, p. 14.

[35]Cf. Milton, *De Doctrina Christiana*, lib. I, cap. xxx: "No passage of Scripture is to be interpreted in more than one sense; in the Old Testament, however, this sense is sometimes a compound of the historical and typical."

[36]Milton, *An Apology for Smectymnuus*.

Milton represented the return to the original prophetic word which, along with inspiration, was identical in his mind with the "liberty to know, to utter."[37] For him once more, the emphasis was placed on the inner word of God and its particular manifestation in the revealed word of scripture. The allegory of the church or the projection into a historical institution of that word had come to be regarded in Catholic Christianity as the way of approaching revelation and the mysteries of the faith. The writings of the prophets came to be interpreted as though the church were a rule unto itself, and had not received its rule originally from the word of free inspiration.[38] In this way, the outward ceremony became the law and the prophets, but Blake rejected the attempt throughout the history of organized religion to substitute religious allegory, the analogy of vision, for the vision itself. He therefore rejected the priestly art and everything connected with it.[39] The notion that a symbolism, by being adopted by a cult, could be the means of reproducing the visionary insight of which it had been the original expression was repugnant to him. It was not repugnant, however, that a work of art should do this, since such a work did not enslave the beholder by pretending to be more than it was—the end-product of creative activity. He associated the rebirth of art in the Renaissance with the renewed emphasis on the word of scripture and the oratory of the preacher. The imaginative freedom of the one and the imaginative freedom of the other were enslaved in his eyes by the pursuit of a systematic rationale of the sphere of fallen nature in philosophy, and of the sphere of divine grace in deism and natural religion.

Luther and Calvin provided a momentary renewal of the oral tradition of the preaching friars and the monastic teachers of the mediaeval period, which shattered the external allegory of the church. But Blake considered Calvin and Luther to have fallen from the literal and individual significance of the scriptures into the dogmatic and moral retrenchment under political authority. The Christian religion was consolidated on its literal level into the warring sects of Protestantism, and the real apocalyptic revolution was effectively

[37]*Areopagitica*. As the prototype of the prophetic word, Christ united preaching with the act of liberation (Luke iv: 18; Isa. lxi: 1–2) and, by implication, with the entire prophetic succession.

[38]Milton, *De Doctrina Christiana*, lib. I, cap. xxx.

[39]*Annotations to Swedenborg's "Divine Love and Wisdom,"* p. 181: "The Whole of the New Church is in the Active Life & not in Ceremonies at all." *The Laocoön Group*: "The outward Ceremony is Antichrist."

avoided. In his own day Blake hoped for such a revolution, and in his eagerness to discern the signs of its approach, he saw in the social upheavals of Methodism, the American and the French revolutions the awakening from the outward ceremony which bound politics and religion together to form the conspiracy of authority and convention. He put into the mouth of Los, the spirit of prophecy, this vision of hope, as he re-created in *Milton* the earlier poet's conception of Christian liberty which had remained unfulfilled in the premature fury of the Reformation.

> Remember how Calvin and Luther in fury premature
> Sow'd War and stern division between Papists & Protestants.
> Let it not be so now! O go not forth in Martyrdoms & Wars!
> We were plac'd here by the Universal Brotherhood & Mercy
> With powers fitted to circumscribe this dark Satanic death . . .[40]

The "dark Satanic death" is man's fallen state and what he sees because of it—the world of "nature." It can only be circumscribed by the observer who has ceased to be utterly dependent on the fixed ratio of the corporeal senses. He cannot do this by means of a religion of allegory and abstract doctrine, but neither can he do it by means of experiment and the empirical generalizations of the natural philosopher. Both of these means ignore the inner powers to which Blake refers—the four faculties or "Zoas" of the prophetic books.

With the decline of authority of the church and the growth of a sceptical attitude towards its allegory, the Christian sects of the Reformation moved away from allegorical illustration to factual and natural adaptation of revealed truth. The result was a further retreat from prophetic religion into the realm of natural religion. Natural religion was, in fact, implicit in all religious allegory, for allegory turned two ways: first, towards the original vision of which it was the expression, and secondly, towards the natural understanding to which it was adapted and from which it derived its imagery for purposes of communication. Allegory also tended to produce identification of the believer with the pattern of his mythology after the manner of the older mystery religions, and by so doing, tended to "Vegetate the Divine Vision."[41] What Blake called the "eternal attributes" of human

[40]*Milton*, 25: 47–51.
[41]*Jerusalem*, 90: 41. Cf. *A Descriptive Catalogue &c.*, Keynes, p. 601.

existence, or the "divine names" could thereby become gods as objects of worship and heroes as objects of emulation. The fanatical devotee could even identify himself with them and be that kind of a maniac who saw himself as his favourite character in religious myth. This was the blasphemy of the natural Selfhood which sought to appropriate what belonged to universal humanity to itself.

> Los cries: "No Individual ought to appropriate to Himself
> Or to his Emanation any of the Universal Characteristics
> Of David or of Eve, of the Woman or of the Lord,
> Of Reuben or of Benjamin, of Joseph or Judah or Levi.
> Those who dare appropriate to themselves Universal Attributes
> Are the Blasphemous Selfhoods, & must be broken asunder."[42]

The appropriation might be extended to one's favourite character in history or literature or even to one's self-portrait, for Blake regarded the whole of man's fallen condition as varying degrees of this madness. The mere fact that the natural man or "Selfhood" always, or at least usually, identified himself with his own role in life subjected him to it and to the Circle of Destiny. Freedom from this fate was the ability to see as vision what was habitually accepted as natural necessity.

The religion of allegory was the contrary of the religion of prophetic vision, and natural religion was its negation. Druidism began, like all cults, as an original derivation from the "Poetic Genius"—the everlasting gospel—and then became a system of allegoric fable which finally confused the prophetic insight of its ancient seers with a ritual of sacrificial atonement. In mediaeval Christianity the same process of separating allegory from vision was apparent. The allegorical mysteries of the faith had been interpreted originally by the rule of right reason, but the rightness of the reason was later based on a doctrinal exegesis accepted by ecclesiastical authority and supported by political power. The practice of a deceit which failed to deceive could not completely survive the intellectual force of the Renaissance and the invention of printing. No sooner had the Reformation accomplished its purpose than the natural light of the new science began to discredit any authority but reason and the senses. Religious allegory was critically examined with reference to natural fact as the approved source of data, and deism signalized the turning to the mysteries of nature, reason and commonsense.

[42]*Jerusalem*, 90: 28–33.

Blake's own attitude towards established Christianity was not that of a heretic who made use of Christian myth to express a rival theological system, but that of a prophet who pointed out that those he called the "Elect" had taken over the Christian religion. His main objection to the allegory of the church was not on the grounds of theological doctrine, but on the grounds that it was merely a husk of original vision with no exclusive right to the title of inspired truth. "That the Jews assumed a right Exclusively to the benefits of God will be a lasting witness against them & the same will it be against Christians."[43] The Christian church was not what it claimed to be: the only vehicle of the word of God universal. For just as the individual could appropriate universal characteristics, so also could communities, races and churches, and so had the Christian church. It had fallen from the vision of the seer into the allegory of the priest whose authority was already being challenged by reason and the new science.

[43]*Annotations to Watson's "Apology for the Bible,"* pp. 7–8.

4. Reason and the New Science

BLAKE RESISTS the tendency of the theologian to lift the vision of God out of its context in the individual perception of the prophet and apostle of the faith, and then exalt it into the authoritative mysteries of the church. He also resists the tendency of the rationalist to lift the vision of nature out of its context in the perception of the individual natural philosopher, and then exalt it into the fixed and unalterable world of natural law. The theologian circumscribes the bounds of heaven by placing the arbitrary limits of his revealed dogma to the appetites of the human soul. The rationalist also circumscribes the bounds of earth by the arbitrary limits of theories and hypotheses. As a theologian, Thomas Aquinas was a rationalist who implemented a revealed doctrine, and he aspired to a transcendent Deity through Aristotle's concept of a "First Cause." This mysterious and super-rational abstraction gave the church the lead in making a system of logic into a system of the universe. The trick was quickly learned by the secular successors and rivals of the scholastic philosophers. The rationalism of the new science made experiment the absolute test of truth; but experiment is limited to the senses, and any reasonable picture of nature must discard as utterly unreliable, and even as impossible, any other kind of perception than that of the organs of sense. The logic of experiment becomes the definitive system of natural reality, and represents a further limitation of man's possibilities. "The desires & perceptions of man, untaught by any thing but organs of sense, must be limited to objects of sense."[1] That he may have some indication of his possibilities, he must first realize that his natural condition is relative and not absolute and unalterable. He must place himself under what Blake calls the "Prophetic character." Otherwise, the relative and the changing in his natural state of "Generation" will consolidate and become absolute for him, and he will find himself repeating "the same dull round over again": "If it were not for the Poetic

[1] *There is no Natural Religion*, I.

or Prophetic character the Philosophic & Experimental would soon be at the ratio of all things, & stand still, unable to do other than repeat the same dull round over again."[2] If what can be changed in man's relationship to his life and his environment remains fixed by the exaggerated inertia of reasonable convictions and conventional commitments, then the risk of turning round indefinitely on the wheel of fate or the circle of destiny becomes greater. For the nature of life cannot be learned by experiment alone, or by what is called experience, and any system of nature or belief which makes it difficult or impossible to see this renders the observer absolutely passive to the conditions in which he finds himself.

Confronted by the apparently unyielding outline of the Newtonian system of nature, Blake can hardly be blamed for despairing of any revolutionary change of outlook in that sphere. The natural philosopher quickly assumed that Newton's description of the world was absolute—in spite of Newton himself—and Blake can only caricature the result in the "Newton" of his prophetic books. His main point, however, is not the need for constant change in the observer's approach to the data of experiment, but the need for the far more radical transformation of the observer's entire angle of vision. It is this ability to change the perspective which distinguishes the "Prophetic character." The experimentalist, however, is betrayed by the logic of his method into making an absolute description out of a collection of experiments, as though he had already arrived "at the ratio of all things." This process consolidates the immediate vision of nature, seen through the organs of perception, into the closed world of nature as formulated by reason and experiment.

The conception of a closed universe may satisfy man's reason, but it fails to satisfy his desires and, in fact, leaves them entirely out of account. Placing the emotions and appetites beneath reason and reason's system of nature can lead only to progressive frustration. "The bounded is loathed by its possessor. The same dull round, even of a universe, would soon become a mill with complicated wheels."[3] In Blake's opinion, the description which the natural philosopher gives of the

[2]*Ibid.* The "Prophetic character" keeps the observer in Generation, but the "Experimental" keeps verging towards what Blake calls the state of "Ulro" where all development or change is rendered impossible by the fixed and unalterable outlook of the observer.

[3]*Ibid,* II.

universal machinery fails to separate the activity of perception from mechanical functions, and yet a complete account of the universe cannot be subtracted from a description of how it is perceived. Unlike the mechanist, Blake distinguishes the psychic functions of love and hate from the motor reflexes of attraction and repulsion. Underlying the organs of sensation are the faculties of perception, and man's perceptions are not ultimately limited to the senses. "Man's perceptions are not bounded by organs of perception; he perceives more than sense (tho' ever so acute) can discover."[4] Even if man's perceptions are bounded by his organs of perception, they are still more bounded by the rational limitations which he has imposed upon them. The phenomena he does manage to perceive are conditioned by the limitations which Blake calls the "ratio." The ratio gives the impression that there is a constant relationship between perceiver and perceived, and the observer can too easily assume that the terms of this relationship are final. If he does so, he closes himself up within his own reflections and reduces himself and his environment to a perfectly ordered and rational cosmos. The tendency to limit and perfect—once and for all—summarizes Blake's view of this kind of thinking and dictates his method of attack which emphasizes emotion and instinct at the expense of the exclusive use of rational means.

Desire or aspiration signifies man's assurance of growth as well as his hope of fulfilment. If the ratio of what has already been possessed is regarded as the fixed limit of his perceptions, he turns away from his inner possibilities or the "Divine Vision" and, observing the ratio only, sees the limits of the universe in terms of the limitations of his own organic perceptions. In other words, he becomes no more than the organ subject to sense-data which he calls the world of nature. Although his desires are limited by his perceptions—since none can desire what he has not perceived—the insatiable nature of even these natural desires and a fundamental discontent indicate to Blake the infinite possession of which man is the lost heir. "The desire of Man being Infinite, the possession is Infinite & himself Infinite."[5] Man's infinite desire can be reflected in the free and open pursuit of knowledge

[4]*Ibid.*

[5]*Ibid.* Compare with this Blake's assertion, in *The Marriage of Heaven and Hell* (Keynes, p. 187), that he printed with "corrosives," by this means "melting apparent surfaces away, and displaying the infinite which was hid."

by the philosopher, but it is actually realized by the seer who is unrestricted by "reasonable" preconceptions. The freedom of the prophet enables him to see through the boundary of the ratio towards the vision of the infinite. Nature itself becomes a vast symbolism which points to its infinite environment—Eternal Existence or "God." "He who sees the Infinite in all things, sees God. He who sees the Ratio only, sees himself only."[6]

Fundamentally, the fixed world of nature is the fixed ratio established between subject and object, and is based on the state or condition of the subjective observer. That growth which is the possession of the seer finds its source in the continued aspiration to see the world of nature as perceived by the imagination and not as conceived by the reason reflecting the ratio. Perception, in this sense, is intensified by means of the imagination, and nature begins to be seen as a vision in the context of unconfined development within the visionary. Blake assumes that some men are aware of their greater possibilities, and desire to realize them. It is to this desire that he refers, and he attributes man's unsatisfied corporeal desires, imprisonment in which is his definition of hell, to his turning away from the "Divine Vision" and his absorption in himself and in the natural world which his limited senses can perceive.[7]

The natural philosopher overcomes the technical limitations of the senses by apparatus, controlled experiment and the application of mathematical norms to his observations. But he does all this by accepting the ratio between himself and his field of observation as invariable and final. There is nothing in the way the Newtonian picture of the world is usually received to suggest a theory of relativity. In fact, the mathematical universe of Pythagoras and Plato becomes an inheritance which is not adopted as the symbol of a heightened degree of intellectual perception, but is directly applied to empirical observation on what Plato would have called the level of appearances. Blake finds it hard to forgive Plato for providing the heirs of the new science with the picture of this kind of universe which has an absolutely

[6]*There is no Natural Religion*, II.

[7]In the third night of *The Four Zoas*, Blake describes the fall of intellect who is Urizen. Urizen's consort, Ahania or Wisdom, warns him not to abandon direction to the charge of Desire (Luvah) who has already turned away from the Divine Vision into Generation. She warns him against the intoxication of the "wine presses" of Luvah (*ibid.*, III, 26–35) lest the "Divine Vision & Fruition" be obliterated.

commensurable structure. The myth of Plato's *Timaeus* has been taken out of the context of the dialectical method, and is being used in a way which, in the opinion of Blake, gives the ratio an abstract validity apart from even the senses. The ratio which is the measure of man's restriction to the senses has become the basis for his interpretation of the world.

In his *Timaeus*, Plato developed the distinction between the sphere of being and that of becoming at some length. Being was changeless, eternal and apprehensible only to thought; becoming was changing, non-eternal and apprehensible to sensation. In its effective application, Blake sees the ontological basis of Plato's world as the ratio abstracted from sensation. What Plato apparently called being, he considers a descent from the world of becoming and growth into the abyss of abstraction. What has become, it is true, can be measured, but what is becoming and is about to become in the future should not be anticipated positively and rationally—if man is to free his powers of perception, and not make a fixed ratio of them.[8] Blake's disagreement with what had come to be accepted as the fundamental contribution of Greek thought places him in an antagonistic position toward the rational tradition of his day. His somewhat irritating dislike of mathematics can be traced to this conviction that the commensurable structure of the philosopher's world is made to follow the pattern of his geometry.

It has already been noticed that there are many points of similarity between the cosmology of Plato and that of Blake. Plato's mythical figure of the Demiurge—who is apparently the incarnation of reason—corresponds to Blake's Urizen. The difference lies in the fundamental emphasis which Blake places on the creative imagination as the first principle of perception. The principle of order or "reason" considered as the principle of ordering what is perceived is creative only when it is subordinated to the root of perception. When it usurps first place and conditions perception, it ceases to be creative, for it limits the growth

[8]In the second book of *Milton* (35: 17–20), Blake speaks of the effect of retaining a belief in an invariable ratio of conditions. The effect is a loss of conscious life, and those who remain under such a Satanic tyranny are described as

> " . . . Shapeless Rocks
> Retaining only Satan's Mathematic Holiness, Length, Bredth & Highth,
> Calling the Human Imagination, which is the Divine Vision & Fruition
> In which Man liveth eternally, madness & blasphemy . . ."

of perception, until what is perceived is assumed to be the limit of the possible. When this assumption has become a conditioned reflex, as it were, the perceiver finds himself in a world of apparently fixed and unalterable conditions which he "discovers" as laws of nature. What Plato described in his *Timaeus* as creation in terms of the operation of reason, Blake describes in his *First Book of Urizen* as the mythical fall of man—also in terms of the operation of reason. But Plato subordinated necessity to reason, the sphere of efficient causes to that of final causes, the physical processes of the natural world to the light of reason in man. Blake considers final causes to have been derived from efficient causes by means of abstraction, and relegates the conception of causality to the logic of abstract reasoning.[9] For him, the sphere of efficient causes is the state of Generation or becoming; and that of final causes is the state of "Hell" or "Eternal Death" where the "become," or the Aristotelian *telos*, has limited the process of growth itself. In spite of the similarities between the Platonic mythology and his own, he pointedly refuses to accept the teleological approach of rationalism.

In harmony with his teleological approach, Plato described the construction of the universe, with the Demiurge as architect and Necessity as contractor. The cosmos was made to follow the order and harmony of a rational master builder in the beginning.

> And thus far, a few particulars excepted, have we shown the fabrications of intellect. But it is likewise requisite to give a place in our discourse to the productions of necessity. For, the generation of the world being mingled, it was produced from the composition of intellect and necessity. But intellect ruling over necessity persuaded it to lead the most part of generated natures to that which is best; and hence necessity being vanquished by wise persuasion, from these two as principles the world arose. If, then, any one truly asserts that the universe was generated according to these, he should also mingle with it the form of an erratic cause, which it is naturally adapted to receive.[10]

[9]Cf. *Milton*, 44 ff. Both Plato and Blake attribute all natural effects to spiritual causes, but Plato's rational *method* disguises the poverty of natural reason to discover what lies beyond the field of natural perception.

[10]*Timaeus*, cap. XVII, 48A (*Works*, trans. Thomas Taylor, London, 1804, II, p. 520). In the earlier work, *The Four Zoas*, Blake's Demiurge is the fallen reason (II, 376–9) or Urizen.

> Then rose the Builders. First the Architect divine his plan
> Unfolds. The wondrous scaffold rear'd all round the infinite,
> Quadrangular the building rose, the heavens squared by a line,
> Trigons & cubes divide the elements in finite bonds.

Cf. Milton, *Paradise Lost*, VII, 221–31; Isa. xl: 12. The mathematical physics of Newton is reflected

The tendency of rationalism to make the universe conform to the categories of thought is implicit in this passage. Although Plato made every effort to protect his conception of reason from being confused with discursive reason or mere opinion, the confusion is bound to occur—from Blake's point of view—when the intuitive perception of truth is not emphasized, but rather the means of formulating it. In short, the technics of thought which Plato developed provide the rational means of formulating the end of knowledge without altering human perception in any way. This formulation of the end of knowledge was carried to its logical conclusion by Aristotle—whom Blake scarcely mentions[11]—and his search for the ultimate *summa* of science took the form of a categorical classification of things in terms of essential and non-essential qualities. But Aristotle was a biologist, and his qualitative science was in abeyance during Blake's lifetime. It is the stress laid on number, weight and measure, derived from the Pythagorean tradition, which Blake associates with Greek ways of thought.[12] That is what makes him see in Greek life an obsession with law, both in the ethical and the metaphysical spheres of speculation. To this obsession with the notion of a commensurable universe comprehensible to the natural reason, he attributes the growth of a naturalistic spirit and an implicit denial of all but organic perceptions. Perception through the five organs of sensation, however, is considered to be better than the abstract knowledge of physical laws and moral duties which follows the assumptions of rational generalization.

In the realm of religion, as already outlined, the ecclesiastical cult was first formed when the original "Divine Vision" became an invisible mystery. In the realm of philosophy, the speculative system was first formed when the same "Vision" became an invisible first cause. Blake was painfully aware that his contemporaries in their haste to get rid

---

in Blake's description of the Urizenic universe (*The Four Zoas*, II, 477–94). But in the later work, *Jerusalem*, the Demiurgic activity is transferred to Los, the symbol of imagination and vision. Along with his spectre and emanation, Los is represented as creating the world of time and space. Perhaps the later work indicates a more sympathetic reading of the Platonic myth. See *Jerusalem*, 91: 31–52, where Los, the visionary, is represented as altering his "Spectre" (50–2) in the apocalyptic movement from fixed temporal conditions—or "every Ratio of his Reason"—to eternal life.

[11]*Marriage of Heaven and Hell*, Keynes, p. 190.

[12]Cf. A. Wolf, *A History of Science, Technology and Philosophy in 16th & 17th Centuries* (London, 1935), pp. 4 ff. See also *The Laocoön Group*: "The Gods of Greece & Egypt were Mathematical Diagrams—See Plato's Works."

of these invisible and mysterious hypotheses were in the process of abandoning themselves to a mechanical order of nature. The deist had cut away the mysteries of the supernatural, but he still retained the husk of moral virtue. The natural philosopher had turned away from the mediaeval version of Aristotelian rationalism, but he had turned towards an *a priori* conviction of the mechanistic structure of the natural world. Blake faced a dilemma: he could not support the ecclesiastical institution of Christianity, but neither could he support its deistical precipitate—natural religion. He rebelled against the arid rationalism of the schoolmen, but he could not accept the mathematical rationalism of Newton nor the empiricism of Bacon. It is not surprising that he thought of his position as "The Voice of one crying in the Wilderness." In his argument to *All Religions are One*, he writes: "As the true method of knowledge is experiment, the true faculty of knowing must be the faculty which experiences. This faculty I treat of."[13]

The faculty which experiences is, of course, the Poetic Genius or that power of imagination in every man which momentarily unites the rational and appetitive with the physical perceptions and the bodily powers of execution in the creative thought and act of art and science. This "true faculty of knowing" is considered to be the real man, and as such, man is essentially a unity both in himself and in his relationship to others. The development of society and of the individual is in direct proportion to the realization of this creative genius and this unity. Conversely, individual and social growth is inhibited by any system of thought or method of experiment which implicitly destroys man's conviction of, and hence his ability to realize, his spiritual birthright.

The mechanistic view of the universe concentrates attention on man as a child of nature and eliminates his spiritual status. Blake sometimes makes the casual reader suppose that he confuses rationalism and mechanism; yet it is not an identity but a close relationship which he suggests. To him, rational generalization abstracts the sphere of nature from the human observer, in the hope of achieving a knowledge of reality undistorted by subjective fantasy. The natural philosopher, however, produces a more perverse distortion than the one he seeks

[13]It must be remembered that "imagination" is defined as the "Human Existence itself," and the term evidently embraces consciousness, whether potential or actual.

to avoid. His error rests on the fundamental consolidation of the relationship between the observer and what he is able to observe. This relationship is accepted as constant and final, and the scale of observation becomes a fixed context described as "natural." This context is forthwith accepted as the ultimate extent of the field of possible knowledge. Thus the ratio or scale of knowledge available to man in the state of Generation is considered to be unalterable. Technical aids to sense-perception do not alter the basic relationship which establishes the observer's state, although they alter the immediate ratio of the organs of perception.

> The Microscope knows not of this nor the Telescope: they alter
> The ratio of the Spectator's Organs, but leave Objects untouch'd.[14]

Objects remain untouched, because the aspect from which they are viewed remains the same. Alteration of perspective is effectively prevented by the definitive nature of rational generalization and the outlook which it develops.

Plato said that the universe was a compound of reason and necessity. In the mythology of Blake, Urizen, the type of reason, who draws the circle of destiny about the universe, is both architect and engineer whose twelve sons are the signs of the zodiac, and who labours to subdue the clash of forces so that he may effectively run the cosmic machinery.[15] The mathematical science of the eighteenth century was, after all, an inheritance from Greek rationalism. This inheritance, however, was divided between those who chose to follow the older organic view and those who chose the simpler, mechanistic outlook. Plato's dialectic was teleological and homocentric, but from Democritus to Epicurus and Lucretius, a trend of thought developed which concentrated on efficient causes and an atomistic approach.[16] Indeed, from the mediaeval period to the end of the eighteenth century, European science moved more decidedly from "reason" to "necessity," from rationalism to mechanism. According to Blake, the process was simply one of disclosing the underlying implications of rationalism. Just as a religion which worshipped a mysterious God was finally unmasked as

[14]*Milton*, 31: 17–18.

[15]*The Four Zoas*, VIIa, 90–1; VIIb, 168–84. Los, the visionary seer, invariably counteracts the work of Urizen, supplanting the mechanical ratio of the heavens with living proportion (VIIa, 465–6):

> Dividing into just proportions, Los unwearied labour'd
> The immortal lines upon the heavens . . .

[16]Cf. Wolf, *History of Science, Technology and Philosophy*, p. 5.

deism or nature-worship, so also, by a more devious route, the rationalism of Plato descended through Aristotle to the mediaeval scholastics, and although apparently rejected by the new science, provided the basis for mechanism.

It would appear that mechanism arose in the mind of the experimentalist a little before he had transferred his sense of the mysterious and the desirable from the works of divine grace to the works of nature. As the interest of the European mind shifted from a preoccupation with the super-rational Deity towards a preoccupation with the data of experiment, there was a period when the natural reason of man enjoyed a special pre-eminence. The time of its gestation was from Bacon to Descartes, and the fulfilment came with Newton and Locke. The former reduced the world to reasonable dimensions, and the latter made man the mirror of nature. Blake lived in the wake of this period, and his writings express the restless intensity of his revolt against it. He was in the habit of laying charges against the new movement in thought by way of its established heroes. In one of Crabb Robinson's opaque conversations with him, Blake is reported to have said: "Bacon, Locke and Newton are the three great teachers of Atheism, or Satan's Doctrine."[17] To this statement, he added his definition of "Atheism": "Everything is Atheism which assumes the reality of the natural and unspiritual world."[18] When such an assumption was made, reason as the instrument of knowledge turned from revelation to experiment.

Thomas Aquinas and the mediaeval thinkers emphasized the reality of the natural world only as the creation of a supernal Deity. He was the true object of reverence, and in so far as he had revealed himself in his Word, the supreme object of scientific inquiry. Reason alone was inadequate for this higher task. The page of revealed truth and the light of divine grace corrected the *ratio naturalis*, and transformed it into the *recta ratio* of the Christian thinker. Right reason survived until the time of Milton as the means whereby the rationalist could learn to know God aright. But when theology ceased to be the synthesis of the sciences, reason ceased to be the instrument of a divine grace, and the Reformed churches turned away from the rationalistic approach of mediaeval Catholicism. The natural world was gradually being

[17]H. Crabb Robinson, *Diary, Reminiscences and Correspondence*, ed. T. Sadler (Boston, 1869) II, chap. II, p. 27.

[18]*Ibid.*

granted an autonomy, and the natural man a prerogative within the universal order of creation. Throwing off the allegory of the church, the secular thinker turned from the *recta ratio* to the *ratio mathematica* to correct and establish the order of his observations. From this kind of mathematical universe to a mechanistic one, there was hardly a step.

Aristotle had originally developed the technics of an organic view which reflected his interest in biology. In one of the prose compositions entitled *A Memorable Fancy*, Blake speaks of bringing in his hand "the skeleton of a body, which in the mill [the reasoning mind] was Aristotle's Analytics."[19] His point is that any philosophy which isolates the logic of classes from the actual perception of particulars takes the life out of thought. Aristotelian logic, as it was taken over by the mediaeval schoolmen, emphasized a mechanism of classification, and like all rational systems was mainly deductive in spirit. As such, it provided the theologian and philosopher with a rational method for the examination of inspired scripture and for the definition of revealed doctrine. It was this inspired scripture, however, which had made the dry bones of the skeleton live, according to Blake. It was inspired scripture which had stressed the point that the natural world was teleologically subordinate to man in the context of his greater destiny. Nature had been created for the sake of man by a super-rational Deity who had conferred upon him, along with the gift of revelation, reason and the senses to make it immediately intelligible. There was, therefore, no mystery about nature, but only about nature's God. Although God was above the reach of discursive reason, the created world was definitely below it, and nature could be examined at once through the categories of thought: substance, essence, form, matter, quality and quantity.

The allegory of the church had given a predominantly human meaning to Aristotelian science. The Reformation was a symptom of the decay of belief in that allegory, and the organic view of the natural world began to pass away along with its rational science. In mediaeval thought, man appeared to be more of an active agent, and nature was passive.[20] Man, if not quite the measure of all things, was at least the

[19]*Marriage of Heaven and Hell*, Keynes, p. 190.

[20]Cf. E. A. Burtt, *Metaphysical Foundations of Modern Physical Science* (New York, 1932), pp. 4 ff.

rationale of all things. Blake agreed with the priority given man as a spiritual being over what he regarded as the fallen world of nature, but he did not agree that the natural man possessed of natural reason was the active agent. He did not, therefore, fall into the trap of the mediaeval thinker who projected his teleological outlook into the phenomena of nature. Regarding nature as immediately intelligible in terms of reason, the latter imposed a subjective pattern of thought on the data of the senses. The reality of objects was what the unaided senses could immediately perceive. Thus, ice, water and steam were severally distinguished as substances, while light and heavy were observed to be qualities. The concept of causality was used to interpret natural phenomena in terms of human purpose, rather than in terms of efficient causes. Heavy objects were thought to tend downward more strongly than light objects, and, hence, to fall faster. The earth itself was the centre of the universe, as it appeared to the eye of the natural man, but the real centre of it was God.

Nothing more strikingly expressed the collapse of this theocentric universe and the homocentric conception of nature than the Copernican revolution in astronomy. When the hypothetical First Cause, or the Divine Sun as Dante envisaged him, gave way before the natural sun of the organic perceptions,[21] the new science turned from the categories of thought toward those which were mathematically commensurable: space, time, mass and energy. This alteration of perspective, although imperceptible in its beginnings, conferred an almost mystical significance on the mathematical formulae which produced certain natural effects. These formulae became the universals of a new logic of experiment, and they eventually provided an apparently positive basis for reorganizing the picture of the world. Blake regarded the new science as a further stage in the imprisonment of the human spirit within the ratio of the five senses. It was, in part, a return to the worship of the Greek gods who were "Mathematical Diagrams."[22] The withdrawal and separation, by the operation of reason, of the commensurable, the

[21]Cf. *Annotations to Swedenborg's "Divine Love and Wisdom,"* p. 133. According to Swedenborg, "The reason why a dead Sun was created is to the End that in the Ultimate all Things may be fixed. . . ." But he added emphatically that "all Things were created from the Lord by the living Sun, *and nothing by the dead Sun*. . . ." Blake's comment follows from his conception of nature as the result of man's limited perceptions through the five senses. "The dead sun is only a phantasy of evil Man."

[22]*The Laocoön Group*.

regular and the predictable for the purpose of systematization, he considered an abstract and dangerous habit of thought. The autonomous science of mathematics was the prototype of all such abstraction, and he viewed with hostility the key role which the *ratio mathematica* took in the development of the European conception of knowledge. With this viewpoint, the sciences could be separated from the evolution of the human spirit and could become the means whereby man's control over other men and the powers of nature would far outstrip his spiritual growth, or even distract him from it. He might even regard such growth as unimportant or too difficult or impossible and the mere figment of the imagination of visionaries!

The transition from the mainly qualitative science of Aristotle to the mainly quantitative one of the Renaissance was, of course, a slow process. The resurgence of the earlier Greek tradition which involved Plato and Pythagoras represented the great stress which was placed on number or quantity by the founders of the new science. This was particularly true of Copernicus and Kepler, whose devotion to the mathematical principles which they applied to the study of astronomy raised it to the height of the first science. Kepler saw the Trinity itself in terms of the astronomical universe, allocating God the Father to the sun, God the Son to the sphere of the fixed stars, and identifying the ethereal medium—which intervened and acted as a kind of *Primum Mobile* impelling the planets around their orbits—with the Holy Ghost.[23] Dante had also established a view of the universe which had represented the spiritual agency of the divine triad, but the celestial spheres were immediately governed by angelic directors. It was only on the border of the universe of matter, in the Crystalline Heaven, that a symbolic picture of God in relation to the celestial spheres was possible.[24] Kepler brought the Deity into the material universe, and

[23]*Opera Omnia*, ed. Frisch (Frankofurti et Erlangae, 1858), I, p. 11: "In globo igitur est trinitas, sphaericum, centrum, capacitas. Sic in mundo quieto, Fixae, Sol, aura sive aethra intermedia: et in Trinitate Filius, Pater, Spiritus."

[24]When Dante gazes into the symbolic image of the point of light with its wheels of fire, he sees the primal triad of angelic orders (*Paradiso*, xxviii, 94–6):

Io sentiva osannar di coro in coro
Al punto fisso che li tiene al li ubi,
E terrà sempre, ne' quai sempre fuoro.

Blake, at the close of his *Vision of the Last Judgment* (Keynes, pp. 651–2), draws a similar distinction between the world of nature and the spiritual world, and asserts that he sees through the one to the other.

there was a noticeable tendency to substantiate the Trinity according to the newer pattern of thought.[25] This was the beginning of what Blake called "Deism" whose followers inferred God from his works.

Kepler asserted that the discovery of mathematical causes was the way to truth for the philosopher, and that all certain and perfect knowledge was mathematical. Quantity was the fundamental feature of things, and he placed it prior to the other Aristotelian categories. He even used the quotation from Plato that God ever geometrizes to show that the human mind is created in such a way that it can only know by quantity.[26] His greatest contribution to the thought of his day was his insistence upon the principle of verifying any mathematical hypothesis by means of direct observation.

It was not surprising that the eager followers of the new science tended to abandon logic for factual data, and to become more absorbed in the collection of facts than in the rational synthesis of them. Following Blake's own line of thought, it was inevitable that the science which had emancipated itself from any kind of revealed doctrine—let alone what he calls "inspiration"—should consolidate out of the chaos of a somewhat uncritical empiricism a mechanistic order of nature. But the first reaction against the deductive logic of Aristotle in favour of an emphasis on induction and experiment was gradually adjusted to that

[25]*Opera Omnia*, I, p. 11: "Sic igitur Sol in media mobilium quietus ipse et tamen fons motus, gerit imaginem Dei patris creatoris. Nam quod est Deo creatio, hoc est Soli motus. Movet autem in fixis, ut pater in filio creat."

[26]In a letter (April 9, 1597), Kepler asserted his conviction that the human mind was capable of knowing the world by quantity and not by quality: "—atque adeo ut vel tandem homo suae mentis vires justo modulo metiatur et intelligat, cum Deus omnia ad quantitatis normas condiderit in toto mundo, mentem etiam homini datam, quae talia comprehendat. Nam ut oculos ad colores, auris ad sonos, ita mens hominis non ad quaevis, sed ad quanta intelligenda condita est, remque quamlibet tanto rectius percipit, quanto illa proprior est nudis quantitatibus, ceu suae origini: ab his quo longius quidlibet recedit, tanto plus tenebrarum et errorum existit." *Ibid.*, pp. 31–2. The authority of Plato was sometimes invoked on behalf of this view, but in the *Republic*, he placed mathematical studies in the same class as that knowledge which came from opinion. It was the dialectic alone which awakened the "eye" of the soul. "This at least no one, said I, will dispute with us: That no other method can attempt to comprehend, in an orderly way, what each particular being is; for all the other arts respect either the opinions or desires of men, or generations, and compositions, or are all employed in the culture of things generated and compounded. Those others, which we said participated somewhat of being, geometry and such as are connected with her, we see as dreaming indeed about being; but it is impossible for them to have a true vision, so long as employing hypotheses they preserve these immoveable, without being able to assign a reason for their subsistence." *Republic*, VII, xiii, 533C ff., in *Works*, trans. Taylor, I, pp. 377–8.

logical balance between the two which came to form the basis of the scientific method of Newton. Blake saw Bacon, however, as the speculative predecessor of Newton, and he usually placed him in the company of Newton and Locke to represent that system of nature which completed the definitive "Philosophy of Five Senses."[27]

There is evidence that Blake read the *Advancement of Learning*, but, with one exception,[28] none of his comments on it survive. In one respect, Bacon appeared to be a better choice than either of the others. Theoretically, neither Newton nor Locke eliminated Providence from the sphere of the natural world. Even Kepler had interpreted planetary movements in terms of the activity of celestial intelligence. Bacon dismissed the notion of a super-rational First Cause, and stated that there was neither a divine mind nor a rational mind attendant on the processes or "forms" of nature.[29] Investigation of nature would eventually yield a knowledge of these forms and would alone reveal an autonomous world of matter whose motions, for all practical purposes, were inherent within itself. He repudiated completely the various philosophic systems which were the rational analogies of the vision of the seer—such as immanentism, transcendentalism, pantheism and theism—and he prepared the way for the complete absorption of the sciences in the realm of efficient causes.

The effect of Bacon, or rather of the scientific naturalism of which he was finally the consecrated spokesman, decapitated scholastic

[27] *The Song of Los*, 48.

[28] Letter to Trusler, Aug. 23, 1799. The quotation, along with its context, suggests that imagination co-ordinates sensation and reason, and also that it precedes the voluntary or appetitive and the rational or discursive. Thus, affection or the will is brought into harmony with reason. "For Imagination ever precedeth Voluntary Motion. Saving that this Janus of Imagination hath differing faces; for the face towards Reason, hath the print of Truth. But the face towards Action, hath the print of Good. . . ." *Advancement of Learning* (1605), p. 47. Blake would find this conception of the imagination congenial. He also thinks of imagination as the co-ordinating faculty (Urthona or Los) but, as noted earlier in this chapter, it is, in addition, the "Human Existence" which perceives more than sense or reason can ever discover. Imagination as vision itself is more than a co-ordinating faculty. Cf. *Annotations to Reynolds's "Discourses,"* p. 244.

[29] E.g. *On the Interpretation of Nature*, cap. 1 (*Works*, ed. R. L. Spedding, J. Ellis and D. D. Heath (London, 1857–74), III, p. 218): "For if any man shall think by view and inquiry into these sensible and material things, to attain to any light for the revealing of the nature or will of God, he shall dangerously abuse himself." Bacon was certainly no Deist! Blake could hardly object to his forthright rejection of any "natural religion," but it was the Baconian outlook, with its concentration on the effects of nature, which contradicted and opposed the prophetic discipline. For a summary of Bacon's position, see F. H. Anderson, *The Philosophy of Francis Bacon* (Chicago, 1948), chap. XXV *passim*.

rationalism. The ontological proof of God tended to disappear, and the existence of a creator became a matter of inference from design in nature. By the end of the seventeenth century, the system of Aristotle had been more or less rejected, and Platonism had either been absorbed into the Cartesian tradition or been isolated from the main stream of thought. The Reformers, for the most part, had turned from a theological rationalism towards an individualistic and atomistic approach to religion. Religion as the history of individual emotion and as the pious success-story of the devotee's good works took the place of the theologies of Luther and Calvin. The undercurrent of "enthusiasm" was submerged in England, for the time being, to emerge early in the eighteenth century with the preaching of Wesley and Whitefield. The terms "reason" and "rationalism" ceased to have any connection with the ontology of the schools, and became associated with the "enlightened" man's acceptance of a vast cosmology based on physics which as a first philosophy, took the place of the mediaeval science of theology.

The emphasis on experiment and the interest in the operations of the human mind from an experimental point of view appealed to Blake, but like other interests and pursuits of the eighteenth century, he found that they formed a parody of his own conception of experiment. As he understood it, experiment was not a lottery for establishing a pattern of natural effects, but a discipline of growth which culminated in a more advanced degree of conscious existence. To abstract from an awareness of thought, emotion and sensation what could be weighed and measured was to reduce the whole truth available to the human faculties as such to the "ratio of the five senses." This kind of "Error or Experiment"[30] eliminated the very existence of the human observer, and made the natural philosopher dismiss those qualities of objects, such as colour and texture, which were derived from his unfortunate presence. The primary or commensurable qualities of things were real, and the secondary qualities merely derivative. The new revelation was limited to a collection of mathematical norms which "corrected" man's perception of nature and his understanding of himself.

Deduct from a rose its redness, from a lilly its whiteness, from a diamond its hardness, from a spunge its softness, from an oak its heighth, from a daisy its lowness, &

[30]*Vision of the Last Judgment*, Keynes, p. 651.

rectify every thing in Nature as the Philosophers do, & then we shall return to Chaos, & God will be compell'd to be Eccentric if he Creates, O happy Philosopher.[31]

At this rate, man was scarcely more than a "ratio" of primary qualities which he perceived in a distorted form through the medium of his senses. In the history of the new science, he had become an insignificant effect of that system of nature which was the ground of reality.

The naturalism of the sciences was reflected in literature, and the reflection could be seen most readily in the change which overtook the method and material of expression. Dante had regarded the fourfold method of formal presentation as the basis of poetic expression.[32] The allegory of the church was also taken over by the poet, whose essential identity with the theologian and the philosopher was asserted in a way which preserved some vestige of the prophetic tradition. In the Renaissance, the connection between the allegorical interpretation of Christian scripture and the fables of the Classical poets continued to be recognized. This connection certainly liberated the poetic imagination, for it permitted the creative artist to see biblical literature as the work of an imaginative tradition and not merely as the material for doctrinal exegesis. But the works within the sacred canon were considered to be factually true, as well as true according to the meaning. The works of the Classical mythologists and of the poets themselves were "true" only according to the meaning. This distinction between fact and fable was a weakness inherent in the notion of allegory itself, from Blake's point of view. Allegory or fable was to be distinguished from "Vision," for the vision of the seer did not represent a previously formulated doctrine, nor did it adumbrate a doctrine whose meaning could be completely and adequately stated in rational terms. It had none of the naturalistic and doctrinal overtones of allegory which had been associated with the thought and outlook of Hellenism. But the history of Greek thought had ended with the collapse of philosophic rationalism which was later taken over by an ecclesiastical organization purveying a definitive doctrine. Although Blake asserted that allegory and fable were essentially visionary,[33] they were still representational to the rationalistic thinker,

[31] *Annotations to Lavater's "Aphorisms on Man,"* no. 532.

[32] Dante, *Il Convivio*, II, i; III, xi–xiv.

[33] Cf. *Vision of the Last Judgment*, Keynes, pp. 637–8: "Fable or Allegory are a totally distinct & inferior kind of Poetry. Vision or Imagination is a Representation of what Eternally Exists, Really & Unchangeably. Fable or Allegory is form'd by the daughters of Memory. Imagination

and they tended to become the mere vehicle of his doctrines. As a means of stating such philosophic truths, the fables of the ancients were regarded highly by Bacon, and since he read most of his own ideas into their myths, he praised them for their insight. By the time of Dryden, however, allegory had already become an artifice rather than an integral part of the method of the literary artist, for the conception of the work of genius as the work of inspiration was no longer seriously entertained.

None of the philosophers who provided the basis for the mechanistic view of man and the universe illustrated the complete break with the notion of visionary perception better than Descartes. His deliberate rejection of what he apparently understood to be imaginative vision in favour of rationalism formed one of the most interesting anecdotes of the period. Evidently, Descartes' decision took the form of a dream which he recorded, along with other experiences, in a booklet called *Olympica* which has since been lost. A summary has been preserved by Baillet in his *Vie de M. Descartes* (1691). In the dream, he was offered the choice of two books: a dictionary or the mere aggregate of knowledge, and a *corpus poëtarum* signifying inspired wisdom. He concluded that the dictionary represented the sciences collected together, and that the work of the poets was the whole of science and wisdom united. Poetic expression contained that which could not be found in the writings of the philosophers, and he attributed this fact to a kind of inspiration which, along with the power of imagination, brought forth the seeds of wisdom. All this was done with an ease and brilliance which could not be imitated by the rational faculty of the philosophers.[34]

On opening the *corpus poëtarum*, he was immediately attracted by a

---

is surrounded by the daughters of Inspiration, who in the aggregate are call'd Jerusalem. Fable is allegory, but what the Critics call The Fable, is Vision itself."

[34]*Œuvres de Descartes*, ed. C. Adam and P. Tannery (Paris, 1908), X, p. 184: "Il jugea que le Dictionnaire ne vouloit dire autre chose que toutes les Sciences ramassées ensemble; & que le Recueil de Poësies, intitulé Corpus poëtarum, marquoit en particulier, & d'une manière plus distincte, la Philosophie & la Sagesse jointes ensemble. Car il ne croioit pas qu'on dût s'étonner si fort de voir que les Poëtes, meme ceux qui ne font que niaiser, fussent pleins de sentences plus graves, plus sensées, & mieux exprimées que celles qui se trouvent dans les écrits des Philosophes. Il attribuoit cette merveille à la divinité de l'Enthousiasme, & à la force de l'Imagination, qui fait sortir les semences de la sagesse (qui se trouve dans l'esprit de tous les hommes, comme les étincelles de feu dans les cailloux) avec beaucoup plus de facilité et beaucoup plus de brillant même, que ne peut faire la Raison dans les Philosophes."

verse from Ausonius: "What way of life shall I follow?" The point at issue could hardly have been put better, and the distinction which Descartes made between the one approach and the other showed a certain comprehension of the vision of the prophet in the work of the poet.[35] But in spite of this comprehension, or perhaps because of it, he rejected the unity which Blake insisted the imaginative vision of the totality of existence alone could give. Instead, he limited himself to that part of life which could be explained by logic and experiment, and abandoned that development of the force of imagination out of which he had asserted the seeds of wisdom came. The metaphysical dualism which his own attitude implied was worked out in terms of a completely mechanistic system of the universe the motions of whose parts were communicated by immediate contact and by the invisible, unextended *res cogitans*. The relationship between the machine of necessity and the spirit of reason was as the relationship between two separate worlds. The rational mind, like Urizen, brooded in isolated majesty over the cosmic machinery. Blake had apparently not read Descartes, but he saw implicit in Bacon what became explicit in Cartesian rationalism: the rejection of the totality of the imaginative vision in favour of the partial, but immediately effective, logic of experiment.

It is Blake's conviction that error will be rejected when it has become determinate or clarified by the mind. In his own imaginative language, he describes the mental act of seeing error and rejecting it as a "Last Judgment."[36] What follows, in any given instance, is the redemption of the mind. But this kind of redemption is impossible when the clarification of imaginative perception is subordinated to what can be abstracted and classified by the reason and stored in the memory. Such a process establishes error, so that it becomes an accepted conviction by which all experiences are interpreted. Prejudice and preconception are characteristic of logical thinking as distinct from

[35]Cf. Descartes, *Cogitationes Privatae*, in *ibid.*, X, p. 217: "Ut imaginatio utitur figuris ad corpora concipienda, ita intellectus utitur quibusdam corporibus sensibilibus ad spiritualia figuranda, ut vento, lumine unde altius philosophantes mentem cognitione possumus in sublime tollere. Mirum videri possit, quare graves sententiae in scriptis poetarum, magis quam philosophorum. Ratio est quod poetae per enthusiasmum & vim imaginationis scripsere: sunt in nobis semina scientiae, ut in silice quae per rationem a philosophis educuntur, per imaginationem a poetis excutiuntur magis que elucent."

[36]*Vision of the Last Judgment*, Keynes, p. 651.

imaginative thinking which includes the desires and the instincts. In this way, reason can provide a continuous defence against new truth and the revolutionary Last Judgment which its recognition effects in the mind. "Reason, or the ratio of all we have already known, is not the same that it shall be when we know more."[37] But the rational habit of reflection which separates or abstracts ideas from their mental images gives an absolute value to the immediate perceptions of sense. Man's present state of existence becomes the absolute condition of all existence. Blake considers this process a rational *tour de force* which will obliterate from the mind of man the possibility of any other state of existence and cause him to fall into a sleep on the Procrustean bed of abstract theory.

Rational abstraction has a very deceptive effect, for it discounts and finally eliminates opposition, until the individual's awareness rejects any unusual experiences which discredit a settled conviction, and thereby prevents their recurrence. Abstract generalizations on conduct influence and infect the direct and "innocent" activity of emotion and instinct within the sphere of religion and ethics. Abstract philosophy enslaves the political activity of nations by dictating the legal preconceptions under which they are to live. Such is the history of man's domination by Urizen. In his *Song of Los*, Blake describes Urizen giving his laws to the nations whereby each succumbed, "Till, like a dream, Eternity was obliterated & erased."[38] The vision of universal nature becomes the world perceived by the five senses, and human nature is made to reflect the shrunken perceptions of men through their own rational abstractions

> binding them more
> And more to Earth, closing and restraining,
> Till a Philosophy of Five Senses was complete.
> Urizen wept & gave it into the hands of Newton & Locke.[39]

The limitations of logical thinking have reduced sensation to a mechanical way of perceiving and knowing, but the simplest enjoyments and the survival of the greatest works of the imagination belie this restricted estimate of man's possibilities.

[37] *There is no Natural Religion*, II.
[38] *The Song of Los*, 35.
[39] *Ibid.*, 45–8.

What is it sets Homer, Virgil & Milton in so high a rank of Art? Why is the Bible more Entertaining & Instructive than any other book? Is it not because they are addressed to the Imagination, which is Spiritual Sensation, & but mediately to the Understanding or Reason?[41]

The kind of thinking which is creative can be the possession of all. Thinking is not necessarily limited to mere habits of thought nor to any logical system of nature.

Blake attributes the atheistical opinions of such contemporary exponents of the new science as the French Encyclopedists to the influence of Bacon. He does not give Bacon credit for disentangling religious dogma from the sphere of scientific observation but associates him with an outlook which discredits inspiration. Commenting on his own earlier annotations to Locke's treatise on the understanding and Bacon's *Advancement of Learning*, he writes:

I felt the Same Contempt & Abhorrence then that I do now. They mock Inspiration & Vision. Inspiration & Vision was then, & now is, & I hope will always Remain, my Element, my Eternal Dwelling place; how can I then hear it Contemned without returning Scorn for Scorn?[41]

According to the Baconian outlook, no divine mind presided over the natural world which could not be seen accurately in relation to any other formal structure but itself. The effect of this outlook was to loosen the philosopher's hold on the whole content of traditional metaphysics. His ontological science of being was given its death-blow by Bacon, or else it became a part of a Cartesian dualism. His epistemology was the sole survivor, for cosmology was finally surrendered to the picture of the world described by Newton. Locke followed in the wake of Bacon and Newton, and according to Blake, he completed the critique of vision and established a "Philosophy of Five Senses."

[40]Letter to Trusler, Aug. 23, 1799.

[41]*Annotations to Reynolds's "Discourses,"* p. 244.

5. The Critique of Vision

THE SUSTAINED EFFORT to systematize and order the structure of the universe was reflected in every sphere of activity at the turn of the eighteenth century. The essential simplicity of Newtonian physics seemed to make it the revealed plan of nature which rewarded and confirmed the belief in the power and unity of the natural order. For a moment it appeared to the contemporaries of Blake that they lived in a universe of which they could grasp the underlying principle by virtue of that "reason" which was "commonsense" in man, and "nature" in the world around him. They felt perfectly equal to the task of coping with their environment without the immediate assistance of divine grace or inspiration. Like Blake's Urizen in the seventh night of *The Four Zoas*, they sought diligently for the "deep pulsation" in themselves and in their world, hoping that it was not too deep, and that they could find and comprehend it.[1] The simple solution appealed to them as being the most profound, and the "ideas" of Locke no less than the "atoms" of Newton gave them a sense of moral security. Although Blake did not agree with the kind of order which the rationalistic mind conceived, he was deeply imbued with the concept of order itself, and he did not reflect in the slightest the attraction which disorder, chaos and the unartificial seemed to have for certain Romantics. Nor did he agree that art was simply nature methodized, as some of the Neo-Classicists maintained. He had much in common with the positive outlook of his rationalistic contemporaries and their effort to make some kind of order out of what they saw.

The cult of reason and nature was, after all, not merely a convenient expedient, nor just a moral ideal. The mathematical rationalism of

[1]At the close of the fifth night Urizen is represented as saying (238): "I will arise, Explore these dens, & find that deep pulsation . . . ." After searching, throughout the sixth night, among the commensurable abysses of the Newtonian universe—a "world of cumbrous wheels"—for the vital force, he finds Orc, the seminal root of nature, at the beginning of the seventh night.

Descartes and the *esprit géométrique* of which Pascal wrote expressed a genuine impatience with the prevailing disorder in the sciences and previous theological sophistry. This impatience was what precipitated the revolutionary discoveries of the new science—with its mechanistic outlook and the calculating machines of Pascal and Leibniz. Newton not only presented the universe as a tidy machine, but he also gave his contemporaries a comprehensible, simple and verifiable account of it. In the sixth night of *The Four Zoas*, Blake also develops the theme of man's rational search for truth. But in his version of the search, the rational means prove to be inadequate, for the natural reason can add nothing to the data of the senses. In fact, the rational mind frequently exchanges the concrete clarity of actual experience for the perverse generalizations of the preconceived order of some abstract system. What has happened before in the interests of a religious allegory is happening again in the interests of the new cult of reason, nature and commonsense. Blake insists that it takes the increasingly uncommon sense of visionary perception to discover the truth in man and his world; the ratio of five senses is merely a distortion of the mind's part in the search. When reason invades the realm of vision, and attempts to infer and generalize about what vision alone can perceive, it only succeeds in perverting man's grasp of the truth and the use of the powers at his disposal.[2]

Newton and Locke represent the two directions which the research of the eighteenth century took. The one provides a cosmological chart and the other a psychological abacus. Although the emphasis is frequently placed on the experimental nature of their labours, the results which they obtained are the answer to a highly speculative outlook. Speculation or reflection, or simply reasoning, as Blake calls it, implies the collection and comparison of mental images for classification or measurement. Classification involves abstracting qualities from things, and collection involves the retention of things—in terms of their qualities—in the memory. The result is that the qualities tend to take on an existence of their own in the mind of the rationalist. Blake counters this tendency by insisting that mere qualities must be related

[2]In his journey towards the northern world of Urthona, Urizen encounters the horrors which are the perversities of the fallen mentality. The world of Urthona is the empty void of original vision, but this void cannot be reconstituted as the world of vision by Urizen who, as the natural reason, attempts to do just that. He creates "many a Vortex" (VI, 184), or takes up many a viewpoint, and fixes "many a Science in the deep."

to the original mental image which is alone real: "Harmony and Proportion are Qualities & not Things. The Harmony & Proportion of a Horse are not the same with those of a Bull. Every Thing has its own Harmony & Proportion, Two Inferior Qualities in it. For its Reality is its Imaginative Form."[3]

Memory and reflection move in the opposite direction to imagination and direct perception. Men are continually turning away from perception towards the indefinite mysteries of nature, seeking a substratum of reality beyond the imagery of perception. To the visionary artist, the proportion of a particular horse is clear, the proportion of horses blurred and "proportion" alone very foggy indeed. To move from the distinct perception of things to the memory of their qualities is to move from light into darkness. Memory and reflection do not lead towards clarity of intellect, but towards the indefinite and invisible conceptions of the natural reason. It is here that Blake disagrees with Locke, who regards perception as the first simple idea of reflection.

> Perception, as it is the first faculty of the mind exercised about our ideas, so it is the first and simplest idea we have from reflection, and it is by some called "thinking" in general. Though thinking, in the propriety of the English tongue, signifies that sort of operation of the mind about its ideas wherein the mind is active; where it, with some degree of voluntary attention, considers anything. For in bare, naked perception, the mind is, for the most part, only passive; and what it perceives it cannot avoid perceiving.[4]

To the speculative mind of Locke, reflection is voluntary and active, while perception alone is involuntary, "for the most part," and passive. To the visionary mind of Blake, perception is based on the imagination which is its first principle and is the *a priori* unity of perception actively using, but independent of, the senses.

By making perception the basis of existence itself, Blake avoids the concept of a substantial reality either inside or outside the observer. The thinker, however, who speculates about the nature of things, separates the perceiver from the perceived, the subject from the object. He finds the ground of reality in himself, in innate ideas, or outside himself, in some form of atomism. The ground of reality, if

[3]*Annotations to Berkeley's "Siris,"* p. 213.

[4]Locke, *Essay Concerning Human Understanding*, Book II, chap. IX, sec. 1. Cf. Blake's *Annotations to Reynolds's "Discourses,"* p. 244.

he is a theist, takes the form of a God who creates from the preconceived plan of the ideas or of one who creates by means of a substance. The former notion is nearer to creation by conception and the latter to creation by invention. Neither of these attitudes can, of course, be completely separated from the other, but it is not difficult to see which one of them Locke favours. After denying the existence of innate ideas, he distinguishes between the secondary qualities which are subjective and the primary qualities which belong to objects apart from the perceiving subject.[5] Locke follows Bacon rather than Descartes, and the naturalism of the former colours his view of the human understanding. Primacy is given to the objective world of the experimenter, and the mind of the subject is reduced to a passive *tabula rasa* which receives impressions from a unit of this objective world. And this world possesses only the primary qualities with which the substratum of matter is endowed. The unit of indivisible substance which is the atom of the natural philosopher can only have been created by the "Deus" who was Fontenelle's divine watchmaker, and whose act of creation was an act of inventive watchcraft, rather than an act of conception in the Platonic sense. Such is Blake's view of the effect of Locke's teaching.

It does not matter to Blake that Locke and Newton insist on a kind of spiritual agency in their description of man and the universe. Along with Bacon, they represent a consolidation of Greek speculation into an experimental philosophy of mechanism which outstrips their powers of perception and makes them like Obtuse Angle, the mathematician in *An Island in the Moon*, who always thinks better with his eyes shut. Worse still, their opinions give the false impression that there is a fundamental change for the better in man's comprehension of the physical world and his relationship to it. But he is still a natural organ subject to sense, as he has been since his fall into the circle of destiny. In his intellect or imagination, he can be an agent, a "Human Existence," but the more he reflects and speculates, the more his intellect falls under the domination of memory and its spectres of

[5]Locke states that the primary qualities of a body produce in the mind the corresponding *ideas*: solidity, extension, figure, motion or rest and number. *Secondary qualities*, however, are not in the objects themselves except as "powers to produce various sensations in us by their primary qualities"; so that, not even *they* are really subjective, although they originate in the act of perception (*ibid.*, Book II, chap. VIII, secs. 9–10).

fading images of sensation and the abstract shadows of these. Intellect, being and imagination are synonyms in Blake's works for creative, clear, definite perception which actively makes use of the imagery of sensation as the common bond of men in the state of Generation. In the language of his symbolism, he asserts that knowledge started to become mnemonic and speculative when the ancients—usually the Greeks—began to worship their gods instead of perceiving them with the eye of imagination. As the memory of the gods was all that was left them, they worshipped mysterious and invisible entities. An entity which could not be perceived in the imaginative vision—or what the Greeks originally called *theoria*—became allegorical and fabulous. As a result, the unity between what could be perceived and what was believed to exist was destroyed, and the speculation on the nature of being apart from perception arose.

The speculator reflecting on the nature of being takes the sum or aggregate of experience from the senses and proceeds to analyse it according to the categories of thought. He then deduces the images of sensation from these representations in the mind, so that what he does perceive comes to be explained and curtailed by classification and measurement. Blake considers that the speculative successors of Plato construe the "ideas" as supreme generalizations from which the Platonic cosmos is deduced according to a mathematical logic. If this seems a wilful misunderstanding of Plato, it is at least a skilful flank attack on contemporary rationalism. To Blake rationalism is a procedure which tends to limit the power of active perception, until a circle of necessity encloses the natural universe, and a circle of destiny limits the life of man. Boundaries to knowledge are the concern of reason, but not knowledge itself, which is from perception, and although the organs of sense indicate man's capacity for vision, they are not that vision. Thought and feeling go beyond the perceptions of the senses, even within the limitations of the ordinary natural state. But according to Locke, perception is not only limited to the senses, it is also reduced to complete passivity, and the only knowledge derived from it which proves finally acceptable is further limited to what can be given a numerical value. This is reason gone mad, "And Urizen, who was Faith & Certainty, is chang'd to Doubt."[6] The journeys of

[6]*The Four Zoas*, II, 315.

Urizen, after his fall from his eternal condition of intellectual vision, illustrate Blake's conception of the end of this kind of rational knowledge: it ends with a universe which is almost entirely void of content, and especially void of conscious life. Being is annihilated when separated from perception, and perception moves towards blindness when separated from being.

In Blake's earlier work, *The First Book of Urizen*, the fallen Demon of intellect is made the original creator of the void which is the ultimate environment of defective thinking. Later, Blake calls this blindness to vision "the Newtonian Voids between the Substances of Creation."[7] For the measurement which fixes the ratio of what can be seen also fixes the measurement of what cannot be seen, and makes the ratio of the five senses the unalterable basis of an absolute picture of the world. By this standard, the existence of anything loses its meaning outside mathematical demonstration and loses also its effective place in the atomic structure of nature. The accuracy with which this point of view describes and demonstrates man's natural condition as a Selfhood accounts for Blake's exasperation with it, for it leaves no alternative. Urizen has utterly subjected his victim, and has given him a system of knowledge which is simply an outline of the terms of his slavery.

Against this kind of slavery which makes no other consistent unity possible for man than his survival as an organism, Blake places the liberating hope of inner growth and fulfilment. Man is born a spectre with all the passive mechanism of conformity to outward accident and environment, but he originates from an eternal "Character" or type of human existence; in this essential principle of his origin lies his hope. He can succumb to the immediate aims of his Selfhood, until the original form of his existence becomes little more than an unrealized possibility. He can also struggle against the natural self with the "New Selfhood" of his character. The struggle provides the means for awakening into activity man's dormant humanity. Even animals, vegetables and minerals possess the impress or mould of development. The entire panorama of the ages is a succession of states eternally created for the planting and growth of the seeds of existence. But they can only grow from the innate form of character within the environment of nature. The roots are in eternity and not in time. "Man is Born Like a Garden ready Planted & Sown. This World is too poor

[7] *Milton*, 41: 46.

to produce one Seed."[8] In his commentary on Chaucer's Canterbury pilgrims, Blake draws the portrait of history from this point of view.

> The Characters of Chaucer's Pilgrims are the Characters that compose all Ages & Nations; as one Age falls another rises, different to Mortal Sight, but to Immortals only the same; for we see the same Characters repeated again & again, in Animals, in Vegetables, in Minerals & in Men. Nothing new occurs in Identical Existence: Accident ever varies, Substance can never suffer change nor decay.[9]

The wheel of destiny can be seen from an immortal perspective, and then it will turn to the advantage of man.

Locke's denial of innate ideas, however, seems to Blake a refusal to accept the very characteristics which could make possible the organization of his existence. "Innate Ideas are in Every Man, Born with him; they are truly Himself. The Man who says that we have No Innate Ideas must be a Fool & Knave, Having No Con-Science or Innate Science."[10] The innate ideas which Locke actually denies in his *Essay* are generalizations derived from sensation. Blake can hardly have objected to the denial of these. His objections are directed against the blank mental tablet which Locke places between the active intellect and the passive memory, between the ephemeral self or reasoning spectre and man's innate genius.[11] The speculative mind is thus cut off from the creative mind, and considered incapable of giving any other content to its ideas than what is provided by the natural environment or by combinations of the ideas themselves. The "Author and Preserver of all things" acts upon the life of his creature solely through the mediation of nature. Earlier in the history of the European spirit, it had been thought possible for reason to become right reason through the direct reception of divine grace. But the door of Plato's cave of the mind has now been shut, so that even the ray of active reason is exchanged for the gloom of natural effects.

Socrates was in the habit of referring to his "daemon" or "genius" which acted as a guide or mentor. Blake considers the genius to be the true man from which the natural man derives his outward form or

[8] *Annotations to Reynolds's "Discourses,"* p. 157.

[9] *A Descriptive Catalogue &c.*, Keynes, p. 635.

[10] *Annotations to Reynolds's "Discourses,"* p. 58.

[11] *Jerusalem*, 36: 38–41:

> Hand stood between Reuben & Merlin, as the Reasoning Spectre
> Stands between the Vegetative Man & his Immortal Imagination.

Cf. Northrop Frye, *Fearful Symmetry* (Princeton, 1947), pp. 14–29.

body. As a first principle, he states "That the Poetic Genius is the true Man, and that the body or outward form of Man is derived from the Poetic Genius. Likewise that the forms of all things are derived from their Genius, which by the Ancients was call'd an Angel & Spirit & Demon."[12] By reducing man's mental life to a series of reflections or images received automatically from sensation, Locke shuts out the transforming power of the active intellect, and apparently denies its existence. Intellectual agency is "the privilege of the infinite Author and Preserver of all things, 'who never slumbers nor sleeps'."[13] The picture of a slumbering creation under a wakeful, though inaccessible creative power would have seemed to Blake a curious parody of his own vision. He also sees the whole of creation as a sleep, but one out of which man can awaken. It is possible to participate in the continual process of creation, and not simply remain subject to it. How can this possibility be realized, if not through the use of that innate genius of growth of which everything partakes?

The spirit of growth is not limited to man; it constitutes the basis of living forms. The acorn which grows into an oak, because it possesses the genius of an oak, and not of a maple or an apple tree, does not speculate how to go about it. Unaware of the process as a means of knowledge, it still possesses a wisdom of its own which gets on with the job, given a suitable environment.[14] Although the acorn contains the form of its future growth, it cannot affect the relationship between the environment and itself; that kind of knowledge is the prerogative of man. If, however, man becomes absorbed in the technical exploitation of the natural environment for his own immediate aims, he forgets his innate wisdom and even denies it. Observing only the effects of a process, he fails to relate his observations to his state of existence, or he ascribes both to the supreme agency of the Inventor of the machinery of atoms which the natural environment has now become. The prevailing description of the atomic structure of the universe in Blake's day seems to leave out any notion of growth as a part of structural development. Change in the relative positions of the atoms is called growth, and change can easily be regarded as accidental,

[12]*All Religions are One*. In the *Cratylus* (398C, *Works of Plato*, trans. Thos. Taylor (London, 1804), V, p. 510), Socrates is made to commend the poets "when they say that a good man after death will receive a mighty destiny and renown, and will become a *daemon*, according to the surname of prudence."

[13]*Essay Concerning Human Understanding*, Book II, chap. 1, sec. 10.

[14]*Vision of the Last Judgment*, Keynes, p. 638.

or as the design of a hypothetical first cause. Newton, of course, gives his support to this atomistic theory: "And therefore that Nature may be lasting, the Changes of corporeal Things are to be placed only in the various Separations, and new Associations, and motions of these permanent Particles."[15] Here is a geometrical diagram unrelated to the specific needs of man's predicament as a human being.

As a human being, Blake insists, man's possibilities lie in developing his powers of perception and not in identifying himself with what he has already observed. If he allows himself to think that his particular degree of perception is unalterable, so it becomes, and he descends from the state of Generation into "meer Nature or Hell."[16] Newton's doctrine of absolute space forms the description of a degree of perception which almost empties the observed world of conscious agency. Such a picture of the world appears to be ultimate, and it can be interpreted as possessing the attributes of deity, uncreated, indivisible, infinite and immutable. Newton himself combats this interpretation, along with the one which ascribes universality to the theory of gravitation—as though mutual attraction were an essential quality inherent in all bodies—but he is still seen by Blake through the eyes of Newtonian mechanists who consider any kind of intelligent agency an unnecessary hypothesis. The views of the latter constitute the "Newton" of the prophetic books. This concept of nature is too much a part of Blake's contemporary background for him ever to take seriously the nature-worship of individual Romantics. Yet any attitude to nature which is lifted clear of its context in human perception and becomes an object of experiment, of worship, or of admiration to the eye of the beholder is bound to develop a body of doctrine or belief which amounts to a denial of vision as he understands it. His point of view is obviously in complete disagreement with both mechanist and pantheist. Even the allegory of the church is better, for it at least provides the philosopher with an analogy of original prophetic vision. Natural philosophy and natural religion provide the philosopher with merely the analogy of the ratio of five senses.

Analogy makes use of representational symbols and, as such, is

[15]*Opticks* (4th ed., London, 1730), p. 376.

[16]*Annotations to Swedenborg's "Divine Love and Wisdom,"* pp. 195–6. Blake's descent into Hell is not the retributive act of an avenging deity, but simply the reduction of the individual to an automatic and mechanical state of existence. Cf. Letter to Cumberland, April 12, 1827. This remark is aimed at the conception of existence apart from perception in terms of an imperceptible particle of "matter" in absolute space.

always one remove from what it attempts to represent, for it is a process of translation and interpretation, and never an act of direct perception. Just as allegory is, by means of reflection and symbolical representation, an analogy of what is directly perceived by imaginative vision, the rational system is, by means of abstraction and generalization, an analogy of what is perceived by the senses. When Newton studied the motions of the heavenly bodies, he wished to find a theory to account for the behaviour of those bodies. In the process, a condition was imposed on the data for the purpose of establishing a systematic analogy. The natural philosophers who followed in the wake of Newton and Locke sought to dispense with abstract universals by returning to facts derived from observation. Out of the facts themselves and their relationships, they hoped a science would emerge which would be formally complete, but still open to new discoveries. This approach to an empirical position involved them in the necessity of assuming *a priori* the objective existence of a consistently uniform world as a matter of fact. The need for the assumption showed the measure of their failure to escape from all hypothetical and rational premises. They might call the generalizations which they derived from their observations "facts," but their fundamental meaning was based on the rational analogy of sense-perception called "nature." To Blake, that reason which is merely the ratio of the senses is always the source of such an analogy, and the result is always another abstract system. In order to move from the generalizations of the rational analogy to the images of imagination, it is necessary to recognize the primacy of perception and existence over any hypothetical world of nature. Both Newton and Locke refused to do this. They did not derive their perceptions from the degree or state of their own existence, but solely from a fixed ratio between an active external world and a passive mind. From this rational hypothesis, they developed a system of nature by analogy.

According to Blake's doctrine of states, nothing can be more pernicious than the assumption that man is relegated to one degree or extent of perception. As the state of existence alters, what is perceived changes. "A fool sees not the same tree that a wise man sees."[17] To assume that what is perceived is the limit of reality and then to proceed to establish a rational analogy of it as a definitive basis for all future

[17]*Marriage of Heaven and Hell*, Keynes, p. 183.

observations seems to Blake the way to remain a fool forever. But as Hume pointed out, the use of analogy to establish the general principles of a system of nature is entirely in accord with the method of Newton: "It is entirely agreeable to the rules of philosophy, and even of common reason; where any principle has been found to have a great force and energy in one instance, to ascribe to it a like energy in all similar instances. This indeed is Newton's chief rule of philosophizing."[18] The system of nature produced by this method is the result of a process of generalization by comparison and reflection. To a theologian who philosophizes in this way, the original vision of the prophet would be the revelation of a mystery, for he would have to relate it at once to a system derived from reflecting on a world of nature. In other words, his analogy of religion or revealed truth would be based on a relationship between the generalizations or "facts" with which reason normally deals and the unknown series of revealed "facts" with which the same reason must also deal.[19] In this way, if the metaphor is not too strained, he would eventually invent a machinery of faith. Bishop Butler's *Analogy of Religion* is such a machinery, and its argument reveals the fundamental dependence of systematic religion on the analogy drawn from nature.

Blake attempts to combat this view and to release the whole conception of prophetic vision from its dependence on nature. Prophetic vision reveals the basis of human existence, and nature, being the limited object perceived by a mere aspect of that existence, is really dependent on, and conditioned by, the limitations of the observer. The expanded power of observation which Blake calls vision should not be translated and interpreted in terms of an analogy drawn from nature, but the entire scheme of created nature should be seen as an analogy of vision. In *Jerusalem*, Los, the visionary faculty of the seer, is man's power of apprehending the world, and is, therefore, represented as its creator. He plants the seeds of the twelve tribes of Israel, symbolizing the zodiacal signs of the constellations, and he also establishes the limitations of the temporal circle of destiny:

> And gave a Time & Revolution to the Space, Six Thousand Years.
> He call'd it Divine Analogy . . .[20]

[18]David Hume, *An Enquiry Concerning the Principles of Morals*, III, i.

[19]Cf. Frye, *Fearful Symmetry*, pp. 382 ff.

[20]*Jerusalem*, 85: 6–7.

The universe of Newton is made the analogy of visionary perception, and priority is given to its apprehension as a mental act, rather than to its discovery as a physical fact. Space and time are conditioned by our apprehension of them, rather than by their effect on us. The present world is not only restricted to what we can see of it, but also to how we look at it, and both form the illusory effect of a limited state of existence.

Berkeley also sees the danger of Locke's *tabula rasa* and Newton's absolute space, but his immediate interest is to confound the doctrines of those he calls "Atheists and Fatalists." "The existence of Matter, or bodies unperceived, has not only been the main support of Atheists and Fatalists, but on the same principle doth Idolatry likewise in all its various forms depend."[21] The Newtonian doctrine of absolute space lends itself to the confusion of real space with God, or to the elimination of divine agency from the field of the universe. Objects can be considered to possess their own agency and to be the cause of their own properties. Further, the belief that the existence of anything can be known apart from perception exaggerates the scepticism of the natural philosopher regarding the senses. He comes to distrust them because of their supposed failure to reveal the nature of things:

> One great inducement to our pronouncing ourselves ignorant of the nature of things is, the current opinion that every thing includes *within* itself the cause of its properties; or that there is in each object an inward essence, which is the source whence its discernible qualities flow, and whereon they depend . . . whereas, in truth, there is no other agent nor efficient cause than *spirit* . . . ."[22]

He is careful to avoid the naïve mistake of some Newtonians who make the description of a natural phenomenon into the explanation of the cause of it. Newton's theory of gravity is recognized to be a description and not an explanation, and Newton himself still continues to identify the cause of gravity with a supernatural agent. But the fact that he describes space in such utterly abstract terms makes it equal to the deity, or at least, exalts it into the eternal environment of divinity. Blake thinks of spatial extension as a limited condition, circular in

[21]Berkeley, *Principles of Human Knowledge*, xciv.

[22]*Ibid.*, cii. Cf. *Milton*, 28: 44–6:

> And every Natural Effect has a Spiritual Cause, and Not
> A Natural; for a Natural Cause only seems: it is a Delusion
> Of Ulro & a ratio of the perishing Vegetable Memory.

form, which is the outline of man's restricted state of existence. The sky-god of space may be the "Pantocrator" and the Creator of all things to Newton, but he is only Satan and the foreman of the celestial mills to Blake.[23] Within the circle of destiny, man is no more than a mill-hand, and he is as subject to circumstance as that pathetic slave of the Industrial Revolution.

In the thought of Berkeley, however, neither the spatial deity of Newton nor the primary qualities of Locke are retained. Considering an idea to mean "any sensible or imaginable thing,"[24] he denies the possibility of isolating a primary quality, since it is impossible to have an idea which cannot be perceived, and hence does not appear with the secondary attributes. It is therefore nonsense to talk about space or matter as existing apart from perception. In his *New Theory of Vision*, he examines the formation of space which he derives from the sense of sight and the sense of touch. There can be no real conception of pure space or extension which can be related to perception in any way.[25] Since the general idea of matter chiefly depends on the primary attribute of extension, it is also eliminated. In Berkeley's universe there can be no deity for whom space is the *sensorium*. When the material *substratum* of Locke's primary qualities woven by the Newtonian concept of absolute space is eliminated, the "Pantocrator" disappears from the "Wheels of Heaven" and becomes "a Spirit who is intimately present to our minds, producing in them all that variety of ideas or sensations which continually affect us, on whom we have an absolute and entire dependence, in short, 'in whom we live and move and have our being'."[26] Berkeley early identifies existence with perception and imagination, but the ultimate basis of perception is the inner agency of spirit which takes the form of the *will-to-perceive*: "While I exist or

[23]*Milton*, 4: 9–11:

> "O Satan, my youngest born, art thou not Prince of the Starry Hosts
> And of the Wheels of Heaven, to turn the Mills day & night?
> Art thou not Newton's Pantocrator, weaving the Woof of Locke?

Bernard Blackstone (*English Blake* (Cambridge, 1949), p. 333. n) compares these lines with a statement in the *Scholium Generale* of Newton's *Principia*: "[Ens intelligens] omnia regit non ut anima mundi, sed ut universorum dominus. Et propter dominum suum, dominus deus παντοκράτωρ dici solet." In Rev. i: 8, Blake's Los is actually being described, for he is both the *alpha* and *omega* of the creative Word, and also the ruler of time.

[24]*Philosophical Commentaries*, ed. A. A. Luce (London, 1944), folio 75, sec. 775, p. 273.

[25]*A New Theory of Vision*, 122 ff.

[26]Berkeley, *Principles of Human Knowledge*, cxlix.

have any Idea I am eternally, constantly willing, my acquiescing in the present State is willing."[27] This brittle conception satisfies a mind in which there is still an urge to establish the causal link between man and his creator, for it is to the will of God that the individual mind finally submits. The greater part of the sensations and ideas which are called the works of nature are not dependent on the will of man or the efficient causes within nature. Their regularity and order along with their beauty and perfection are effected both immediately and finally by a divine agency within the mind.

It is in this way that Berkeley tries to guard the concept of causality with reference to nature, and to place spirit in the position of being the only efficient and final cause. Subtly but unmistakably, however, the logical grammar of causes draws him away from the actual language of perception—in spite of his protestations—and his view of the divine will draws him away from prophetic vision into a system of philosophy. The fire which is seen is not the cause of the subsequent pain but the sign or mark which forewarns the perceiver of its power and property. These signs compose the letters of an alphabet which are for our information and for the understanding of the language of God. So far, the signs show a striking resemblance to the "signatures" of Boehme.[28] But the point at which Berkeley diverges from the views of both Boehme and Blake is where he associates an understanding of the divine language with a study of final causes, or infers the attributes of the first cause from his works and approaches him as the author of nature.[29] He seems to confuse the rational analogy of what is perceived with the fundamental activity of perception itself. The imaginative idea fades before the rational hypothesis of causal agency, and God is evidently conceived as will, rather than perceived as the totality of human existence, or as man.

Berkeley's formal exposition makes it appear to Blake that he approaches the deity more through the abstract ratio of perception than through actual perception. In this, he ostensibly follows the dialectic of Plato whose antitheses of sense and intellect noticeably affect the productions of his later years. Earlier Berkeley could write:

[27]*Philosophical Commentaries*, folio 79, sec. 791, p. 279.

[28]Jacob Boehme, *Signatura Rerum*, chap. I, secs. 14–15; chap. IX, sec. 3. Berkeley does claim to avoid the subjection of the mind to the service of "general grammar-rules" (*Principles of Human Knowledge*, cviii; and cf. lxvi).

[29]*Principles of Human Knowledge*, lxvi, cvii, cviii.

"Sensual Pleasure is the Summum Bonum. This is the Great Principle of Morality. This once rightly understood all the Doctrines even the severest of the Gospels may clearly be Demonstrated."[30] The moral overtones may suggest that calculus of pleasure and pain which seems to appeal to certain contemporary writers on ethics. But the frank reliance on an active discipline based on direct perception is closer to Blake than the consistent onslaught which the same writer makes on the senses in his *Siris*.

It was the Platonic doctrine, that human souls or minds descended from above, and were sowed in generation; that they were stunned, stupified, and intoxicated by this descent and immersion in animal nature; and that the soul, in this ὀνείρωξις or slumber, forgets her original notions, which are smothered or oppressed by many false tenets and prejudices of sense. Insomuch that Proclus compares the soul, in her descent invested with growing prejudices, to Glaucus diving to the bottom of the sea, and there contracting divers cloaks of seaweed, coral, and shells, which stick close to him, and conceal his true shape.[31]

Blake never denies that sensation when entirely dependent on the natural data of experience is the deprivation of vision. He does, however, make a distinction between the stupefaction of sense in the fallen state and the notion that the senses are the cause of that stupefaction. The cause of man's slumber is his fallen condition in which his powers of thought, affection and sensation have all suffered. The way to awaken them into their original unity does not lie in the direction of a denial of one of them in favour of the others. Sensation is not less reliable than thought or emotion, and Blake pointedly associates the awakening vision of the whole man with "an improvement of sensual enjoyment."[32]

What Berkeley calls the "original notions" of the soul cannot be

[30]*Philosophical Commentaries*, folio 74, sec. 769, p. 271.

[31]Berkeley, *Siris*, 313. This passage is quoted by Blackstone (*English Blake*, pp. 88–9). He relates it to a passage in the fourth night of *The Four Zoas*. Tharmas, the symbol of man's original power over the field of experience, is overwhelmed by the fall into Generation, and his original "body" is overwhelmed by the ever-changing sea of sensation (IV, 132–36).

"... The Eternal Man is seal'd, never to be deliver'd.
I roll my floods over his body, my billows & waves pass over him,
The sea encompasses him & monsters of the deep are his companions.
Dreamer of furious oceans, cold sleeper of weeds & shells,
Thy Eternal form shall never renew, my uncertain prevails against thee."

[32]*Marriage of Heaven and Hell*, Keynes, p. 187.

recaptured by the logical mind, and Blake's annotations to the philosopher's *Siris* show an impatience with a form of expression which gives the impression that this is possible. Man's "true shape" is to be realized by the active use of all his faculties, and these find their unity in the imagination. The prototype of man's existence is not to be conceived as an intellectual phantom, but as a supremely corporate and organized life. Berkeley, however, insists on describing the deity in whose image man has been made as one who "knoweth all things, as pure mind or intellect, but nothing by sense, nor in nor through a sensory."[33] The description is philosophically adequate, and even edifying, but it leaves man out. Blake puts him back in by redefining "pure mind or intellect" as "Imagination or the Human Eternal Body in Every Man." More determined than the philosopher to maintain the complete interdependence of knowledge, being and perception, he constantly refers all statements regarding "spiritual agency" back to the imagination. Just as definite in his rejection of any conception of pantheism as Berkeley, he still remains conscious of the latter's tendency to purify the notion of the supreme being and to abstract the divine image or idea from the human imagination or that conscious root of what is conceivable to man. After Berkeley's remark that "Plato and Aristotle considered God as abstracted or distinct from the natural world," Blake writes: "They also considered God as abstracted or distinct from the Imaginative World, but Jesus, as also Abraham & David, considered God as Man in the Spiritual or Imaginative Vision."[34] Although Berkeley is never in danger of placing a *tabula rasa* between *esse* and *percipi*, he makes use of the ratio of what is perceived as the way to knowledge. He sees the basis of all perception in the rational conception of a Divine Perceiver whose will constantly creates the activity of consciousness. Blake sees the basis of all perception in the imaginative unity of sense and intellect which culminates in his perception of the "Divine Image."

Berkeley speaks of the higher and lower faculties of the soul, and thinks of an ascent or gradual evolution to the highest. The perceptions of sense provide subjects for the imagination, and by a process of rational abstraction these become objects for the understanding. Imagination is made to reflect the objects perceived through the

[33]*Annotations to Berkeley's "Siris,"* p. 203.
[34]*Ibid.*, p. 212.

senses, and it is only by means of the activity of rational judgment that the understanding is provided with knowledge. Blake sees this entire process as one act of insight, with the four factors in the process acting as a unit, for they are not divided into "higher" and "lower." The logical thinker, using the "reasoning negative," is always in between two contraries, sense and intellect, and consequently thinks in terms of a movement from one to the other. This movement usually tends to exclude one of the contraries at the expense of the other. And yet a horse is best understood by direct observation, and not by reasoning about its characteristics or deciding about its essential horseness: "Knowledge is not by deduction, but Immediate by Perception or Sense at once. Christ addresses himself to the Man, and not to his Reason."[35] In direct perception lies the root of existence, and although there are degrees of existence according to the extent of perception, the active understanding of the individual is not increased by exclusively rational means.

Berkeley's earlier emphasis on sensation and perception seem to give way, in his later works, to the supreme priority of reason over the senses. The old dualism of soul and body emerges from the pages of his *Siris*, as he refers to Proclus on the two sorts of philosophers.

> The one placed Body first in the order of beings, and made the faculty of thinking depend thereupon, supposing that the principles of all things are corporeal: that Body most really or principally exists, and all other things in a secondary sense, and by virtue of that. Others, making all corporeal things to be dependent on Soul or Mind, think this to exist in the first place and primary sense, and the being of Bodies to be altogether derived from, and presuppose that of the Mind.[36]

Blake also considers the natural body as a derivative of mind, but he is convinced that the separation of body and mind in the act of reflection makes a rational abstraction of mind and a physical mechanism of body. This viewpoint forces the philosopher to reflect on an exceedingly ethereal kind of "spiritual agency" or frankly to place the root of being and perception in the realm of mechanical functions. In the logical dualism, Blake notices an effect which he resists. The effect is inescapably bound up with the way reason operates: mind becomes vague and indeterminate, however important its activity may be, while the really corporate existence of the individual is based on the

[35] *Ibid.*, p. 214.
[36] *Siris*, 263.

senses alone. Paradoxically, but understandably, he counters this effect by asserting the corporate existence of the soul as a "Spiritual Body" to which the mere mechanism of organic functions, or the "Natural Body," is an obstruction.[37] The actual obstruction is the reasoning process which does not lend itself to a complete understanding. His own outline of the fall of man into the state of Generation does not refer to the submerging of the higher faculties by the lower, but rather to the contraction of the eternal "Senses" into the five channels of natural perception. But because philosophy separates the higher faculty of reason from the lower faculty of sensation, spirit has become ghostly or nondescript to the speculative thinker, and reason itself tends to become what Blake calls the "reasoning Spectre"—the mere reflection of the natural organ subject to sense.

Blake is aware that neither Plato nor Berkeley is talking nonsense, but he is convinced that speculative thought distracts and blinds the eye of man's imaginative understanding. He agrees with Berkeley's remark derived from Themistus that: "it may be inferred that all beings are in the soul. For, saith he, the forms are the beings. By the form everything is what it is. And, he adds, it is the soul that imparteth forms to matter . . . ."[38] But there is no use talking about form unless it can be apprehended by "Sense or the Eye of Imagination." While this eye is blind, eternal life is a mirage, and the higher realm of the intellect a delusion. By adopting a rational position regarding the relationship between sense and intellect, Berkeley has denied in practice what he has maintained in theory—the unity of perception and existence. Theoretically, he continues to maintain the link by the intervention of an infinite Perceiver as intelligent cause. Theoretically also, he endeavours to maintain a distinction between the naturalistic conception of cause and effect and his own conception of "signs" and the things signified, but he seems to cut the natural phenomena explained free from the totality of man's perceptions. These phenomena form a rational discourse which is "the immediate effect of an Intelligent Cause."[39] He appears to be interested in the fact that God speaks grammatically. Blake is more interested in the fact that he

[37]*Annotations to Berkeley's "Siris,"* p. 218.

[38]See *ibid.*, p. 219: "This is my Opinion, but Form must be apprehended by Sense of the Eye of Imagination. Man is All Imagination. God is Man & exists in us & we in him."

[39]Berkeley, *Siris*, 254.

speaks idiomatically and to every individual in his own dialect.[40] The phenomena of nature are seen by Berkeley as a logical grammar of cause and effect and not as a series of recurrent visions which are vital and intimate realities.

In spite of these differences between the seer and the philosopher, Berkeley's concept of nature comes nearer to being that of an inspired masterpiece than that of a work on logical analysis.[41] Natural phenomena form among themselves a sign language, symbols of the thoughts which the universal mind would impart to us.

> It is the searching after and endeavouring to understand this language (if I may so call it) of the Author of Nature that ought to be the employment of the natural philosopher; and not the pretending to explain things by *corporeal* causes, which doctrine seems to have too much estranged the minds of men from that Active Principle, that Supreme and wise Spirit, "in whom we live and move and have our being."[42]

Berkeley's closing genuflexion is not the least of his failings in Blake's eyes. It is not the fact that God is made to speak grammatically and philosophically, but that he is also made to speak with an Oxford accent that annoys him. The emergence of the bishop who is trying to be edifying as well as instructive irritates him as he thumbs over the pages of *Siris*. Berkeley's ethical opinions with their emphasis on not resisting political authority are to be found in his *Passive Obedience*, a treatise which is supposed to be based on the "principles of the law of nature." However, he still sees the nature of vision, if not the vision of nature, from a viewpoint not unlike Blake's. He does not read Plato for his metaphors nor merely for the charm of his language, but is convinced of the immediacy of vision and revelation in the mind of man. Ultimately, he is in the great tradition, like Plato and Milton and the ancients: "The Ancients did not mean to Impose when they affirm'd their belief in Vision & Revelation. Plato was in Earnest: Milton was in Earnest."[43]

Bacon, Newton and Locke, it seems to Blake, isolated the whole notion of vision from the knowledge which is immediately possible and reliable. By doing so, they thought to establish man's supremacy

[40] *Annotations to Berkeley's "Siris,"* p. 215: "Jesus supposes every Thing to be Evident to the Child & to the Poor & Unlearned. Such is the Gospel."

[41] Berkeley, *Siris*, 251–2.

[42] Berkeley, *Principles of Human Knowledge*, lxvi.

[43] *Annotations to Reynolds's "Discourses,"* p. 195.

over nature, but such a supremacy is bought at the price of an outward conformity to general laws and techniques. Inwardly a slave to a condition of being, the individual can only turn his technical achievements to the expression of his own inner poverty. In the growth of "enthusiasm" in both religion and politics and in the erratic individualism of the romantics, Blake hopefully looks for a recognition of man's primary task: the rediscovery of himself.

The third Book of *Jerusalem* is dedicated "To the Deists," and it closes with a summary indictment of Locke's rationalism. Earlier, Hand has been used as the symbol of the "Reasoning Spectre" standing "between the Vegetative Man & his Immortal Imagination."[44] Reason, desire and the senses have been separated from the active existence of the human imagination and have finally formed the three-brained creature which Hand has now become—a creature whose head, heart and loins have been given to nature, the harlot Rahab. For the new method of knowledge rejects or ignores the inner frontier of the human spirit and completely depends upon the outer frontier of natural objects. Scholastic rationalism has hitherto placed a religious allegory founded on revelation between man and the mystery of his own existence, so that insight into essential qualities can only be obtained by rational inference through the classification and definition of objects perceived by the senses. The method of the new science, however, as Locke interprets it, has reduced man's mental life to the empirical process of sorting and sampling the imagery of sensation, although Locke himself makes no very convincing effort to explain the agency which accomplishes this work. Knowledge is, at worst, a confused set of impressions, and at best, an orderly arrangement of these within the limits of a pattern of probability approved by men of sense, and in accord with the recognized order of nature. "Knowledge then seems to me to be nothing but the perception of the connection of and agreement, or disagreement and repugnancy, of any of our ideas."[45] Such a theory of knowledge restricts the activity of the mind to collecting and comparing the images of sensation. It ignores what Blake calls "Ideas" which are perceived and known directly from man's existence as an intellectual agent, and only mediately through the senses.

[44]*Jerusalem*, 36: 38–41.

[45]Locke, *Essay Concerning Human Understanding*, IV, i, 2.

> Therefore rejecting Ideas as nothing & holding all Wisdom
> To consist in the agreements & disagreements of Ideas . . . [46]

But knowledge can surely be what man makes of his impressions and not just what they make of him. In the midst of this triumph of reason, nature and commonsense, Blake welcomed the enthusiasm of the Methodists and the political revolutionaries. He has also been placed among the Romantics, although his resemblance to them went no farther than a shared belief that man could be an individual undertaking an adventure and not merely the object of a cosmic experiment.

[46] *Jerusalem*, 70: 7–8.

6. Enthusiasm and the Romantic Revolt

IN LOCKE'S DESCRIPTION of the process of reflection, he gave expression to a theory of knowledge which was becoming the established outlook of the natural philosopher of his day. Blake was certainly interested in the developments following the technical methods of the new science, especially when they directly affected the conditions of human life. But he was also most interested in the outlook which the natural philosopher developed in himself and in the increasing number of those whose way of thinking he influenced. One of the main characteristics of this outlook seemed to be a professed incredulity and a consistent suspension of belief. This might be a distinct advantage for the incessant collection of new facts and for the interpretation of natural law, but it reduced the individual's active life to one long experiment with temporal circumstances. In addition, the sceptical spirit obviously weakened belief in the religious allegory of the church, unless scepticism was rigorously restricted to the realm of natural philosophy. Bacon had evidently adopted the latter course, for he definitely described the true contemplation of nature as a movement from doubt to certainty: "if a man will begin with certainties, hee shall end in doubts; but if he will be content to beginne with doubts, he shall end in certainties."[1] By professing to confine this method to natural philosophy, he became one of the most celebrated examples of the growing separation between religious belief and natural knowledge. The profound contradiction which this outlook implied irritated Blake; beliefs and facts, the understanding of life and the knowledge of things were utterly separated and approached by totally different

[1] *Advancement of Learning* (London, 1605), Book I, p. 26. Cf. *Annotations to Reynolds's "Discourses,"* p. 61: "The Great Bacon—he is Call'd: I call him the Little Bacon—says that Every thing must be done by Experiment; his first principle is Unbelief, and yet here he says that Art must be produc'd Without such Method. He is Like Sr Joshua, full of Self-Contradiction & Knavery."

methods. Although the rationalist could gradually dispense with the religious allegory and evolve a religion of nature, the roots of the allegory he discarded were of immediate importance to those who were less gifted in worshipping ethical principles and natural laws. Some of these began to reaffirm their belief in one or other of the established churches by a return to the religion of faith and good works.

Toward the end of the seventeenth century, the reaction against the zeal of the reforming age produced an indifference to religion and even a decided prejudice against it. Such conditions formed the background of the pietistic movement in Germany, of quietism in France and of the religious societies in England. These various revivals of the religion of piety and good works were alike both in their purpose and method. They attempted to awaken an interest in religion within the bounds of the established church, which they considered to be too dogmatic and remote from the personal problems of the laity. They were interested particularly in establishing religion on the truths of the inner life without denying or changing the fundamental doctrines of their respective churches. They emphasized the value of acts of devotion and charity. The fate of the religious societies in England illustrated what happened to pietism when it remained embedded within the confines of an organized church and continued to retain a vested interest in a useful and edifying system of education. The support of high church dignitaries who had been at first suspicious and even openly hostile to the movement showed that it was really an effort to renovate rather than to renew, to refurbish rather than to recreate, the means and the ends of the established church.

Becoming aware that irreligion and immorality were associated with the prevailing ignorance among the mass of the people, the clergy began to make common cause with the societies and to reduce to a pious parody Blake's maxim "That to Labour in Knowledge is to Build up Jerusalem, and to Despise Knowledge is to Despise Jerusalem and her Builders."[2] Ken, who had been made Bishop of Bath and Wells in 1684, was in the habit of questioning beggars on their knowledge of religion, and he found them so ignorant that he was forced to conclude that the only chance of improvement was in raising up a new generation who should be better taught. Part of the legacy of

[2] *Jerusalem*, 77, Preface.

Puritanism had been the conviction that religion meant the contempt for all other learning than that of sectarian dogma. The newer outlook was given expression by Robert South in a sermon delivered in Westminster Abbey in 1692.

This Emanation of Gifts from the Spirit, assures us that Knowledge and Learning, are by no means opposite to Grace; since we see Gifts as well as Graces conferred by the same Spirit. But amongst those of the late Reforming Age (whom we have been speaking of) all Learning was utterly cryed down. So that with them the best Preachers were such as could not read, and the ablest Divines such as could not write. In all their Preachments they so highly pretended to the Spirit, that they could hardly so much as spell the Letter. To be blind was with them the Proper Qualification of a Spiritual Guide, and to be Book-Learned (as they called it) and to be Irreligious were almost Terms Convertible. None were thought fit for the Ministry but Tradesmen, and Mechanicks, because none else were allowed to have the Spirit. Those only were accounted like St. Paul, who could work with their hands, and in a literal sense, drive the Nail home, and be able to make a Pulpit before they preached in it.[3]

Blake would have considered South's attitude commendable, had it not been pressed into the service of "state religion." As it was, the effect of this kind of movement was to judge the productions of literature according to a general ethical standard. Such a standard might appear just and fair to reason and to the legislator, but it fell short of the scope of the imagination and individual conscience. "Is not every Vice possible to Man described in the Bible openly?"[4]

Nevertheless, individual conscience did play a part in the religious societies, and the importance which it was given foreshadowed the coming of evangelical enthusiasm. The insistence on the new birth and on its expression in works and actions which, in the opinion of

[3]Robert South, *Twelve Sermons upon Several Subjects and Occasions* (4 vols., London, 1698), III, pp. 547–8. Cf. Thomas Bray, *An Essay towards Promoting All Necessary and Useful Knowledge* (London, 1697), p. 12: "And as for our younger Gentry, I cannot think but it would tend extreamly to furnish their Minds also with that useful Knowledge in History, Travels, Humanity, Agriculture, and all such Noble Arts and Sciences, as will render 'em serviceable to their Families and Countries, and will make 'em considerable both at home and abroad: And that it will very much keep 'em from idle Conversation and the Debaucheries attending it, to have choice Collections of such Books dispers'd through all the Kingdom, and waiting upon 'em in their own Parlors, as will ennoble their Minds with Principles of Virtue and true Honour, and will file off that Roughness, Ferity and Barbarity which are the never failing Fruits of Ignorance and Illiterature."

[4]*The Laocoön Group.*

many, might appear unreasonable and even contrary to good manners anticipated the arguments and beliefs of Wesley and the Methodists. But the ultimate achievement of the societies was to provide a programme for moral rearmament. It was left for the Methodists to develop on a larger scale the enthusiasm latent in these beliefs. Blake hopefully associated this new movement with the regeneration and awakening of man. Always scanning the horizon for some sign of a religious or social explosion which would awaken the individual from his constant preoccupation with the compromise and distraction of his natural existence, he found the zeal and energy of Wesley and Whitefield congenial. When Cary abandoned his previous statement that Blake was mad and considerately pronounced him an "enthusiast,"[5] he was using a term which connected him not only with the Methodists but with anyone who refused to accept a purely rational outlook.

Perversity, wilfulness and extravagance were the words frequently used to describe Blake by some of the people he met in society, but it was not merely perversity nor enthusiasm which drew forth his praise of Wesley and Whitefield. He thought of Calvin and Luther as having fallen from the literal and individual interpretation of the prophetic word into a dogmatic and moral retrenchment under political authority. In the first book of *Milton*,[6] Los, the spirit of prophecy, calls this to the remembrance of his two sons: Palamabron, the type of the Redeemed, and Rintrah, the type of the Reprobate. Both of these types represent the two classes of men who require neither miracle nor a new birth to remind them of eternal life. The Elect, however, require both of these incentives, and to the Elect Wesley and Whitefield are sent as witnesses.[7] Blake hopes that they will effect a revival of that faith which is "the substance of things hoped for, the evidence of things not seen."[8]

[5]Alexander Gilchrist, *Life of William Blake* (Everyman ed., London, 1942), chap. XXXV p. 321.

[6]*Milton*, 25: 47–55.

[7]The main characteristic of the Elect, as Blake uses the term (*ibid.*, 27: 32–4), is the need for the miraculous which takes the form of an exclusive revelation. The danger is that the Elect will become attached to this revelation as the definitive expression of eternal truth. In his letter to William Law (Jan. 6, 1756), Wesley admitted as the basis of argument "no writings but the inspired" (*Letters*, ed. J. Telford, 8 vols., London, 1931, III, p. 332). Blake's admiration for Law and Boehme would certainly have made him class Wesley himself with the Elect in this argument.

[8]Heb., xi: 1.

> The Witnesses lie dead in the Street of the Great City:
> No Faith is in all the Earth: the Book of God is trodden underfoot.
> He sent his two Servants, Whitefield & Wesley: were they Prophets,
> Or were they Idiots or Madmen? Shew us Miracles!
> Can you have greater Miracles than these? Men who devote
> Their life's whole comfort to entire scorn & injury & death?[9]

Thinking, no doubt, of Wesley's fifty years of horseback-riding and of his tireless activity, Blake ignored the Holy Club and the abstinence from frivolous amusements and assessed the Wesleyan conception of faith as an approach to his own "liberty of both body and mind to exercise the Divine Arts of Imagination."

He was always aware, however, that the opposition between faith and reason among his contemporaries fell short of his concept of complete intellectual liberty. For the rationalist distrusted the faith of the enthusiast, and restricted passion and enthusiasm to the five senses. The enthusiast tended to distrust all secular knowledge which had not been given the perspective of religious faith. Religious faith usually remained on the defensive, in this struggle to capture the mental outlook of the age, and the defenders frequently collapsed into a negative attitude of self-denial and abstinence.

> We are told to abstain from fleshly desires that we may lose no time from the Work of the Lord: Every moment lost is a moment that cannot be redeemed; every pleasure that intermingles with the duty of our station is a folly unredeemable, & is planted like the seed of a wild flower among our wheat: All the tortures of repentance are tortures of self-reproach on account of our leaving the Divine Harvest to the Enemy, the struggles of intanglement with incoherent roots.[10]

Such was the extent of the ascetic delusion of the religious enthusiast and the persistent rational error which he retained in the form of an opposition between spirit and the senses. That there was such an opposition Blake admitted, but it could not be resolved by negating one of the contraries. The contraries could only be resolved by being brought together in an "enthusiasm" which included them both, and which was that vigour of spirit inseparable from every active enjoyment. "I know of no other Christianity and of no other Gospel than the liberty both of body & mind to exercise the Divine Arts of

[9] *Milton*, 24: 59–63; 25: 1–2. Cf. *Jerusalem*, 52, Preface: "Foote in calling Whitefield, Hypocrite, was himself one . . . ."

[10] *Jerusalem*, 77, Preface.

Imagination. . . ."[11] His inclusive conception of liberty formed a contrast to Wesley's pious restrictions and his political conservatism which reminds one more of Luther's position than Blake's. Blake still supported what he called "true enthusiastic superstition" in preference to deism and its reasonable pretence to moral virtue. Deism was an ethical allegory translated into axiomatic principles, and it gave political and social authority the appearance of reason, nature and commonsense. Even when he seemed to be most revolutionary, the deist, such as Voltaire and Rousseau, was merely seeking a reshuffling of social organization, so that enlightened self-interest—or what Blake called the "Selfish Virtues of the Natural Heart"—could have even greater scope.

Always a friend to the improvement of social conditions, Blake nevertheless detected a sinister basis to the deist's pursuit of liberty: it was the professed belief that freedom could be brought about by a change of circumstances and education alone. This was either rational self-deception or moral hypocrisy. The mediaeval monk and the contemporary Methodist at least recognized the need for a change of heart to make the best circumstances effective. They also recognized that man's natural condition was insufficient, and that faith was not born out of a moral metaphor. But the faith of the Methodist could not always be distinguished from an emotional aberration which Blake satirized in *An Island in the Moon*.[12] Whatever the perversities of religious feeling to which Methodism might lead, it remained as a witness to the need for a more profound revolution, and one which rational commonsense could not provide. The need was not satisfied by the enthusiasm of the pietists by any means, but reached out to the mystic lore and enigmatic writings of theosophers and seers of every description.

Religious enthusiasm was the start of an awakening out of the circle of destiny, with its "Twenty-seven Heavens & their Churches"—the "Monstrous Churches of Beulah." It was the expression of a desire to get beyond dogma and ritual to understanding and action—from the "Synagogue of Satan" to the "Everlasting Gospel." "Beulah"

[11] *Ibid.*

[12] "Ah, Mr. Huffcap would kick the bottom of the Pulpit out with Passion—would tear off the sleeve of his Gown & set his wig on fire & throw it at the people. He'd cry & stamp & kick & sweat, and all for the good of their souls." *An Island in the Moon*, chap. IV.

itself was the state of mystic ecstasy as well as that of sexual delight, midway between the awakened understanding of Eden and the involved turmoil of Generation. It was the state where self-will had been subdued but not yet annihilated, and was associated not only with the Methodists such as Whitefield and Hervey but also with the quietists, Fénelon, Madame Guyon and the Spanish mystic St. Teresa.[13]

Although it has only confused the study of Blake's works to place them in a mystical or theosophical tradition, there is much more similarity between his prophetic books and the writings of Paracelsus, Boehme and Swedenborg. The followers of Boehme in England, especially William Law, formed a part of Anglican pietism which Blake evidently regarded with great interest. He was reported to have called Boehme a divinely inspired man, and he praised the diagrams which Law added to his translation of Boehme, saying that Michelangelo himself could not have done better.[14] On the writings of Swedenborg, however, he commented at much greater length.

Blake treated the Swedish seer as one half-converted from the camp of the enemy. He found it difficult to forget that Swedenborg had been a natural philosopher, and that he had turned from the systematic explanation of the natural universe to a factual survey of heaven and hell. Besides, he took on the role of the apostle of the new age with a cardinal's mixture of humility and superior authority, and dispensed justice with the air of Plato's philosopher-king. The moral judgment as a system of rewards and punishments had taken its tyrannical place in the vision of Swedenborg, and the legal code of retribution which formed the basis of a city or kingdom in the natural world was projected into the sphere beyond it.

Again, consider the wickedness prevalent among men: unless the wicked were restrained by the penalties of the law, no city or kingdom could stand. Man is, as it were, a community in miniature. Unless he is disciplined physically, after death he would be chastised or punished; and this would continue until he ceased to do evil from fear of punishment, although he could never be brought to do good for its own sake.[15]

[13]See the reference to these quietists in *Jerusalem*, 72: 45–52. See also *Milton*, 41: 16–18. In *Milton*, 24, above, Wesley and Whitefield are identified with the two "witnesses" of Rev. xi, Moses and Elijah.

[14]H. Crabb Robinson, *Diary, Reminiscences and Correspondence*, ed. T. Sadler (Boston, 1869), II, chap. II, p. 27.

[15]Swedenborg, *True Christian Religion*, chap. IX, no. 531. According to Crabb Robinson

Like the Druids and the succeeding legislators of Greece, Swedenborg had a conception of spiritual discipline which reflected natural conditions and the absolute rule of necessity. Any such "community in miniature" could only be ruled by what Blake calls the "laws of Babylon" or the code of retributive justice. This is the persistent error of the Elect who turn the free community of prophetic vision into a collection of "Reprobates," and put Babylon in place of Jerusalem.

> O Swedenborg! strongest of men, the Samson shorn by the Churches,
> Shewing the Transgressors in Hell, the Proud Warriors in Heaven,
> Heaven as a Punisher, & Hell as One under Punishment,
> With Laws from Plato & his Greeks . . .[16]

Although Swedenborg found that the ruling love was what ultimately determined the place of the individual in the spiritual and celestial worlds, he made the mistake, as far as Blake was concerned, of trying to explain what was beyond logic, logically. Divine Providence could not be explained in rational terms derived from natural conditions without creating the misunderstanding that Providence was only omniscient when everything was preordained. In attempting to correct the doctrines of the various churches, Swedenborg had fallen under their influence.

The Swedenborgian system of correspondences was the rational counterpart of Blake's visionary mythology, but the two points of view which these systems reflected were as different as a geologist and an artist. The former was always emphasizing the reality of what he saw and establishing his credentials as a witness, while the latter emphasized what was doing the seeing and never forgot that, as a witness, he was simply another seer. Swedenborg was continually

(*Diary*, II, chap. II, p. 27), Blake said of Swedenborg: "He was a divine teacher. He has done much good, and will do much. He has corrected many errors of Popery, and also of Luther and Calvin. Yet Swedenborg was wrong in endeavouring to explain to the rational faculty what the reason cannot comprehend." The rational order of Swedenborg's visions was not appreciated by Thomas Taylor the Platonist (1758–1835) who was not alone in associating them with the effects of contemporary enthusiasm. Speaking of the work of Hesiod (*The Mystical Hymns of Orpheus*, trans. Thomas Taylor (London, 1824), p. xx n.), Taylor wrote that "his Theogony, when considered according to this exposition, will be found to be beautifully consistent and sublime; whereas, according to modern interpretations, the whole is a mere chaos, more wild than the delirious visions of Swedenborg, and more unconnected than any of the impious effusions of methodistical rant."

[16]*Milton*, 24: 50–3. Cf. *ibid.*, 41: 11–12. It is just possible that Swedenborg is the "Wicker Man of Scandinavia" who has so puzzled Blake's critics.

separating the rational content or meaning of what he saw from its visionary form, and then giving this meaning a general or abstract significance. The difference between Swedenborg's "correspondence" and Blake's symbolic "image" was the difference between a definition made for the reasoning mind and a symbol which was left for the whole understanding. Blake agreed that the life of man was to be understood by image and sign, and that these corresponded to man's entire human existence and to his universal environment, but no one could be taught to see for himself while he was expected to learn by rote. Swedenborg's method of abstracting the contents or index from the book of vision made it possible to imitate the seer's insight outwardly in reasoning and talking—like a monkey on a string.

> Thus Swedenborg boasts that what he writes is new: tho' it is only the Contents or Index of already publish'd books.
>
> A man carried a monkey about for a shew, & because he was a little wiser than the monkey, grew vain, and conciev'd himself as much wiser than seven men. It is so with Swedenborg: he shews the folly of churches, & exposes hypocrites, till he imagines that all are religious, & himself the single one on earth that ever broke a net.[17]

Although Blake attributed Swedenborg's "confident insolence" to the philosopher's habit of systematic reasoning, the latter's doctrine of correspondences was still a blunt declaration by a different type of mind of the very basis of his own visionary art.

In his *Heaven and Hell*,[18] Swedenborg declared that everything in nature and in the body of man corresponded to certain spiritual things. Ignoring the four levels of interpretation current in the Middle Ages and the Renaissance, he asserted that the science of correspondence—unknown to the primitive Christian communities—had been the

[17] *Marriage of Heaven and Hell*, Keynes, p. 190. Swedenborg described Noah as the parent or seed of the ancient church (*Arcana Coelestia*, no. 788), but he made Shem represent internal worship, and Japhet external worship (*ibid.*, no. 1140). Blake said that they represented Poetry, Painting and Music in his *Vision of the Last Judgment* (pp. 80–1), and he let his reader go on from there. There was no place to go with Swedenborg but to a dictionary of his correspondences. His followers have compiled several of these. Cf. George Nicholson, *A New and Comprehensive Dictionary of Correspondences, Representatives, and Significatives, Contained in the Word of the Lord* (London, 1800). Nicholson claimed (p. xxiii) that his dictionary provided "the only infallible rule for unsealing the divine mysteries in the word of the Lord, and for furnishing the Christian world with an authentic, genuine and sublime system of theology." Cf. Swedenborg, *True Christian Religion*, nos. 201–7.

[18] Nos. 87–105.

universal science of the ancients, forming a language which communicated with the angels of heaven.[19] This science of sciences flourished in the kingdoms of Asia among the magicians and seers of those countries, until it was communicated to Greece in the form of the oldest myths of Greek literature. With this account of the origins of a universal symbolism may be compared Blake's description in *The Marriage of Heaven and Hell* of the origin of religious ritual from the tales of the ancient poets.[20] Whereas Swedenborg developed his argument with an eye on the moral degradation of man and his consequent loss of knowledge, Blake ascribed to the restrictions of a priesthood who had lost the power of vision the ignorant idolatry of succeeding generations. Swedenborg explained the relationship between the language of symbolism and the rites of the Hebrew religion, and he related the prophetic word to the development of their ceremonies. But he admitted that organized religion eventually culminated in idolatry and finally in atheism. These last two stages were the result of a confirmed belief in nature apart from the teaching of the Word. Of natural religion and its supposed independence from any inspired doctrine, Swedenborg wrote:

> Nor do the writers on natural religion derive their knowledge from themselves; they merely confirm by rational declarations what they have learnt from the church which has the Word. It is possible that some of them do not believe what they are supposed to have proved.[21]

[19]In a letter to Flaxman (Sept. 21, 1800), Blake declared that his mind was filled with books and paintings of old which were "the delight & study of Archangels."

[20]Cf. *Vision of the Last Judgment*, Keynes, p. 638: "Let it here be Noted that the Greek Fables originated in Spiritual Mystery & Real Visions, which are lost & clouded in Fable & Allegory, while the Hebrew Bible & the Greek Gospel are Genuine . . . ." From the purely philosophical point of view, Immanuel Kant showed how easy it was to establish metaphysical dogma on the basis of such visions as those of Swedenborg. In his *Träume eines Geistersehers* (1766), the celebrated founder of the critical philosophy satirized the construction of a metaphysical system in which all that was required was the acceptance of concepts derived from visions, as though they were conclusive. This process consolidated vision into dogma, and developed the allegory of a church or sect, but there could be no ultimate finality to vision, for it was the expression of the seer's continuous development. However, fear of ridicule may have prevented Kant from admitting how much his own thought was influenced by that of Swedenborg. Cf. Frank Sewall, "Kant and Swedenborg on Cognition," *New Church Review*, V, no. 4 (Oct., 1898).

[21]*True Christian Religion*, no. 273. Cf. *ibid.*, no. 12: "In the spiritual world I have seen men who, from things visible in this world, have so confirmed their belief in nature that they have become atheists . . . . Let everyone, therefore, beware of confirming his belief in nature; let him confirm his belief in God; the means are not wanting."

Both Swedenborg and Blake took a similar course in their description of man's "progress" from divine wisdom to profane knowledge. Both agreed that the lost language which was the prophetic word should be restored, but both did not agree on the best means of doing this.

It was inevitable that the writings of Swedenborg should form the basis of a cult, and in 1788 a "New Church" was organized in London. In this way, he gave the promulgation of his doctrine the imprimatur of a new revelation and sought to establish the immediacy of inspiration through a specially ordained link in the prophetic tradition. His followers were, therefore, privileged to accept, conserve and defend a revealed mystery, an arcane doctrine of correspondences—a dictionary of symbols rather than a literature of visions. Blake recognized in Swedenborg what he deplored in Milton: the effort to give coherence and stability to a religious revelation in terms of a "higher" rationalism.[22] Even Milton's later voluntarism was reflected in the priority Swedenborg gave the will in his scheme of redemption, for the will was the being of man's life, and the understanding the manifestation of that life. Hence, the aspiration of the understanding, while it was united to the unregenerate will or Selfhood, proved to be inconclusive until man was given a new will. It was the will which impelled the understanding to think. If the words "desire" or "energy" had been substituted for "will," Blake might have agreed, but for him, the term "will" suggested the perverse activity of the Selfhood, and when applied to God, the arbitrary power of an omnipotent tyrant. "There can be no Good Will. Will is always Evil; it is pernicious to others or suffering. If God is anything he is Understanding. He is the Influx from that into the Will."[23] Blake wished to emphasize that man's redemption was not limited to any specific revelation or special grace, but was also an attainment through the development of his understanding. He liberated the notion of redemption from being a religious

[22]*Milton*, 24: 39–54. According to the Swedenborgians, however, Blake's anti-rationalism was sheer perversity, when it did not indicate a fundamental lack of balance. Cf. J. Spilling, "Blake, Artist and Poet," *New Church Magazine*, VI (London, 1887), p. 259: "With the former [Swedenborg] the Reason and the Vision were equal. With the latter [Blake] Vision overpowered and overmastered Reason."

[23]*Annotations to Swedenborg's "Divine Love and Wisdom,"* fly-leaf, Keynes, p. 736. "Understanding or Heaven" was what man created beyond the natural self, and it was acquired "by means of Suffering & Distress & Experience." "Will, Desire, Love, Pain, Envy" were of the Selfhood, although "Desire" and "Love" were used in a less restricted sense as well.Swedenborg's "new will" corresponded to Blake's "New Selfhood" (*Jerusalem*, Preface) in some respects.

monopoly and related it to the growth of every faculty. Swedenborg's subordination of the understanding to the will tended to produce a cult of authority which Blake sought to avoid, because he saw in it the seeds of a theological determinism not unlike the Calvinist doctrine of predestination.

In his annotations to Swedenborg's *Divine Providence*, Blake was concerned with the deductions made from the concept of a general Providence. In his struggles to relate the divine omniscience to the temporal state of man, Swedenborg experienced some difficulty. It was perhaps not his fault, but the fault of his deductive method, which made the relationship sound very much like predestination. His logical exposition betrayed him into placing heaven or all that was good in opposition to hell which was all that was not good. Man's freedom of choice consisted in his choosing one or the other according to his ruling love, and his ruling love dictated in which he was to be "enrolled." To this Blake retorted: "What is Enrolling but Predestination?"[24] Swedenborg was not content to let the realm of paradox which contained that of logic remain itself, but was always subjecting it to the logical form of exposition which was obviously incapable of expressing it. After stating that every man lived after death according to his life on earth, and that his place was assigned to him either in heaven or in hell, be proceeded to state that both these acted as one "Form" and that no one could occupy another place in that "Form" but his own. It followed that from infancy to death, and after, his place was foreseen "and at the same Time provided."[25] Abandoning all such logical deductions, Blake maintained the paradox of the utter bondage of the natural man, and the possibility of his freeing his spirit in this or in any other world. As a natural creature, man could choose not to be negative and passive, but to awaken his human existence. Otherwise, he possessed no choice, for he had denied what Blake called the Poetic Genius and what Swedenborg called the

[24] *Annotations to Swedenborg's "Divine Providence,"* pp. v, 82, 254, 434. In his *Heaven and Hell* (no. 313), Swedenborg stated that "the inner mind is formed for the reception of all things of the world; and those who receive the world without at the same time receiving heaven receive hell."

[25] *Annotations to Swedenborg's "Divine Providence,"* pp. 280–1. To this Blake retorted: "Devils & Angels are Predestinated." Man was neither a devil nor an angel, unless he gave himself up to one or the other completely, but Swedenborg seemed to think that man became one or the other after the death of the body, and that his life was henceforth utterly determined by his condition. Blake considered this kind of predestination "more Abominable than Calvin's" (*ibid.*, p. 434), and called it "Cursed Folly."

divinity of his Lord. Rejecting Swedenborg's *post mortem metamorphosis* of man into an angel or a devil, Blake contended that man as an existence was limited to neither heaven nor hell, for both these "places" were visionary states like the world of nature. Swedenborg was undoubtedly aware of all this, but the discursive form of his exposition betrayed him into a separation of the two contrary states of man. Each of them was made to appear as an eternal lot or portion to which the individual was forever allocated by the foresight of divine Providence. In his last annotation to Swedenborg's *Divine Love and Wisdom*, Blake brought the paradox into its paradoxical unity beyond the subordinate conditions of logical thinking. "Heaven and Hell are born together."[26]

By saying that they were born together, he sought to cut through the duality of soul and body, of what Swedenborg called the externals and the internals of the mind, and reach creative mind itself—the ground of the seer's perception or the Poetic Genius. This conception was the only "divinity" in Blake's thought, and when Swedenborg wrote, "The Negation of God constitutes Hell, and in the Christian World the Negation of the Lord's Divinity,"[27] he commented, "The Negation of the Poetic Genius." Like Swedenborg, he conceived of God as Divine Man whose appetitive nature was infinite love and whose understanding was infinite wisdom. Unlike Swedenborg, he did not represent either heaven or hell as supreme states, but as the fallen conditions of man's affections and his understanding. The perception of unity in human thoughts and affections constituted individual redemption, just as the separation of thought and affection constituted the distinction between soul and body, spirit and matter, heaven and hell: "Thought without affection makes a distinction between Love & Wisdom, as it does between body & spirit."[28] To overcome this distinction in one's self was to be redeemed from the unprofitable search for good and evil, and to be liberated for actual regeneration. *The Marriage of Heaven and Hell* is a satire on the moralist's desperate search for absolute right and wrong. As a parody of Swedenborg's *Heaven and Hell*, it forms a part of Blake's effort to free the theme of redemption from religious morality before it is completely smothered by theological conservatism and progressive naturalism.[29]

[26]*Annotations to Swedenborg's "Divine Love,"* p. 458.

[27]*Ibid.*, p. 14.

[28]*Ibid.*, p. 15. Cf. *Vision of the Last Judgment*, pp. 91–2.

[29]Cf. James Spilling, "Blake the Visionary," *New Church Magazine*, VI (London, 1887), p. 210:

Literary historians have called Blake a "Romantic." With certain specific Romantics he may be said to have had some connection, but to read his works in the context of most of the romanticisms of the period would distort them completely. His case against the exclusive use of reason was not on account of its emphasis on order, but because he was convinced that reasoning alone would reduce the reasoner to chaos. He never asserted the claims of the ego above those of society, but denounced the ego as the Selfhood, and considered the claims of society as of the most pressing interest and importance. All his writings and paintings were addressed to a public which ignored him, and he wrote nothing for the purpose of self-expression. He appears in the pages of Gilchrist, his biographer, as a man of considerable charm and dignity, who frequented the haunts of society eagerly and as often as he was invited. He was about as gloomy as a circus-barker, and as melancholy as Falstaff. In this respect, he is to be distinguished from Cowper for whose biography by Hayley he did four engravings, and in whom he saw the "Divine countenance."[30]

Apart from his "Divine countenance" or "genius," Cowper suffered from an apparently incurable religious melancholy. He was the best example in the century of the combined impact of the mechanistic philosophy of nature and evangelical Calvinism on a sensitive mind. He was caught between two forms of fatalism, and he retreated from both into a childlike appreciation of nature. Blake robustly dismissed the mechanistic universe of the Newtonians as a rational *tour de force*, and he ridiculed the doctrine of predestination as an error based on theological rationalism. But Cowper did not possess Blake's ground of vision, and he shifted nervously from the aimless search for natural security to desperate reflections on the ways of Providence. A somewhat romantic appreciation of nature came to be an escape from the burden of reflection, but nature only relieved his desperate conviction

"By fits, he was Swedenborgian and non-Swedenborgian. At times the clear placid reason of the apostle of the New Church annoyed him. Blake hated reason . . . . In fact, in a letter which we now have before us, Dr. Garth Wilkinson tells us that Charles Augustus Tulk, one of the most earnest and original of New Church thinkers, often conversed with Blake. 'Blake', says Dr. Wilkinson, 'informed Tulk that he had two different states; one in which he liked Swedenborg's writings, and one in which he disliked them. The second was a state of pride in himself, and then they were distasteful to him, but afterwards he knew that he had not been wise and sane. The first was a state of humility, in which he received and accepted Swedenborg'. We can readily believe this statement, as it serves to explain much in relation to Blake's attitude to our great seer which is otherwise inexplicable."

[30]Letter to Hayley, May 24, 1804.

that he had been condemned by divine foreordination. He who considered that the "designs of Providence are inscrutable"[31] could, in another letter, remark:

> Man often prophesies without knowing it; a spirit speaks by him which is not his own, though he does not at the time suspect that he is under the influence of any other. Did he foresee what is always foreseen by Him who dictates what he supposes to be his own, he would suffer by anticipation, as well as by consequence; and wish perhaps as ardently for the happy ignorance, [to] which he is at present so much indebted, as some have foolishly and inconsiderately done for a knowledge that would be but another name for misery.[32]

He was the perfect example of one who had been betrayed by false prophets, and by their false conception of prophetic knowledge. In these circumstances, his immediately personal faith was at once the source of his joy and his despair. He still clung to the belief in an inscrutable deity, and yet wrote his *Olney Hymns* to the personal Jehovah of the Hebrew prophets.

His effort, which is reflected in the hymns, to retain belief in the face of despair made him a kind of hero for Blake. The ancient conception of the divine mania was associated with the need for a refuge from the mechanistic and empty universe of natural philosophy. In his *Annotations to Spurzheim's "Insanity"* (p. 154), Blake counters the doctrine that the primitive feelings of religion or enthusiasm are the cause of insanity with the following note on Cowper: "Cowper came to me and said: 'O that I were insane always. I will never rest. Can you not make me truly insane? I will never rest till I am so. O that in the bosom of God I was hid.' " To be "*truly insane*"—the true madness, the divine mania of antiquity is here identified with mental health and the ability to balance the inner life with temporal affairs: "You retain health and yet are as mad as any of us all—over us all—mad as a refuge from unbelief—from Bacon, Newton and Locke." Blake himself had found the refuge from unbelief neither in the conception of an inscrutable Providence, nor a transcendent first cause, nor in a childlike faith in the moral order of nature, but in the original Christian conception of the essential unity of anthropomorphic God and theomorphic man. He was more of a humanist than a Romantic, for he did not fall away from the pattern of thought which retained

[31] William Cowper, Letter to Rev. John Newton, Dec. 17, 1781.

[32] *Ibid.*, June 23, 1780.

that conception in the Renaissance into either the theory of the Great Chain of Being or the romantic cult of nature.[33]

The cult of nature was one indication in the Romantic movement of an inner poverty of spirit, a search, in one form or another, for an *anima mundi* as the means of regaining the natural vitality and faith of childhood. A deluded mysticism was indicated in this attempted retreat from experience into a lost innocence, a reversal of the direction which the affections and the thoughts travel from the first environment of nature through that of society towards self-realization. If the Neo-Classical preoccupation with reasonable methods and the toys of mechanism failed to carry the totality of man's powers to maturity, so did the Romantic revolt in favour of the higher insight which was supposed to be above commonsense and was often beneath it. Living in an age of revolutions, the outstanding Romantics were aware of an inner force which, in Blake's cultural cycle, was the prelude to the realization of man's creative powers, individually and socially. The original revolutionary impetus, however, inevitably fell from its first aim into the wasted effort of individual dissipation and political tyranny. The revolutionary wars, like the earlier wars of religion, served to illustrate the subjection of the creative energy of a new enlightenment to its natural counterpart—the will to power. The characteristic assertion of the will which distinguished the Romantic's search for truth in man, nature and society usually completed a circle. Wordsworth's youth began with a search for power rather than knowledge, but from a political revolutionary, he became a recluse, and finally, a conservative. Unfortunately, in Blake's eyes, Wordsworth's creative energy persisted only too often in the form of a subjection to the natural man and his memories.

Although Blake considered Wordsworth the greatest poet of his age, he was disturbed by the apparent passivity towards nature reflected in such words and phrases as "sensibility," "emotion recollected in tranquility" and "the influence of natural objects." Believing that the

[33]The subject of several of Cowper's hymns is Blake's Jehovah who is the original image of the individual in his "Divine" or "Human" nature. *Jehovah Our Righteousness* reflects the despair of Cowper and his conviction that he is unable to gain personal redemption. It may also be compared with Blake's attack on the self-righteousness of the moralists. The celebration of Jerusalem as the original city of the redeemed in the hymn, *Jehovah Shammah*, is comparable with Blake's epic conception in *Jerusalem*. The hymn called *Jehovah Jesus* contains the substance of a remark in *The Marriage of Heaven and Hell*: "Know that after Christ's death, he became Jehovah."

only active agent was spirit, and that the seer was the only true poet, he resented the intrusion of reflection and memory into the creative process. The imagination which was dominated by these was permissive and passive, rather than imperative and active. Commenting on Wordsworth's sub-title, *Poems Referring to the Period of Childhood,* Blake writes: "I see in Wordsworth the Natural Man rising up against the Spiritual Man Continually, & then he is No Poet but a Heathen Philosopher at Enmity against all true Poetry or Inspiration."[34] In one of his subsequent notes, Blake emphatically asserts that imagination has nothing to do with memory, for he obviously connects memory with the retention of general or abstract ideas derived from the fading images of sensation. The poet who regards memory as the prime source of his work is a bad philosopher and not really a poet at all. The accumulation of experiences and impressions may seem to form an essential part of his own work, but the memory of past incidents on which recollection is based destroys the immediate present of inspiration. Recollection and reflection are distracting, and to raise up past incidents to induce certain states of emotion and thought is to raise up the natural or temporal man against the spiritual or eternal man. Memory reaches back into the past, and reflection projects the sum of experience into future plans, but the inspired present is not this kind of receptacle for past memories and future conditions. The moment of vision includes temporal experience without being dominated by it, just as the moment of action includes previous practice without being prevented by it. Memory has to do with passive recollection, while inspiration is itself active and immediate recognition. Memories connected with the child's sheltered world of nature and home formed part of Wordsworth's practice of recollection but this redigestion of one's own childhood is very different from Blake's visionary recognition of the actual state of childhood in his *Songs of Innocence and Experience.*

The distinction between vision or recognition and memory or recollection is Blake's distinction between nature as a visionary state of existence and nature as the only condition of existence. To recollect is to remain within the circle of destiny and to look forward and backward along the direction of time's arrow; to recognize is to see the circle of destiny in perspective, and nature as the imaginative vision within the mind of the seer.

[34]*Annotations to Wordsworth's "Poems,"* p. 1. Also pp. 374–5.

Some see Nature all Ridicule & Deformity, & by these I shall not regulate my proportions; & some scarce see Nature at all. But to the Eyes of the Man of Imagination, Nature is Imagination itself. As a man is, so he sees. As the Eye is formed, such are its Powers.[35]

It would seem, at this point, that both Blake and Wordsworth are talking about the same vision of nature, but Blake emphasizes the action of perception as the ground of the vision, and Wordsworth, the "Presences of Nature."[36] Wordsworth was, after all, less of a seer and more of an observer, and therefore, less of a poet and more of a philosopher. He laid great stress on the power of natural objects to reveal the spirit that produced them, and even to provide him with his conceptions.

> The external universe,
> By striking upon what is found within;
> Had given me this conception.[37]

Although perfectly aware that Wordsworth considers natural impressions alone incapable of giving him his conceptions, Blake disagrees with the latter's consistent emphasis on the active power and ministry of nature. For those who have not even begun to see nature, nature is certainly a ministry, but the poet is supposed to be superior to a spiritual moron. Nature as a panorama of objects limits the vision of the seer and can neither enrich nor strengthen it. "Natural Objects always did & now do weaken, deaden & obliterate Imagination in Me. Wordsworth must know that what he Writes Valuable is Not to be found in Nature."[38] Seeking strength and the conviction of a moral order in his environment by a process of recollection and retrenchment, Wordsworth is using natural objects as firm ground for his thoughts and affections. Blake, already in possession of visionary health and stability, is impatient with Wordsworth's search for security and moral poise. When Wordsworth speaks of his wish to have the temporal sequence of day following day united by the sense of security which he calls "natural piety," he attaches himself to the natural environment in the status of a dependant. This attachment puts both nature and himself in a very false position as far as Blake is concerned.

Wordsworth's tendency to regard the natural environment as an analogy of its spiritual counterpart within himself might have reflected

[35]Letter to Trusler, Aug. 23, 1799.

[36]Wordsworth, *The Prelude*, i, 464.

[37]*Ibid.*, viii, A 765–7.

[38]*Annotations to Wordsworth's "Poems,"* p. 44.

his earlier desire for power and the disappointment which followed it. Disillusionment perhaps prompted him to turn from society to nature, and seek the ground for self-realization in nature rather than in man. Looking for the creator of nature rather than the creator of man, he "surpassed" the conception of the anthropomorphic God who had created man in his own image, and worshipped a deity whose attributes were in the powers of nature. Blake associates these powers with the plurality of gods in the heathen mythology: "Solomon, when he married Pharoah's daughter & became a Convert to the Heathen Mythology, Talked exactly in this way of Jehovah as a Very inferior object of Man's Contemplation. . . ."[39] Wordsworth's search for a sound basis and a norm for action was an endeavour to surpass man, and at the same time, to turn again and see in him as a social entity and in nature something of "kindred permanence."[40] This attempt to see man's creative possibilities through the active mediation of nature brings forth Blake's uncompromising opposition. Wordsworth "fitted" the external world to the mind, and the mind to the external world, in a way which reminds Blake of the natural creature who is merely an organ subject to sense and not of creative mind at all: "You shall not bring me down to believe such fitting & fitted. I know better & please your Lordship."[41]

In spite of the disagreement with Wordsworth and his concept of nature, Blake recognizes the clarity of imaginative perception in the actual poetry of his contemporary. The ability to see, however it may be subordinated to what is seen, has a way of overcoming the immediate plans and limitations of the poet's Selfhood or natural self. The actual seer or spiritual self is the imagination which makes use of the corporeal understanding. But when the seer attempts to see only with this kind of understanding or reason, or permits its restrictions and conditions to dominate and explain what he does see, he fails as a seer. Blake detects this failure in Wordsworth's reliance on the natural field of perception instead of on the plain act of perception itself.

[39]*Annotations to Wordsworth's "Excursion,"* p. xi.

[40]Wordsworth, *The Prelude*, xiii, A 42.

[41]*Annotations to Wordsworth's "Excursion,"* pp. xii-xiii. The sentimental piety of Wordsworth who sought his natural morality and his sense of man's destiny from the birds and the bees excites Blake's scorn, if not his contempt. "Does not this Fit, & is it not Fitting most Exquisitely too, but to what?—not to Mind, but to the Vile Body only & its Laws of Good & Evil & its Enmities against Mind."

The undistracted and independent act of perception is the basis of Blake's "work of art." What he calls "spiritual sensation" is an enlarged and heightened ability to perceive—an ability not to be traced to any datum of existence such as nature, but to be identified with the development of human existence. Existence is the same as perception, and the field of natural objects is a datum of perception and not its ultimate source. A real work of art expresses human existence and not some natural force or power. The language of such art is the same as the immemorial language of the seer which translates the apparent data of natural existence into the speech of a prophetic orator. Blake obviously thought of himself as a "true Orator" in whose rhetoric the forms of nature became the figures of speech of an inspired vision. Unlike the Aristotelian Thomas Aquinas who treated rhetoric and poetic as mere subdivisions of logic,[42] he reflected the other and earlier use made of these arts to express scriptural truth according to its visionary types or symbols. Abelard, for instance, was of the opinion that the intention of divine scripture was to teach or to move after the manner of an oration.[43] Blake evidently intended his prophetic books to be read in this fashion, and to him they were undoubtedly his contribution to "the Word of God Universal." As such, they can never be really reconciled to either the Neo-Classical or the Romantic canons of taste. His images and metaphors are like those of Isaiah and the writer of Revelation. His belief in inspiration is concrete, individual and unmetaphysical, reminding one of the "daemon" of Socrates and the Jehovah of the Hebrew prophets. In his preface to *Jerusalem*, he writes:

> When this Verse was first dictated to me, I consider'd a Monotonous Cadence, like that used by Milton & Shakespeare & all writers of English Blank Verse, derived from the modern bondage of Rhyming, to be a necessary and indispensible part of Verse. But I soon found that in the mouth of a true Orator such monotony was not only awkward but as much a bondage as rhyme itself. I therefore have produced a variety in every line, both of cadences & number of syllables. Every word and every letter is studied and put into its fit place; the terrific numbers are reserved for the terrific parts, and the prosaic for the inferior parts; all are necessary to each other.[44]

[42]Thomas Aquinas, *Posteriorum Analyticorum Aristotelis Expositio*, I, i, 6 ff.

[43]Peter Abelard, *Commentaria super S. Pauli Epistolam ad Romanos*, Prologus: "Omnis Scriptura divina more orationis rhetoricae aut docere intendit aut movere."

[44]*Jerusalem*, 3, Preface. Blake's Swedenborgian critic, James Spilling ("Blake the Visionary," p. 209), seized on Blake's "taking dictation" as evidence that he was more or less a passive

Freedom of utterance takes this form of an inspired oration emancipated from the outward convention of literary composition, so that the inner integrity of the author's vision may be exactly maintained. Both in art and politics, Blake asserted the supremacy of internal over external organization, and he "took dictation" from the organized spirit within him—the Poetic Genius or the human existence itself.

Strictly speaking, the literary tradition of which he considered himself a part was finished by the time of Milton, and in this respect, he was more closely allied to the Renaissance than either the period of Neo-Classicism or that of the Romantic revolt. Revolt or revolution was the culminating stage in his cyclic myth, and it always expressed the emergence of the real from the outer husk of appearance and convention; it was the actual taking effect. Both the spirit of enlightenment and revolution burned in him as intensely as in any of his contemporaries, but they were content with a relatively superficial kind of revolution—the kind that altered external conditions and man's apparent relationship to them. Blake was more ambitious, and he sought to redeem the entire perspective of history by an apocalyptic revolt in the ground of the human mind. For the typical enlightened philosopher, the human mind was a datum of nature, and in its powers and possibilities limited and unalterable. For Blake, however, the only hope of any revolutionary change in man's natural and social environments lay in a redemption of his own inner chaos. Wordsworth never approached this conception of revolution more closely than in his description of the transformation of natural chaos into the ordered vision of eternity within one mind:

---

amanuensis. "He wrote what he was 'commanded by the spirits' to write. Swedenborg did not so. Our commissioned seer would not write anything that he was commanded to write by either angels or spirits; in fact, they dared not command him; he only wrote that which was revealed to him by the Lord while he was reading the Word (Swedenborg, *Divine Providence*, no. 135). The distinction is broad and marked. It accounts for the sweet reason of Swedenborg, and the dark mysticism of Blake." Blake practically anticipated this criticism in the following lines taken from the Preface quoted above—lines in which he invokes the source of his inspiration as "that God from whom all things are given."

Again he speaks in thunder and in fire!
Thunder of Thought, & flames of fierce desire:
Even from the depths of Hell his voice I hear
Within the unfathom'd caverns of my Ear.
Therefore I print; nor vain my types shall be:
Heaven, Earth & Hell henceforth shall live in harmony.

Tumult and peace, the darkness and the light—
Were all like the workings of one mind, the features
Of the same face, blossoms upon one tree,
Characters of the great Apocalypse,
The types and symbols of Eternity,
Of first, and last, and midst, and without end.[45]

In this respect, Blake was both a Romantic and a revolutionary, but his enthusiasm never led him into the delusion that the end justified any means, nor into the more engaging delusion that a utopian end required no very drastic means to accomplish it.

[45]*Simplon Pass*, 15–20.

7. Visionary Politics

NEVER A PRACTICAL POLITICIAN nor one whose interest impelled him to take an active part in the revolutionary activities of his day, Blake was nevertheless fascinated by these activities, and the part they played in the development of his thought was considerable. Just as he tried to achieve in the intellectual sphere a balance between reason and desire, and in religion, a marriage of heaven and hell, so politically, he endeavoured to see the social community as a form which would permit the free interplay of the moral sense and creative activity. In his youth, he was an enthusiastic revolutionary who saw in the American and French revolutions the dawn of a new age and the historical analogy of his own cyclic myth with its stages of fall, oppression in the fallen state, last judgment and redemption. It was under the influence of this kind of enthusiasm that he created his mythical figure of Orc—the type of revolution and energy. In his later prophetic books, however, he emphasized the necessity of individual redemption before any political revolution could hope to realize the renewal of any nation or people. But this later development was one of clarification rather than of change, for he did not limit man's possibilities to the conditions of his social environment. The fundamental ground of revolution in human affairs lay in the visionary state of the individual, and the root of all tyranny and oppression was ultimately man's imprisonment in the circle of historical destiny. Blake's notion of liberty could hardly be restricted to the overthrow of a traditional monarchy in favour of the "rights of man." He obviously did not believe in progress based on reason, nature and commonsense, for he was convinced that such "progress" was bound to be circular. The hitherto unknown goal which a Condorcet thought inescapable, he regarded as unattainable as long as man's perspective remained unaltered. The same historical pattern would remain, and the same types of social organization would succeed one another.

In the earlier prophecies of *Europe*, *America* and *The French Revolution*, however, Blake is not mainly concerned with the pattern of recurrence, but with the possibility of revolutionary renewal within the immediate present of historical time. As he understands it, revolution is the political counterpart of man's individual desire to liberate himself from a previous cycle of development and make a fresh start. On the threshold of this new beginning in the process of time, Orc, who is the spirit of revolutionary energy, is born of Los and Enitharmon, who are man's inner perception of time and space. The temporal field of history gives birth to the spirit of renewal, and this is an eternal event. As the first born of Enitharmon, Orc rises from the depths of man's natural needs, and revolution starts from the exasperation of the misused and distrusted energies of the governed. Like Dionysus he arises, but like Prometheus he is immediately bound by the limiting conditions of his natural state and obscured by the clouds of Urizen's reasonable traditions and preconceptions.[1]

But although Orc is born into time, he is an immortal, and his ultimate origin is eternal. With that naïve presumption which Blake always associates with energy and desire, he seizes the "Trump of the last doom" and tries to "awake the dead to Judgment." Pitied by the responsible and experienced Urizen, whose "iron tube" he cannot blow, he becomes the spirit of frustrated energy and falls into the course of "finite revolutions."

> Thought chang'd the infinite to a serpent, that which pitieth
> To a devouring flame; and man fled from its face and hid
> In forests of night: then all the eternal forests were divided
> Into earths rolling in circles of space, that like an ocean rush'd
> And overwhelmed all except this finite wall of flesh.
> Then was the serpent temple form'd, image of infinite
> Shut up in finite revolutions, and man became an Angel,
> Heaven a mighty circle turning, God a tyrant crown'd.[2]

As the "image of the infinite," the cyclical movement of the state of Generation contributes to man's possibility of achieving the inner, radical revolution, and it is from the standpoint of this possibility that Blake sees the political upheavals of his day.

[1] *Europe*, 24–8; 138–45.
[2] *Ibid.*, 86–94.

To the eye of the prophetic revolutionary, the force of political revolt shows up government as an analogy of man's predicament in the natural universe. Man has lost his humanity and has become a creature or "Angel" within the circle of time. Subjected to the tyranny of a divine king and the government of "Heaven," he is caught in a net of conditions. As long as he sees these natural conditions as the inevitable basis for his continued existence, he will reproduce his slavery to them in the form of his governments. In short, both political theory and practice will always reflect the limitations of his own finite horizon. The widening of this horizon cannot be accomplished by any government or by any political technique, and Blake evidently hopes that the revolutionaries of his day will at least realize the importance of this fact. He is, however, very much aware of the change in the fire of Orc when it enters the world of man's fallen perceptions, and becomes "a devouring flame." He is also aware that the revolutionary distrusts and fears the naked force of revolt at least as much as any reactionary, and the established rebel is Orc subdued by Urizen once again. By this means, the energy of desire meets the negative boundary of expedient conditions, the general fear of reprisals and the dogmatic outline of the political programme. The conquest of Orc by Urizen gives to Orc the form of the serpent, a form which Blake associates with eating the fruit of the Tree of the Knowledge of Good and Evil. Every government must claim to know what fallen man cannot know, according to Blake—what is good and what is evil. To pretend to this knowledge is the basis of political authority, and the pretence is the necessary fiction of the ruler. Political rule seems to be based on the abstract authority of a perfect constitution or on the divine right of kings. Between these extremes of tyranny, Blake finds nothing to choose, and his expressed views on politics frequently warn against exchanging the tyranny of kings for the tyranny of the state.

Shortly before his death, in fact, he noticed that the fear of disorder had already produced a reaction in favour of complete conformity. In a letter to George Cumberland, he wrote that "since the French Revolution Englishmen are all intermeasurable by one another: certainly a happy state of agreement, in which I for one do not agree."[3] Revolution—like the creative activity of the artist—was the continual

[3]April 12, 1827.

drive towards freedom of life and existence, and in the same letter he made use of the phrase "Republican art" which expressed the kind of liberty which he wanted in politics. It was that kind of liberty which found a place for every honest man's opinions as the expression of the citizen's existence, and such political freedom implied the existence of the prophet within the form of the state. Blake is to be distinguished from the authors of ideal republics such as Plato, More and Bacon and also from the political theorists of his own day whose belief in progress was founded on their prediction of the perfect state in which natural rights and natural liberties would prevail. The whole utopian ideal assumed that the natural man could be disciplined and governed by reason in his own best interests. Blake saw in this assumption the old struggle to force the duty of the citizen into the mould of the moral virtues which would reduce him to a social entity in a closed society. The utopian theorists appeared to believe that the natural man could be made better, if he would submit to a programme of rational education. The political naturalists, such as Rousseau, believed that he would become better by reason of his own nature, if only he could be liberated from unnatural and fabulous traditions to partake of the freedom of reasonable institutions. As the issues at stake became clarified, Blake separated his faith in humanity, which he shared with, say, Tom Paine, from the cult of nature and reason, and translated liberty into the consistent effort on the part of man to free his humanity from the abstract values of natural reason and the limitations of self-interest. He confirmed and enlarged his enthusiasm for the revolutionary force by seeing it as the historical analogy of the mental revolution or "apocalypse" of which it was also the outward and visible sign.

In the words of his song which closes the Preface to *Milton*, Blake expresses his hope for the "New Age"—a hope which will end in the building of Jerusalem in "England's green & pleasant Land." The end is to be effected, not by the external pressure of a technique imposed by reason, nor by the enthusiasm of the revolutionary force, nor even by the drive of man's instinctive needs, but by art—that is, by the use of the creative imagination. The imagination unites the man of intellect, the man of feeling and the man of instinct in a way which makes communication in the interests of a common aim possible and fruitful. Unlike the utopians, whose origin stretches back to More and finally to Plato, Blake is convinced that the stone rejected by these builders should be the very one to be placed at the head of the corner. Plato professed to exclude the poets from his republic, and he created a hierarchy of guardians to impose the perfect rule of intellect. More ironically established a government of talent over an isolated and protected community. Both Plato and More assumed that a common understanding already existed in the minds and hearts of their citizens. Blake speaks neither with the philosophic majesty of Plato nor with the irony of More, and he is fully aware that what he has to say requires constant struggle against any preconceived ideal of perfection. The preconceived ideal of perfection exists in the reasoning memory as a model for the present and a programme for the future, but imagination gives both past and present an immediately revolutionary significance.

When the imagination sets about recreating the form of man's social environment—the political unit—it gives that unit its original human form. Everything that man can create or imagine is contained in man, man considered not as a furtive animal of a natural environment but as the individual ground of that humanity which is the divine original of his creator: "Man can have no idea of any thing greater than Man, as a cup cannot contain more than its capaciousness. But God is a man, not because he is so perceiv'd by man, but because he is the creator of man."[4] The fundamental mistake in politics—as in religion—lies in man's constant attempt to go outside his original capacity into the abstractions of a super-state which ignores the real roots of individual life. Just as the superhuman deity ends by being a non-human abstraction, so also the political leviathan of the theorists puts the state in a false relationship to man's actual possibilities. The myth of the state as it was rationally conceived by eighteenth-century philosophers is untrue to Blake, because it is untrue to the visionary imagination. Such a state purports to be an improvement on the state of nature, and yet it is to arise out of the context of natural conditions. To Blake, however, man does not start from a point of origin within nature, but rather from one which is within himself. His reference to England, France and America as original human forms is more than a poetic trick of personification. Revolution is the beginning of a political act of self-realization, and in a very real sense he sees the body politic as the ground of this kind of fulfilment—that is, as the field for realizing

[4]*Annotations to Swedenborg's "Divine Love and Wisdom,"* p. 11.

man's humanity. If, however, man persists in seeing himself as a fragment of what he can see of his natural environment, he limits his possibilities to the state of nature. Attempting to construct the nation on the basis of his natural needs, he encounters the limitations of his Selfhood and its inevitable habit of seeing its own interests as different from the neighbour's. Until man can learn the immemorial lesson which lies at the root of his existence, revolution will be followed by the counter-revolution of exasperated authority trying to correct errors by a programme, a constitution, a code of moral restrictions. Begun always with high hopes, political revolt contains the seed of its own shipwreck, and like France's National Assembly, the revolutionaries attempt to remove from the community what they have not removed from themselves.

> They murmuring divide; while the wind sleeps beneath, and the numbers are counted in silence,
> While they vote the removal of War, and the pestilence weighs his red wings in the sky.[5]

As long as man remains a mirror of his natural conditions, revolution remains no more than the mirror of his unrealized hopes.

For Plato, these hopes take the apparent form of a programme in the mind of the philosopher. But the ideal state of justice is a possibility in the political sphere only as an analogy of the perfected philosopher himself who is already an inhabitant of its eternal original.

> But in heaven, probably, there is a model of it, said I, for anyone who inclines to contemplate it, and on contemplating to regulate himself accordingly; and it is of no consequence to him, whether it does exist any where, or shall ever exist here. He does the duties of this city alone, and of no other.[6]

Plato's city is an exemplar of the just man, and it takes the form of the three faculties represented by the three classes of citizens. But Plato seems to eliminate the visionary imagination which has given him his creation—once it has been created. Here lies the difficulty of utopian rationalism: how to retain the creative genius which has created the perfect conditions. Without this genius, the *Republic* becomes an ideal programme to be enforced, and ceases to be a vision which can be realized. Blake obviously believes that the original city can be continually realized by the revolutionary imagination. He avoids the

[5] *French Revolution*, 246–7.

[6] *Republic*, ix, 592B (*Works*, trans. Thos. Taylor (London, 1804), I, p. 437).

closed programme of regimented perfection which can be seen in Plato's apparent desire to *make* his ideal city the model for human institutions. Plato ostensibly describes a state which is the intelligible original of the cosmic order formulated by reason. This is not Blake's way of realizing the unfallen city at all, but is rather the way to a closed society ruled by guardians. He makes no compromise between what can be realized and what can be enforced, and in this respect avoids the influence of the contemporary political theorists who are busy devising programmes for achieving the perfect state.

Since the myth of the state created by Rousseau and his followers is based on the natural goodness of man, the original political unit is connected with the memory of primitive tribalism. Blake avoids associating his eternal city with any such state of nature, and his dislike of Plato's system of education is founded on his conviction that in a wholly rational community intellectual activity will collapse into a code of "moral virtue." Plato's intention may not have been to arrest growth or to return to nature, but rather to formulate the conditions of growth in terms of a goal which lies entirely beyond the social community. Blake, however, interprets Plato's emphasis on an ethic imposed by the state as a distrust of growth and as a return to natural law and natural morality. All formulations of conditions for action arising from rational reflection rely on memory rather than on inspiration. The term "memory" itself, as Blake uses it, implies an attachment to the past, and therefore, a fear of change. For Blake, Plato's nature is the commensurable structure of the universe encompassed by the ratio of the five senses which reduce it to the ordered cosmos of the Platonic *Timaeus* and the Newtonian *Principia*—a "Mathematic Form" which is "Eternal in the Reasoning Memory."[7] Plato's *Republic* with its discussion of justice and injustice, of good and evil, is founded on this kind of order which seeks to bring abstract perfection to bear on concrete activity. His city is in the reasoning memory of his philosopher and not in his imagination.[8] Blake associates abstract perfection as reflected in the moral laws of statecraft with the natural man's fear of change. His own radicalism is a revolt against this "Heathen or Platonic Philosophy, which blinds the Eye of Imagination, The Real Man."[9]

[7]*On Homer's Poetry & on Virgil.*

[8]Cf. *Jerusalem*, 74: 10–13.

[9]*Annotations to Berkeley's "Siris,"* p. 241.

He was a strange radical even for the eighteenth century, and yet all the phrases of the revolutionaries can be found in his works, which he describes as an "Endeavour to Restore what the Ancients call'd the Golden Age."[10] Is not this "Golden Age" identical with the hopes of the contemporary "primitives"? On the contrary, Blake never looks back in memory to a period when man lived in pastoral simplicity and in complete accord with natural law. He does not hold the central fiction of the primitivist: that the natural world is the work of a benevolent "Deus" whose benevolence is reflected in the impulses of the natural heart and in the thoughts of the unperverted mind. The unperverted mind has never been the natural possession of man, because man has never been, nor can he be, as man, wholly natural. Blake was no Arcadian who longed for the lost unity of a primeval society, for his original city exists neither in the past nor in the future but in the eternal present. However, after quoting the antiquarian's description of the early Britons as men who were "wiser than after-ages," he does say that "The Primeval State of Man was Wisdom, Art and Science."[11] But he refers to a state of mind, or more accurately, a state of existence, which cannot be induced by the restoration or preservation of institutions, nor by the invention of others. The restoration involves an upheaval, a radical change, in the "State of Man" as an individual and as a political entity. Such a change is the real revolution which will transform the monster Leviathan into the man, Albion.

Blake's political views develop from the radical enthusiasm of his earlier works to the apocalyptic fulfilment of his later ones, and he maintains a direction which leaves mundane politics far behind. The earliest works, however, express the patriotism of an Englishman who has learned his politics from Shakespeare. In them there is also an ironical insight into the moral complacency which the Whigs had inherited from the Puritan régime. The Whig party which consisted of the dissenters and those Anglicans of the middle class interested in political and economic expansion was the party of progress and of enlightenment. It represented a break with the past and with those traditions which had supported the older landowners and gentry. Like the young Swift, Blake evidently admired the energy of such a faction, but unlike him, he never became interested in the party as such. In

[10]*Vision of the Last Judgment*, Keynes, p. 639.

[11]*A Descriptive Catalogue &c.* (no. V, The Ancient Britons), Keynes, p. 608. *Jerusalem*, I, Preface, 3.

King Edward the Third—written between 1769 and 1778 during the Tory government of Lord North and the active participation of George III in political affairs—Blake gives evidence of a growing antipathy to the kind of liberalism which championed economic expansion as a moral duty and which was, at the same time, left of centre. The setting and form of the play reflect the influence of Shakespeare and the Elizabethans. In the opening lines, the king is represented as praying to a somewhat jingoistic deity to look after the interests of his Englishmen, and he appears to be most concerned about the depredations of the French on the supplies of English merchants.[12] The interdependence of political ambition, commercial enterprise and religious zeal is recognized, and the liberty to expand is "the charter'd right of Englishmen."[13] War as the instrument of policy founded on the ambition of princes begins to draw both irony and condemnation from a writer who, in later years, declares that war is "Energy enslav'd" and "Heroism a Miser."[14]

The form which Blake's development took illustrates his maxim that error can only be recognized when it has been clarified. The representation of conventional opinions on politics and an energetic and somewhat apocalyptic mode of expression are present in this early work. Opinions which express eighteenth-century views on politics are suggested in a line or a phrase. After the bishop has connected the success of industry with religion, he piously remarks that, while sitting in council with his prince, his thoughts take in "the gen'ral good of the whole," and he closes with the advice:

> Be England's trade our care; and we, as tradesmen,
> Looking to the gain of this our native land.[15]

Blake leaves this heroic opportunism and the "tricks of the world" to the bishop, the prince and the merchant, while he cuts his revolutionary path "into the heaven of glory."[16] The beginnings of this path can be seen in some of the symbols which emerge from the text of the earlier

[12]Cf. D. V. Erdman, *Blake, Prophet against Empire* (Princeton, 1954), pp. 60 ff. The external evidence which Erdman provides for regarding *King Edward the Third* as an example of irony is certainly adequate. The internal evidence in the fourth scene is at least suggestive. There is some doubt whether Blake was keeping a straight face, and that is enough for the present purpose.

[13]*King Edward the Third*, Scene [1]: The Coast of France, 9.

[14]*The Laocoön Group*.

[15]*King Edward the Third*, Scene [2]: English Court, 29, 34–5.

[16]*Ibid.*, Scene [3]: At Cressy, 272, 274.

works. "Conscience" and "Reason" become the inverted "Hell" and "Heaven" of the satirist and, finally, "Los" and "Urizen" in the pattern of the prophetic books. The song of the minstrel at the end of *Edward the Third* makes use of the legend of Trojan Brutus as the founder of the British race, but the ancestral symbol is to be abandoned in favour of the more inclusive "Albion" used in the same song and in the *Prologue to King John.*

In the *Prologue to King Edward the Fourth*, Blake has already turned his back on any glorification of war and military courage. Political exploitation and its victims form his subject. His vision of the chaos and destruction of war as it affects the individual and the nation end on an ironic note, for the responsibility for war is placed at the door of the "Ministers" of "Heaven"—the "Kings and Nobles of the Land."[17] The revolutionary is beginning to make an appearance, and in the *Prologue to King John*, the struggle of the patriot against the tyrant transcends mere national pride. The closing lines contain imagery which may even suggest a release from the social evils of oppression and war into an earthly paradise not unlike that of the philosophers. There are also overtones from the book of Job, and the description of the unfallen state preceding creation "when the morning stars sang together."[18] The inner revolution of the imagination and the outer revolution of the political order continue to intermingle, until they finally reach their visionary unity in the later works. Blake's radicalism still retains much of the denunciatory fury of the Puritan and the cant of the Whig. In *Gwin, King of Norway*, the monarch is accused of the exploitation of the peasantry who, like the Jacquerie, are aroused to combat tyranny. Gordred is significantly described as a giant, the symbol of the social revolution and of the revolutionary force of liberty which later becomes Orc. The struggle between liberty and tyranny takes on the imagery of both history and nature, and in the prophecies becomes the epic struggle of Orc against Urizen to burst the fetters which enslave the mind of universal humanity. As he moves towards the apocalyptic visions of *The Four Zoas*, *Milton* and *Jerusalem*, the prophetic radical also moves in his imagination from the

[17] *Prologue to King Edward the Fourth*, 15–16.

[18] Job xxxviii: 7. In the *Prologue to King John*, "the stars of heaven tremble"—and later, Albion's "sons shall joy as in the morning." "Albion" is not yet the male progenitor, and is little more than another name for England.

tyranny of politics to that of the historical cycles—and then, towards the ultimate tyranny of the circle of destiny.

The revolutionary liberty which he has celebrated as the effort to throw off the yoke of political faction becomes the force of imaginative vision liberating human existence from the perception of an overwhelming world of nature and the cycles of generation. The extent of the Newtonian universe is the basis of the deistical belief in a Supreme Being whose power is measured by the vastness of space, and whose wisdom is the accumulation of endless time. Blake considers deism or natural religion to consist of a glorification of self-interest, pride and moral virtue. The so-called humility of the true deist who worships the sky-god of empty space—a deity who is intolerant ot anything or anybody outside the reasonable scope of his devotee's restricted understanding—such humility disguises a profound contempt for humanity. Blake was suspicious of the potted benevolence of the deist, and he called the genuinely humanitarian Paine a "better Christian" than Bishop Watson who, in his opinion, was a deist at heart.[19] Voltaire would have sneered at the bishop, and he was ostensibly engaged in eliminating bishops from the earth, but he was still, according to Blake, one of those "who would in certain Circumstances have been Christians in outward appearance."[20] Although Blake quoted from Voltaire's *Essai sur les mœurs et l'esprit des nations*, the satirical *Micromégas* clarified the deist's view of the contemptible insignificance of man, the inhabitant of a small speck of dust in universal space. Both the traveller from Sirius and the Saturnian related the value of human life to the eternity of endless time and the infinity of endless space: experience was measured by the clock.[21] Such a point of view was absurd to the writer of the *Proverbs of Hell*, for whom the "hours of folly are measur'd by the clock; but of wisdom, no clock can measure."[22] Not every deist carried the implications of his position as far as Voltaire, and it was really because of men like Paine[23] that

[19]*Annotations to Watson's "Apology for the Bible,"* p. 120.

[20]*Vision of the Last Judgment*, Keynes, p. 649.

[21]Voltaire, *Œuvres* (Paris, 1827), LIX, p. 184.

[22]*Marriage of Heaven and Hell*, Keynes, p. 183.

[23]Paine recognized the tone of contempt in the writings of Voltaire. "His forte lay in exposing and ridiculing the superstitions which priestcraft, united with statecraft, had interwoven with Governments. It was not from the purity of his principles, or his love of mankind (for satire and philanthropy are not naturally concordant), but from his strong capacity of seeing folly in its true shape, and his irresistible propensity to expose it, that he made those attacks. They were,

Blake saw in the American and French revolutions an attempt to liberate the human mind from the tyranny of statecraft buttressed by organized religion and vested interest.

Revolution is primarily the sign of the intellect's desire to cast out error and, in the words of the Apocalypse, "to make all things new." Only in a subsidiary sense is it an effort to throw off one form of government for another. In *The French Revolution*, the aim is the clarification of political error in the form of the king, the bishop and the landowning aristocrat—symbolized by the so-called Duke of Burgundy,[24] an invention of Blake to complete his pattern. Clarification takes place as a struggle between the forces of reaction which are the forces of the Elect and those of the revolutionary Reprobates. Necker, the type of the common man in his indictment of the excesses of monarchy, Sieyès, the abbé of the people, and Orléans, the nobleman turned revolutionary, are placed in opposition to the attempt to exalt the caste system into a fixed analogy of the celestial order. The struggle between these two contraries becomes in the mind of Blake the awakening of man's intellect after its slumbering tour along the arc of six thousand years, the cyclical unit of his myth. This recreation of a historical event in terms of a complete cycle of history marks the beginning of that union of literal fact and imaginative myth which distinguishes the later prophetic books. Side by side with *The French Revolution* and *America*, he wrote the so-called minor prophecies. The gradual process of synthesis which his complete works reflect, had by this time reached the stage immediately preceding the more comprehensive effort displayed in *The Four Zoas, Milton* and *Jerusalem* where the theme is lifted above history. Meanwhile, revolution stirs his imagination, and he sees the fall of the Bastille as the removal of the most significant symbol of submission.

It is in *America*, however, that the actual symbols of the later prophecies begin to make their appearance. The "Preludium" introduces the muse of history, "the shadowy Daughter of Urthona"[25] who is addressed by the revolutionary force in the person of Orc. Blake's muse of history is the daughter of the cosmic clock—the ticking measure

---

however, as formidable as if the motives had been virtuous: and he merits the thanks rather than the esteem of mankind." Paine, *Complete Writings*, ed. P. S. Foner (New York, 1945), I, p. 299.

[24]*French Revolution*, 247–54.

[25]*America*, "Preludium," 1.

of man's fallen sense of time—"shadowy," because history seen as the mere passage of time can clarify nothing in the imperceptible blur of the unknown future passing swiftly through the unrealized present into the lost past. Also the "Dark Virgin," she remains untouched by any other kind of experience than that provided by the stubborn defence of established forms of thought and practice—the iron maiden of silent desperation and jealous stupidity. Orc is the only lover who can awaken her and make her fruitful. As the eternally youthful wisdom of inexperience, he alone can break the chains which are the hypnotic spell of inertia cast by her father, the spirit of time unredeemed. To awaken her out of the dumb silence of the inevitable and necessary is the task of this "terrible boy," the titanic force of elemental life, capable, like most children, of frightening his elders into a panic of corrective discipline. Orc is finally crucified by Urizen in the seventh night of *The Four Zoas*, but he is allowed to romp his fiery way through *America*, until he begins to burn up the limitations of man's fallen condition entirely.

> Stiff shudderings shook the heav'nly thrones! France, Spain & Italy
> In terror view'd the bands of Albion and the ancient Guardians
> Fainting upon the elements, smitten with their own plagues.
> They slow advance to shut the five gates of their law-built heaven
> Filled with blasting fancies and with mildews of despair,
> With fierce disease and lust, unable to stem the fires of Orc.
> But the five gates were consum'd, & their bolts and hinges melted;
> And the fierce flames burnt round the heavens & round the abodes of men.[26]

America ends with the threat of an apocalyptic renewal of existence itself.

The same work also expresses another aspect of Blake's sympathy with the American Revolution. Washington and the other revolutionaries are represented as meeting on the coast of America "glowing with blood from Albion's fiery Prince,"[27] and the inference is clearly that the revolting colonies have done nothing more than put into practice what England has taught them. Like many of his contemporaries, Blake sympathized with the colonists, and he objected strenuously to the Tory policy which had precipitated the war. In the

[26]*Ibid.*, "A Prophecy," 219–26 (Keynes, p. 208).
[27]*Ibid.*, 5 (Keynes, p. 202).

satirical mood of *The Marriage of Heaven and Hell*, the Tories are symbolized by Albion's Angel who confronts Orc.

> "Blasphemous Demon, Antichrist, hater of Dignities,
> Lover of wild rebellion, and transgressor of God's Law,
> Why dost thou come to Angel's eyes in this terrific form?"[28]

In passages like this, Blake succeeds in uniting the different aspects of a political outlook with that wider context which gives his perspective to the particular historical moment. Orc who is also the "Terror" is the symbol of those instincts which the tyranny of Urizen has "perverted to ten commands,"[29] and he becomes man's Promethean saviour who consumes the lifeless past with the fire of his liberated energy.

In the cancelled plates of *America*, however, the demon Orc appears not only as the preliminary force which culminates in freedom of action but also as the type of the visionary power

> seen even by mortal men,
> Who call it Fancy, or shut the gates of sense, or in their chambers
> Sleep like the dead.[30]

The revolutionary is the political analogue of the prophet, but the obsession with deism and the desire to make man "Righteous in his Vegetated Spectre" causes certain political "prophets" to fall from prophetic energy into fanaticism, from being liberators into being tyrants. Although Blake gave little evidence of having read any work of Rousseau, except perhaps the *Confessions*,[31] a disciple of that apostle of the natural man illustrated the effect of deistical virtue and political power on the career and attitude of a revolutionary. Not only did Robespierre succumb to a rigorous delusion which cost him his life, but he changed liberty into tyranny with an incorruptible zeal. In his speech concerning the aims of the Committee of Public Safety, he declared that the fundamental principle of democratic government was virtue, and that virtue was the love of country and its laws. If, however, the basis of popular government in peace was this kind of virtue,

[28]*Ibid.*, 56–8 (Keynes, p. 203).

[29]*Ibid.*, 61 (Keynes, p. 203).

[30]*Ibid.*, cancelled plates, 63–5 (Keynes, p. 210).

[31]Cf. *Jerusalem*, 52, Preface: "Rousseau thought Men Good by Nature: he found them Evil & found no friend. Friendship cannot exist without Forgiveness of Sins continually. The Book written by Rousseau call'd his Confessions, is an apology & cloke for his sin & not a confession."

in revolution, virtue and terror became the same thing: "Terror is nothing else than swift, severe, and indomitable justice; it flows, then, from virtue."[32] Terror was obviously a part of the revolutionary spirit operating in the fallen world of man's perceptions, and Blake could see that the real prophet would never become a politician without risking his integrity and his sense of direction. The outcome of such a *tour de force* was the translation of the allegory of the *civitas dei* into a despotism of liberty. The actual freedom of the eternal city could not be enforced by unregenerate man as a utopian plan for his social and political life.

The concept of the state as a copy of the *civitas dei* was an error of the totalitarian theocracies which Blake calls "Druidism," and deism is the secular precipitate of Druidism. Deism had survived in the form of "Greek Philosophy" which taught that the natural man could be both virtuous and free in his political life—a theory which Robespierre's argument that obedience to the Committee was obedience to "one's better self" was evidently intended to bring into effect.[33] It would therefore be wrong to confuse Blake's "Albion" with any political pretensions of the British people and suppose that he identifies his symbol with the state. Albion begins as a symbol of Britain's past as seen in the imagination—a patriarchal ancestor like the biblical Jacob who united in himself the whole history of his progeny. But the symbol finally becomes the totality of an entire temporal cycle seen as the primal man whom we meet in so many early myths. Blake does not give his creation a significance which would support the fallacy of the race born to rule by divine right. Apart from other considerations, it was his radicalism and his sympathy with men like Paine which

[32]"Rapport sur les principes de morale politique qui doivent guider la Convention nationale dans l'administration intérieure de la République, fait par Robespierre, au nom du comité de salut public, à la séance du 5 février [17 pluviôse] 1794." Quoted by P. J. B. Buchez and P. C. Roux, *Histoire parlementaire de la révolution française* (Paris, 1834–8), XXXI, p. 276: "Si le ressort du gouvernement populaire dans la paix est la vertu, le ressort du gouvernement populaire en révolution est à la fois la vertu et la terreur: la vertu, sans laquelle la terreur est funeste; la terreur, sans laquelle la vertu est impuissante. *La terreur n'est autre chose que la justice prompte, sévère, inflexible; elle est donc une émanation de la vertu*: elle est moins un principe particulier qu'une conséquence du principe général de la démocratie appliqué aux plus pressants besoins de la patrie." Following Rousseau, he could remark earlier (p. 274): "Heureusement la vertu est naturelle au peuple, en dépit des préjugés aristocratiques."

[33]Cf. Mark Schorer, *William Blake: The Politics of Vision* (New York, 1946), p. 212 n. See also *Jerusalem*, 52, Preface.

helped him avoid the pitfall of becoming the oracular prophet of Anglo-Saxon supremacy. He was not interested at all in political supremacy but in an awakened enlightenment, and he despised any system of thought which led to a logic of power.

In this respect, he defended Paine's *Age of Reason* as an honest criticism of a Christianity which had become dedicated throughout Europe to the interests of states and princes. Although he would take exception to Paine's admiration for "the vast machinery of the universe," he sympathized with the revolutionary's straightforward humanitarianism. With much of Paine's criticism of orthodox Christianity, he agreed. Reading the Christian scriptures as natural fact and as authentic history was as nonsensical to the one as to the other, and Blake was equally irritated by ecclesiastical emphasis on the crucifixion. The result had been, as Paine remarked, that the cross had become "the object of dismal admiration."[34] In his *Annotations to Bishop Watson's "Apology for the Bible"*—which was an attempt to refute Paine—Blake comments (p. iii): "Paine has not attacked Christianity. Watson has defended Antichrist." Calling the bishop "a State trickster," he indicates in nearly every note that "State Religion" is the source of Watson's denunciation of Paine, and not any conscientious sense of duty to the public. By clarifying the bishop's motives to his own satisfaction, Blake defines his position on the relationship between the church and the state. The ceremonial laws which were developed from the attempt to make a politically effective weapon out of a mystery cult have been inherited by the state. These along with the penal laws court transgression and are the most "oppressive of human codes" (p. 25). "Given under pretence of divine command," they are the source of the collaboration of church and state. The destruction of this combination was one of the professed aims of the revolutionaries, and it receives Blake's wholehearted support. The liberty which both he and the revolutionaries embrace is a liberty of conscience. Had not Paine declared that his own mind was his church?[35]

It is one thing, however, to liberate the individual's mind from its bondage to church and state and quite another matter to liberate the individual from his slavery to nature so that he may realize the free conscience which Blake identifies with "genius" and "imagination."

[34]*Complete Writings*, I, pp. 471–2.

[35]Paine, *Complete Writings*, I, p. 464.

But the free conscience is not the portion of the natural man as such. For the natural man, moral virtue is still necessary and is, in fact, the *sine qua non* of his political liberty—a freedom which depends upon a legal and moral defence against worldly licence.

> Many Persons, such as Paine & Voltaire, with some of the Ancient Greeks, say: "we will not converse concerning Good & Evil; we will live in Paradise & Liberty." You may do so in Spirit, but not in the Mortal Body as you pretend. . . . You cannot have Liberty in this World without what you call Moral Virtue, & you cannot have Moral Virtue without the Slavery of that half of the Human Race who hate what you call Moral Virtue.[36]

Blake was fully aware that the defence against licence could too easily become an exasperated despotism of terror, and Paine had hardly finished his *Age of Reason* before he himself was imprisoned by Robespierre. His release came from America, the country of hope for both Blake and Paine. But it is neither to America nor to any other political state that Blake looks for that freedom which can exist only "in Spirit."

> I am really sorry to see my Countrymen trouble themselves about Politics. If Men were Wise, the Most arbitrary Princes could not hurt them. If they are not wise, the Freest Government is compell'd to be a Tyranny. Princes appear to me to be Fools. Houses of Commons & Houses of Lords appear to me to be fools; they seem to me to be something Else besides Human Life.[37]

Neither princes nor legislative assemblies are the ground of his political science. Just as the use of the imagination in the acts of life is the very existence of the individual, so also the imagination of a nation—its arts—is its "existence." Here, the thoughts and aspirations of a people find their expression, and it is in the arts that the "political scientist" possesses the touchstone for knowing the state of the nation.

With the firm conviction that the activity of which the arts were the visible sign was the state of the nation Blake wrote his *Public Address.* In it, he emphasizes that the arts are not merely an indication of educated taste, nor are they for the amusement and edification of an intelligentsia, nor for the support and delectation of authority. "Let us teach Buonaparte, & whomsoever else it may concern, That it is not Arts that follow & attend upon Empire, but Empire that attends upon

[36] *Vision of the Last Judgment,* pp. 92–5 (Keynes, p. 650).
[37] *Public Address,* Keynes, p. 629.

& follows The Arts."[38] Recognizing the essential and the prophetic value of art, he took into consideration its political effect in arousing and maintaining the morale of a people without surrendering its integrity and its liberty to the arrogant assumptions of authority. The conventional rituals of social intercourse had formed an important subject of study for the citizen in antiquity. The effective cultivation of the arts for the purpose of moulding the citizen is the concern of humane letters. It was their use to support political policy which degraded the states of Greece and Rome in the eyes of Blake. It was their use to support the power of an established priesthood which disgraced the Egyptians, the Druids and those who destroyed the liberty of the arts in the interests of a closed socials cheme. Blake endeavoured to restore freedom and health to them by avoiding the aestheticism of the connoisseur on the one hand and the decadence of public taste on the other. His efforts were, in his own eyes, those of an ardent patriot and one who felt his duty to the public.

Having this sense of social responsibility, he optimistically grasped at every sign of a turn in contemporary political and social affairs which might indicate the realization of his hopes for his country and Europe. Even before the treaty with Napoleon, signed at Amiens in 1802, he hoped for a peace which would bring his wish to fulfilment. In a letter to John Flaxman dated October 19, 1801, he wrote: "The Reign of Literature & the Arts commences. Blessed are those who are found studious of Literature & Humane & polite accomplishments." With an astonishing vigour of mind and heart, he never succumbed to cynicism nor even to the disappointment which Plato had apparently experienced before he was moved to formulate a political straight-jacket for society. Blake was, however, just as convinced an enemy of mimetic art, with its representational symbolism and the inability of its adherents to see the difference between the work of the creative imagination and the imitation of the objects of nature.[39] He did not choose to do Plato's condemnation of the mimetic arts full justice—a condemnation which was directed against the consideration of art as mere amusement. The refusal of the philosopher to admit such art into his ideal republic along with his insistence that artists should be responsible to superior authority for the moral effect of their works

[38] *Ibid.*, Keynes, p. 626.
[39] *Ibid.*

caused Blake to forget that Plato regarded the ancient poets as the children of the gods.[40] But Plato could see that the Athens of his own day had forgotten the gods, and he gave every appearance of retreating into the conception of a closed and guarded society.

Blake did not feel what Wordsworth called the "weight of too much liberty,"[41] but he did feel the weight of mediocrity, the limited bias of personal interest and the prejudices arising from the fears of the political animal. Immediate personal interests distracted the individual from realizing his real possibilities, and these were projected into the aggressive policies of the state and into commercial expansion. The theme of Mandeville's *Fable of the Bees* reflected this perverted picture of society—society in its fallen condition. The term "fallen" in the works of Blake always describes the collapse from a possible unity of thought and desire into a disunity of separated elements or selves pursuing interests which, through fear and prejudice and habit, they see as different from the interests of others. Mandeville's work was a commercial supplement to the political science of Hobbes who had asserted that the basic principle of the state was security against fear. *The Fable of the Bees* was immediately concerned with the state as a security against want. In any such society, art became a luxury product, and Mandeville evidently thought of it as a kind of social disease which somehow indicated political health.

It is not this kind of art alone, however, which is diseased in the opinion of Blake; it is the mercantile state which has succeeded in reducing art to a commercial luxury. The enterprising search for individual and national freedom from fear and want is the basis of the fallen society, where freedom cannot be maintained without the heavy hand of moral sanctions or the ethics of the successful merchant. Yet once these moral sanctions are most successful, the promised freedom turns out to be a mirage, for the state which is founded on fear and want can only collapse or decline when both of these are nearly eliminated "for the greatest number." To forestall immediate decline, commercial interest is usually forced to supply new wants, and political policy a new fear—the fear of being an individual apart from the

[40]Plato, *Republic*, II, 366B. The reference is obviously to the inspired poetry of Orpheus and Musaeus, and not to the comic and tragic poets of his own day, nor to the myths put into the mouths of heroes by such as these in the past. In his *Sophist*, Plato drew a sharp distinction between divine and human poetic (265E), and also between a divine and a human imagery (266B ff.).

[41]*Wordsworth, Miscellaneous Sonnets*, "Nuns fret not at their convent's narrow room . . . ," 13.

collective average. The satire of Mandeville brought out the curiously false basis which supported commercial enterprise, and the work of Hobbes the prejudice of fear which nourished the political leviathan.

In his *Songs of Innocence and Experience*, Blake's imaginative conception of the two states of the human soul bears a direct relation to his views on political theory and practice. The childhood state of innocence which he recreates is the sense of security in nature and in the tribal environment of the family. But when the individual gains experience, he is educated into the mistake of seeking his lost sense of security in the sphere of social relationships, and, ultimately, in the enforced security of the state. There can, however, be no return to childhood through the regressive attempt to make everyone feel natural and "at home." Rousseau, assuming that the mind was a *tabula rasa*, had prescribed an education in natural morality so that this *tour de force* might be effected. It is Blake's opinion that there is no such thing as natural morality, since morality is a code of conduct abstracted from actual experience, and man's real nature is not in his environment but within himself. He is also unable to admit that there is any such thing as enforced security, which seems to him a contradiction in terms. There is left only the actual growth of each individual from natural to human relationships which supersede and correct mere social conformity. Being neither a romantic nor a cynic, he sees no way except the inner growth of individual character as the solution to the problem.

Inner growth is the transformed political science, the "Science of Sciences," which demands "firm & determinate conduct"[42] consistent with creative activity. As an individual and as a society, the human existence is identical in its interests and in its needs, and it remains to determine for one's self that identity which really exists between the individual and the group. Growth of character is synonymous with the growth of the imagination which is the form of individual life. Blake uses the term "Art" to signify the means whereby this growth can be achieved. It certainly cannot be achieved by herding into states under the impulse of fear and the desire for protective security. After reading Bacon's statement that "the increase of any state must be upon the foreigner," he writes: "The increase of a State, as of a man, is from internal improvement or intellectual acquirement. Man is not

[42]*Public Address*, Keynes, p. 629.

improved by the hurt of another. States are not improved at the expense of foreigners."[43] The rejection of any outward sanction as a means to this kind of improvement, either individually or collectively, is a rejection of arbitrary statecraft. It is also the rejection of the great instrument of statecraft in the nation of shopkeepers—unlimited mercantile expansion. Blake is convinced that commerce undertaken with the motives of Mandeville's bees will destroy the arts which are the means of "internal improvement": "for Commerce Cannot endure Individual Merit; its insatiable Maw must be fed by What all can do Equally well; at least it is so in England, as I have found to my Cost these Forty Years."[44] If Blake condemns the empire of commerce, he does so because of its tendency to uniformity, not because it develops individual enterprise. He does not despise wealth, but he distinguishes between wealth as a means of enriching life and wealth as an end in itself.

Blake is the contrary, not the negation, of the political views of Plato and Dante, and he reverses their utopian rationalism. In his *Republic*, Plato describes the decline of the state from the rule of justice. From the aristocratic life of intellect, the individual and the community are represented as falling under the tyranny of desire. Blake brings the prophetic revolutionary back in at the nadir of this cycle, and converts Plato's tyranny of desire into his own vision of the tyranny of reason. He puts blood into the conservative utopia and brings it to life, not by reversing the poles of the state but by placing them in balance. The radical is not exalted to the top of the heap, and the conservative reduced to the bottom; instead, they both act as contraries in an active equilibrium. The conservative Elect and the liberal Redeemed are to be held in tension by the prophetic Reprobate. He will resist tyranny in the spirit of the revolutionary Orc, and inspire leadership in the spirit of the prophetic Los. For Orc is the demonic form of Los, and the arts of communication are the instruments of the prophet who contains both. Blake's temper gives both of them their fullest expression in his *Public Address*: "Resentment for Personal Injuries has had some share in this Public Address, But Love to My Art & Zeal for my Country a much Greater."[45]

[43]*Annotations to Bacon's "Essays,"* Keynes, p. 768.
[44]*Public Address*, pp. 51–7 (Keynes, p. 622).
[45]*Ibid.*, p. 58 (Keynes, p. 623).

8. Genius and Imagination: The Alchemy of Vision

THE SUPREMACY OF REASON over the feelings and the senses in any work of the imagination produces what Blake calls fable or allegory. The supremacy of the senses results in the imitation of nature, and the supremacy of the feelings in the sectarian art of the bohemian. But his own art—which he calls vision—unites in the imagination these other approaches, and he makes use of a symbolism which is a particular application of the universal language of the imagination. He does this in a way which is rigorously accommodated to the source of his creative activity, and he emphasizes what he is doing with a point of view, rather than what he is saying with a medium of expression. The medium of expression, however, is given a frame of reference by this very point of view, for Blake was no obscurantist. "Obscurity is Neither the Source of the Sublime nor of any Thing Else."[1] He has no intention of creating a cryptogram, but he does intend to arouse the faculties of the reader to relate one image to another in somewhat the same manner that we relate one word to another in ordinary discourse. Once this is accomplished, the reader sharpens an insight which Blake has induced in him, and becomes aware of the workings of an "Art" which is "The Whole Business of Man."[2]

Blake was, however, separated from his time by this conception of art as the language of vision, and not as mere representation of natural objects. The interest in linguistic study which had begun to flourish before the end of the eighteenth century made use of an analytic method which was utterly at variance with his. The followers of Locke tried to abstract words or symbols from their meanings and to create an exact language which would prove suitable for communicating rational generalizations. Language was to be reasonably reconstructed, once man could be broken of the habit of involving the irrational in

[1] *Annotations to Reynolds's "Discourses,"* p. 194.

[2] *The Laocoön Group.*

his speech. This programme presented the philosophers of the Enlightenment with another means of eliminating the superstitions of revealed religion and of carrying forward the work of Locke by explaining the operations of the human mind in natural and rational terms. For Condillac the operations of the mind were explained by the principle of verbal association, just as the revolutions of the stars were explained by the theory of gravity.[3] The contemporary philosopher was obviously thinking of the development of language from the primitive imagery of the instincts and the feelings to the cultivated abstractions of reason, from untutored impulse to speculative reflection.

Blake opposed such a conception of the ascent of man from early barbarism to enlightened self-interest. In *The Marriage of Heaven and Hell*, originally conceived as a satire on Swedenborg, his attack becomes a somewhat angry shout of laughter at the rational pomposity of the age. A rationality confined to sense and reflection is the new panacea, the new alchemical formula for transforming all baser metals into gold. In fact it is assumed that the process of understanding is to be a rational organization of the energies of man and the forces of nature. From Blake's point of view, unorganized energy does not exist, and energy organized by reason is energy rendered passive or subverted. Reason and energy are contraries, unless the former becomes the negation of the latter, but the dialectic of actual understanding does not proceed by one absorbing the other. The moment this negative activity occurs, the real process of understanding ceases, and the "Elect"—whether an individual or a group—remains shut up in the closed circle of a rational "Heaven." Such a "Heaven" will be ruled by the successor to Milton's "Governor or Reason" who was called "Messiah," and it will be inhabited by the rational millenarian who wants to be forever reasonable and right:

> The history of this is written in Paradise Lost, & the Governor or Reason is call'd Messiah.
>
> And the original Archangel, or possessor of the command of the heavenly host, is call'd the Devil or Satan, and his children are call'd Sin & Death.[4]

[3]At the close of his *Essai sur l'origine des connaissances humaines*, the Abbé de Condillac claimed to have done what Locke did not do: to have gone back to the first operation of the soul, analysed the understanding and discovered the necessity of signs and the principle of the association of ideas. Locke had merely introduced the method of Newton into the study of man. Condillac proposed, as he indicated by the sub-title of his work, to reduce *à un seul principe tout ce qui concerne l'entendement.*

[4]*Marriage of Heaven and Hell*, Keynes, p. 182.

One year after Blake had etched these words, an apostle of reason and nature was repeating the old story across the Channel. The Puritan millenarian had given way to the deistical utopian, but the Messianic claim was still there. Robespierre, in a report on the principles of political morality which should guide the National Convention, identified the prerogative of the general will with the indestructible power of reason. Reason was represented as the almighty interpreter which would translate the collective will into social action.[5] This political principle was enforced by the necessary and inevitable "justice" of the guillotine.

The rationalist, however, cannot contain the tension of Blake's "Mental Fight,"[6] and he succumbs to the programme or the cult—some reasonable delusion which will suppress the uncertain and uncomfortable struggle in himself and his neighbour. This very suppression he gradually mistakes for maturity in himself and progress in the state of society. Youth declines into middle age, and revolution falls back into reaction. But the triumph of the gods of rational form over the titans of exuberant energy always proves to be a Pyrrhic victory and the prelude to a greater and more lasting defeat. Particularly in his earlier works, Blake traces this recurrent pattern of failure, masked by success, to the Greeks' subversion of the titanic energies of man in a reasonable endeavour to "save the appearances" and organize the civilized state. Although the end was apparently praiseworthy, the method brought about the decline of the ancient world. The ultimate denial of liberty is implicit in the attempt to identify individual freedom with reasonable limitation and the doctrine of the mean.[7] The error

[5]P. J. B. Buchez and P. C. Roux, *Histoire parlementaire de la révolution française* (Paris, 1834–8), XXXI, p. 289: "Nous provoquons sur tous les objets de ses inquiétudes, et sur tout ce qui peut influer sur la marche de la révolution, une discussion solenelle; nous la conjurons de ne pas permettre qu'aucun intérêt particulier et caché puisse usurper ici l'ascendant de la volonté générale de l'assemblée, et la puissance indestructible de la raison."

[6]The love of combat can take two forms: the inner form, leading to a degree of self-mastery, and an outer form, leading to a more or less effective conquest of immediate conditions. Blake refers to both in the well-known lines of his Preface to *Milton*:

I will not cease from Mental Fight,
Nor shall my Sword sleep in my hand
Till we have built Jerusalem
In England's green & pleasant Land.

[7]The Classical maxim—"nothing in excess"—is answered with aphorisms such as these from the *Proverbs of Hell*: "The road of excess leads to the palace of wisdom. No bird soars too high, if he soars with his own wings. Every thing possible to be believ'd is an image of truth." Finally, the *Proverbs* end with a conclusive "Enough! or Too much," for Blake sees the doctrine of the

of Classicism was first revealed in the stand ostensibly taken by Homer and the poets who ordered the world of epic experience by a reasonable and natural interpretation of original prophetic vision.[8]

The visions of the Greek seers were systematically rationalized into fable and allegory, and the gods gradually became the symbols of the superiority of reason over the passions. The consequent separation of the sublime from the pathetic made the Greek and the Roman look for his deities on Olympus and in the temple, and for his thrills in the theatre and the arena. Higher and lower are equivocal terms, and to make reason the "higher," and the appetites the "lower," part of man was equivocation *par excellence*. For Blake, creation by means of the imagination can only take place when they are both retained as contraries within the field of individual experience. The visionary imagination is not derived from either the rational or the appetitive; they are derived from it. Blake therefore calls the first principle of perception neither reason nor desire but "Imagination" or the "Poetic Genius." He identifies this Genius with the Jehovah of the Hebrew prophets, and holds that their language of vision was stolen and perverted by the Hellenic poets whose type was "Homer."

This concerted attack on reason discloses the poverty of imagination which Blake attributes to his contemporaries. For them, the initial association of ideas in the mind is thought to be improved, corrected and rendered suitable to become the material of knowledge by rational thinking. But Blake considers that imagination alone gives a clue to the union of perception with its original source. Creative imagination contains the conflict of the contraries and consummates the marriage of heaven and hell, of reason and desire. Because the visionary dialectic of imagination is the basis of understanding and the ground of the "Mental Fight," he identifies it with its source in prophetic vision or the Poetic Genius. In this sustained process of struggle and search,

---

mean as a ludicrous example of Greek equivocation. How can one know the mean, except as a word in the books of the philosophers, until he also knows what exceeds it?

[8]In his *Notes on the Illustrations to Dante*, Keynes, p. 700, Blake speaks of "Homer" as "the Poetry of the Heathen, Stolen & Perverted from the Bible." Like Dante, Homer had accommodated original vision to man's natural needs, his racial prejudices, his political and moral sanctions. As theologian rather than poet, Homer naturalized the gods who—in the earlier Samothracian theogonies—were the celestial regents of the planets. The Olympians were brought within the sphere of reason and nature, and the ground was prepared for the reasonable systems of the philosophers.

individual genius is realized. The expression of Blake's own thought is never the completed and static distillate of confirmed opinion. The activity of individual genius is not indicated by what one gets from heaven, but rather by what one is able to continually wrest from hell, for it is out of the "Abyss" that heaven is formed. To the Elect, however, the heaven of reason and memory always appears to remain triumphant. "It indeed appeared to Reason as if Desire was cast out; but the Devil's account is, that the Messiah fell, & formed a heaven of what he stole from the Abyss."[9] Blake sees paradise regained and understanding achieved by the adventurous descent into the hitherto unknown, and not by rational rumination on the already known. Genius is realized through the art of transforming energy and reason into the work of creation. Such work produces "gold tried in the fire"[10] and is itself the reward of this visionary alchemy.

In his *Song of Los*, Blake represents Palamabron, the type of the inspired artist, giving "an abstract Law" to Hermes Trismegistus, the traditional founder of alchemy. The Hermetic art was much studied by the Alexandrian Greeks, and it included astrology, medicine and magic, as well as alchemy. It is the alchemical *magnum opus* which, in some respects, resembles Blake's conception of the work of art. Theory, however, had become separated from its root in the perception of the seer, and had taken the form of an elaborate series of rituals which were supposed to be based on a working hypothesis of the relationship between man and the field of his experience. The vogue of the Hermetic art during and after the Renaissance attracted those who sought in a vague mysticism the answers to questions which neither traditional metaphysics nor natural philosophy provided. Forms of Cabbalism, astrology and magic continued, along with alchemy, to furnish a mysterious exhilaration for the dilettante and the misguided, while they provided a lucrative profession for the quack. But underneath this exterior of fraud and deception still lurked the quest for intrinsic power and real knowledge. For the Cabbalist sought the Tetragrammaton, or the Name of God, as the source of unity between man and the world; the astrologer, speaking of constellations and planets, struggled to find a relationship between the powers of the soul and the forces of nature; and the alchemist's search for gold was the search for a lasting good transmuted, as it were, from the dross of natural existence.

[9]*Marriage of Heaven and Hell*, Keynes, p. 182.

[10]Rev. iii: 18.

Unfortunately, the symbolism of each of these systems usually degenerated into a scholasticism more abstract and general in its application than any of the despotic orthodoxies which it was supposed to supersede. The symbolism of Blake, however, is an image of truth which is both independent and original; its independence is founded on the fact that each individual must approach experience for himself, and its originality is derived from the ultimate unity of his particular experience with the universal experience of mankind. The individual point of reference of symbolism seems to have been forgotten by most Hermetic philosophers whose occult correspondences formed a traditional lore of half-understood truths. This errant mysticism supplanted actual understanding, and its deceived adherents pretended to have recovered a lost science, when what they had gained was the husk of an Egyptian cult—a pseudo-magical formula for uniting heaven and earth.

By criticizing the Hermetic philosophers, Blake also criticizes that part of natural philosophy which aimed at the same end—the conquest of nature by the application of analytical formulae, emphasizing demonstration at the expense of perception, and seeking to reduce the knower of the field and the field of experience to a fixed "Ratio" or set of consistent norms. In effect, he rejects the Aristotelian analytics of definition by means of genus and species. This kind of rational generalization from the general to the particular and from the particular to the general produces, in his eyes, a clothes-horse of characteristics, but does not reveal the essence or "character" of anything. The analysis of a living organism reveals its skeleton, not its essence; definition by means of class-characteristics imposes the judgments of one man's system on others.[11] Such is the limitation of natural reason that it can know only by established relationship or "Ratio" between particulars, and cannot perceive the essential character of the particulars.

The mathematical method which succeeded that of Aristotle reduced natural knowledge to a demonstrable set of levers operating as references in space. Descartes was so convinced that this was the true picture of natural reality that he was obliged to introduce his *res cogitans* as a distinct, if somewhat diaphanous, existing principle. The Cartesian outlook frequently led to a subsequent denial of this principle, since it

[11]Cf. *Marriage of Heaven and Hell*, Keynes, p. 190. Blake calls "Aristotle's Analytics" the "skeleton of a body."

required too great an effort of will, obscured by fantasy, to believe in it. For the complete dualism of soul and body tended to discredit the whole notion of spiritual agency, and Newton did not help matters by supposing that the operation of the divine will was to be found in a universal spirit of gravity. It appears to Blake that this method of knowledge leaves unexplained even the most obvious level of sense-experience. Knowledge as he understands it can only "come to pass by an improvement of sensual enjoyment,"[12] leading through the senses to the root of perception.

> But first the notion that man has a body distinct from his soul is to be expunged; this I shall do by printing in the infernal method, by corrosives, which in Hell are salutary and medicinal, melting apparent surfaces away, and displaying the infinite which was hid.[13]

Understanding by means of "corrosives" is Blake's alchemical process for disclosing the imaginative form of things (that is, their essence or "character"). "Genius" is realized in the observer to the extent that he can use the "Ratio" and not be limited to it and to the skeleton of commensurable relations.

The Hermetic alchemist laid claim, however, to a more penetrating general system of knowledge than that of any natural philosopher. *His* analysis went further and was supposed to penetrate deeper into the secrets of nature. But the mystery of his symbols often fascinated the devotee without enlightening him, and left him a caricature of the experimenter whom he hoped to outstrip. What might be called the external method of these deluded followers of Hermes committed them to traditional rites of awe-inspiring solemnity, and consoled them with occult phenomena of an unusual nature, so that they imagined themselves heirs of the promise and more knowing than other men. The vogue of secret societies during and after the Enlightenment has already been noticed. Blake does not spare them in his *Island in the Moon*, and his attitude seems to be that they represent an unhappy mixture of abstract theory and his own prophetic theory of the discovery and the awakening of individual genius. Their astrological and magical calculations were attempts to provide general rules for developing their powers of observation beyond the usual limits. They were evidently trying to imitate the effects of what Blake calls vision prematurely, and

[12] *Ibid.*, Keynes, p. 187.
[13] *Ibid.*

acted as though they possessed a general technique for discovering the elixir of life. Their activities are represented by the "stupendous Works" of the Spectre of Urthona who endeavours to convert Los, the prophetic visionary, to his will before the apocalyptic ending of *Jerusalem*.

> The Spectre builded stupendous Works, taking the Starry Heavens
> Like to a curtain & folding them according to his will,
> Repeating the Smaragdine Table of Hermes to draw Los down
> Into the Indefinite, refusing to believe without demonstration.[14]

Real vision is individual, definite and determinate, but the folding of the heavens into various patterns—as general systems of nature—and the reduction of the meaning of experience to the general prescription of a *tabula Smaragdina*[15] are illusions of reason: "What is General Nature? Is there Such a Thing? what is General Knowledge? is there such a Thing? Strictly Speaking All Knowledge is Particular."[16] Systematic generalization is not the basis of knowledge at all, for knowledge which can be conceived apart from the development of all the faculties of the individual perceiver is, at best, transitory theory and, at the worst, despotic dogma. Before man can hope to know anything else, he must first know himself.

Both the poetic works of Blake and the alchemical treatises of the Hermetic philosophers, however, are based on the possibility of a

[14]*Jerusalem*, 91: 32–5.

[15]The *Smaragdine* [Emerald] *Tablet of Hermes* was an alchemical summary of the *magnum opus* published in the sixteenth century (Gebri Arabis, *De alchemia*, Norimburgae, 1541, p. 363). It was translated in *The Mirror of Alchimy* (London, 1597), pp. 16–17. Thomas Taylor (Proclus, *Theology of Plato*, London, 1816, II, p. 194 n.) gave the following translation: "It is true without a lie, certain and most true, that what is beneath is like that which is above, and what is above is like that which is beneath, for the purpose of accomplishing the miracle of one thing. And as all things were from one through the mediation of one, so all things were generated from this thing by adoption [i.e. by participation]. The sun is its father, and the moon its mother. The wind carried it in its belly. The earth is its nurse. This is the father of all the perfection of the whole world. Its power is entire when it is converted into earth. You must separate the earth from the fire, the subtil from the thick sweetly with great genius. It ascends from earth to heaven, and again descends to the earth, and receives the power of things superiour and inferiour. Thus you will have the glory of the whole world, and thus all obscurity will fly from you. This is the strong fortitude of all fortitude, because it vanquishes every subtile thing, and penetrates all solid substances. Thus the world was fabricated. Hence admirable adoptions will take place of which this is the mode. I am therefore called Hermes Trismegistus possessing three parts of the philosophy of the whole world. That which I have said concerning the work of the sun is complete."

[16]*Annotations to Reynolds's "Discourses,"* p. 61.

balanced union of the human faculties. Although most of the alchemists presumably practised for the external purpose to which the experiments were said to lead—the production of gold—this was not considered by its more devoted students to be its main aim. For them the aim was twofold: the resolution of all the materials into the *prima materia*, or first substance, and the inner union of the faculties. In this way the alchemist attempted to find a unity in both the subjective and objective aspects of human experience. His task in the laboratory was symbolic of an inward search, and the transmutation of metals became the transformation of his own spirit. He based his hopes and his calculations on analogy and correspondence, and his outlook reflected the essential unity of man, the microcosm, and the universe, the macrocosm. In his attempt to establish a meeting point between man and his world, the alchemist looked for substances in nature which would correspond to the substances in his own nature and effect the aim of his inner quest. Such men as Agrippa and Paracelsus were in search of a relationship between two constants: the human soul and material substance, and they found it, or thought they did, in a doctrine of occult correspondences. In his criticism of Swedenborg, Blake shows an admiration for the alchemical systems of Paracelsus and Boehme, but he adopts neither.

> I must Create a System or be enslav'd by another Man's
> I will not Reason & Compare: my business is to Create.[17]

Creation through the act of perception and expression through his art give him the imagination as the prime agent and the basic point of reference between body and soul: "Man has no Body distinct from his Soul: for that call'd Body is a portion of Soul discern'd by the five Senses, the chief inlets of Soul in this age."[18] Perception unites the two constants in the imagination which is man's human point of view, and Blake ignores the alchemist's search for the prime substance as the basis of the "great work."

But it would be doing the alchemist little justice if his approach were not viewed with the greater understanding which some of the alchemical visionaries undoubtedly possessed. Their main fault in Blake's eyes is their incurable obsession with a general recipe for the great work of transmutation in themselves and in the world. Paracelsus'

[17]*Jerusalem*, 10: 20–1.
[18]*Marriage of Heaven and Hell*, Keynes, p. 182.

theory of concordance assumed a definite correspondence between man's physical and psychic properties and various substances in nature. Boehme developed the same doctrine in his description of what he called "signatures," while Swedenborg introduced the whole notion once again as the forgotten "science of correspondences." Caught between the qualitative science of Aristotle and the quantitative science of the mathematicians and the empiricists, the alchemist became both artist and experimenter, using his imagination to unite the perceptual and the commensurable. In Blake's language, he attempted to unite both art and science in wisdom—the state of man in the age of gold of which the gold of his search was the symbol. When he spoke of the transmutation of metals, he thought the mineral kingdom was the extreme bound of the natural universe, and represented the penetration of potential life to the margin of existence. He also thought of the refinement of man's natural possibilities in the realization of human existence—Blake's final identification of natural forms with the human.

> All Human Forms identified, even Tree, Metal, Earth & Stone: all
> Human Forms identified, living, going forth & returning wearied
> Into the Planetary lives of Years, Months, Days & Hours; reposing,
> And then Awaking into his Bosom in the Life of Immortality.[19]

The "Life of Immortality" is the actual achievement of the identification underlying the accidental forms of nature. The realization of this essential image of creation superseded the dualism of the apparent constants—soul and substance, human and non-human. Like Blake, the alchemist also made use of the doctrine that man was the microcosmic image of the macrocosm, and hence that all created forms were, in their identity, human. Unlike Blake, however, he applied this *analogia hominis* to the realm of natural substance.

The spirit of alchemy attempted to unite Hermetic philosophy with experiment, and it reflected the conviction that, behind the phenomena of human experience, there were general laws which reason could discover and through which both psychological and cosmic events

[19]*Jerusalem*, 99: 1–4. In the English version of his *Aurora* (London, 1659, chap. v, pp. 12–13), Paracelsus spoke of "a certain perfect substance" which could be "lifted up out of Vegetable substances into Mineral, and out of Mineral into Metalline perfect substances into a perpetual and divine Quint-essence concluding in itself the essence of all Celestial and Terrestrial Creatures."

could be controlled. Paracelsus, who concentrated more on the inner aspect of the art, took what he called the three principles of substances and related them specifically to the constitution of man.[20] These principles were salt, sulphur and mercury, and they were said to produce life from the *ens primum* of matter or *alcahest*. This was the primary being of matter—Blake's original root of desire in the person of Orc—which, in the alchemist himself, eventually developed the free will and the imagination. Just as the *ens primum* was the ground of potential life within the substance of the natural universe, the mercurial faculty of desire affecting the imagination was the basis of potential genius within the life of man, and the three principles of substances were analogous to the human faculties. Salt was the irreducible basis, the body and the instincts, which Blake symbolizes by Tharmas. Mercury or quicksilver was the alchemical symbol for the psychic substance, *spiritus vitae*, the faculty of will and desire which Blake expresses through Orc and Luvah. Sulphur was the analogue of man's *spiritus* which he explicitly connects with Urizen, the intellectual or rational faculty.[21] These component virtues and principles could only be "completed" by a knowledge of the ground of their operation —in man, the imagination or visionary power which Blake symbolizes by Los. In the creative artist this power operated to the fullest extent, in the original thinker to a considerable extent, but in the dogmatic rationalist only to the extent of indexing the work of the other two. Dante and Shakespeare are representatives of the first class, Paracelsus

[20]Paracelsus, *Paramirum*, lib. i (*Opera Omnia*, Genevae, 1658, I, p. 35). In his *De Naturalibus Rebus* (cap. IV, *ibid.*, II, p. 188), he states: "Man consists of three things: sulphur, mercury and salt. Whatever exists anywhere also consists of these, neither more nor less. These are the body of every individual thing, whether possessed of sense or not." *Imaginatio* is defined as the celestial or supercelestial body of the stars in man (*Dictionariolum Paracelsicum*, *ibid.*, III, App., p. 16). The *alcahest* is a preparation from mercury (*ibid.*, p. 13).

[21]*Book of Urizen*, chap. III, 2; chap. IV[b], 2, 3. The fall of Urizen produces "whirlwinds of sulphurous smoke," and he is seen by Los as "the surging, sulphureous, Perturbed Immortal." The changes of Urizen form a consolidation of the fallen state of the mind. His "phantasies" become "sulphureous fluid"–

And the sulphureous foam, surgeing thick,
Settled, a lake, bright & shining clear,
White as the snow on the mountains cold.

This particular work ends with the image of "the salt Ocean" into which Tharmas sinks at the beginning of *The Four Zoas* (I, 70). Tharmas, who is the body and the instincts, is also the originator of the automatic, cyclical flow of natural life which takes the form of the universal round of existence or the "Circle of Destiny" (I, 65–9, 80–2)—the "Sea" of created nature (80–5). The alchemists also spoke of salt as the "Great Sea" from which the physical body was derived.

and Boehme of the second, and Swedenborg with his eighteenth-century rationalism the third.

> Thus Swedenborg's writings are a recapitulation of all superficial opinions, and an analysis of the more sublime—but no further.
>
> Have now another plain fact. Any man of mechanical talents may, from the writings of Paracelsus and Jacob Behmen, produce ten thousand volumes of equal value with Swedenborg's, and from those of Dante or Shakespear an infinite number.
>
> But when he has done this, let him not say that he knows better than his master, for he only holds a candle in sunshine.[22]

The use of the creative imagination in the arts is a continual participation in the vision of the prophetic Reprobate who never ceases to believe.

Paracelsus illustrated the tenuous distinction which separated the alchemist from the fraud: the one who found the actual basis for his "experiments" in the mind and the one who was solely influenced by the pursuit of immediate results. A contrast might be drawn between Jonson's Subtle and Shakespeare's Prospero; the satirical caricature of the one might be seen as the distorted image of the other. Subtle's fraudulent behaviour was based on the exploitation of the same general theory which, seen in the right perspective, liberated Prospero from his spirits and his enchantments—or as Blake would say, from the deformities of his "Selfhood." This Selfhood or spectre is the natural man who is composed of the limitations or "dross" which bind his imagination to the effects of nature. The subjection and final destruction of the spectral self, like riding a bronco, require not only skill and courage, but also continual alertness. The process of mastery and final liberation is based on a process of awakening—an awakening into Blake's freedom and unity of the mind which is the unfettered imagination or the human existence itself. When Prospero compared the apparent world of nature to the "baseless fabric of this vision" and himself and his auditors to "such stuff as dreams are made on" (that is, as spectres of a sleeping humanity), he echoed the entire theme of Blake's prophetic books.[23]

[22]*Marriage of Heaven and Hell*, Keynes, pp. 190–1. Both Milton and Swedenborg are of the class of the "Elect" or those who accept the dead letter of their visions and their beliefs. It was Milton's matter-of-fact use of imagination which formed a prelude to the natural religion of the deists and affected, according to Blake, the visions of Swedenborg (*Milton*, 24: 39–54).

[23]Shakespeare, *The Tempest*, IV, i, 151, 156–7.

The structural pattern of these prophecies is fourfold and consists of four "States of Existence." There is the awakened state of Eden which is eternal existence viewed *sub specie temporis*. Eden signifies "pleasantness," for it is the original paradise in which enjoyment is complete and one joy does not absorb another. The repose of Eden is Beulah where the dialectic of the contraries is resolved—where heaven and hell are contained in equilibrium or "married," as the name implies. Here the possession of one truth does not mean the negation of its contrary. But the contraries are discriminated as lover and beloved, and their enjoyment which Blake compares with the love of the sexes takes on an isolation which is the beginning of the fall into Generation. In the state of Generation, the contraries are separated by the "reasoning negative," and their relationship assumes the nature of a conflict both within man and outside him in the field of his experience. There is, however, still a balance between the subjective and the objective aspects of experience, until finally, the ultimate state of Ulro is reached where the subject becomes nothing but an effect of the natural field, and the fall is completed. The outline of this pattern is developed in the *Book of Urizen*, and in the original state of man, the channels of perception are said to have been flexible and unconditioned by a fixed ratio between the observer and the field of observation.

> Earth was not, nor globes of attraction.
> The will of the Immortal expanded
> Or contracted his all flexible senses.
> Death was not, but eternal life sprung.[24]

Once the fall begins to take place, however, the conditions of each state tend to close man off from the one superior to it. Urizen, the rational faculty, makes a virtue of necessity, and makes the fallen conditions of man's life the basis for systematic knowledge.

Although man is betrayed by his reason into accepting conditions as unalterable and terms as final, the remnants of his imagination keep him from utter submission. Unlike abstract reasoning, the imagination reaches out to the feelings and the instincts, and can affect the whole man. In the work of the imagination, Blake finds the alchemical elixir which will undo the work of the fall and be the means of

[24] *Book of Urizen*, chap. II, 1, 1–4. The parenthetical reference to "globes of attraction" emphasizes Blake's attitude to the Newtonian theory of gravity and the mechanistic system of nature which reduces man to a mere aspect of the natural world.

redemption. His theme is the awakening from the sleep of Ulro to what he calls "Eternal Life."[25] Imagination provides the means and is itself the end of this process, for its work partakes of the nature of restoration and also of discovery. But there is nothing regressive about this method, and it is partly to guard against such an interpretation that Blake rejects memory from his conception of the imagination. He is neither a primitivist who tries to regress into the past nor a utopian who holds high hopes for progress into the future; the development to which he refers is not limited to the circle of time. He can still state that the moderns are "in a less distinguished Situation with regard to mind"[26] than the ancients. This implies that the ancients were more inspired by the imaginative vision which was an active participation in man's unfallen condition.

Although invocation as an ancient and formal rite intended to produce in the invocator a state of mind receptive to inspiration is not specifically used by Blake, he does use an invocatory form to indicate that the work of creation is also the work of inspiration and not the usual art of self-expression.[27] Both the ancient Greek poets and the Hebrew prophets apparently wrote as though they had a divine commission. Thomas Taylor, in his notes to his translation of Iamblichus, offered the opinion that inspiration, since it came from natures who were free from the obscurities of mundane existence, had ceased in the arts before the fall of Rome: "And as to the poets that have lived since the fall of the Roman Empire, it would be ridiculous to suppose that they possessed this highest enthusiasm, as they did not believe in the existence of the sources from whence it is alone genuinely derived."[28] But Taylor certainly appeared to be a follower of what has already been called the priestly school, and he attached a significance to the revival of ancient rites and ceremonies which Blake did not. The paternal institutes Taylor sought to renew constituted the cultivation of those "eternal principles or characters of human life"[29] which Blake said had appeared to poets in all ages and were, for example, expressed in the Canterbury pilgrims of Chaucer. They were the originals of the inspired artist and could be related to the characters

[25] *Jerusalem*, 4: 1–2.

[26] *Annotations to Watson's "Apology for the Bible,"* pp. 6–7.

[27] See the opening lines of *Milton* and *Jerusalem*.

[28] Iamblichus, *On the Mysteries*, trans. Thomas Taylor (Chiswick, 1821), p. 359.

[29] *A Descriptive Catalogue &c.*, Keynes, p. 601

of any of the ancient myths. The work of the prophetic poet is an original mythology created in conformity with these archetypes, and any work which cannot be related to this visionary symbolism is not a work of genius at all.

The imaginative work is an original derivation, and yet, at the same time, it conforms to a universal symbolism—a language which is man's own, for it is the native speech of his universal humanity.

> As all men are alike in outward form, So (and with the same infinite variety) all are alike in the Poetic Genius . . . . No man can think, write, or speak from his heart, but he must intend truth. Thus all sects of Philosophy are from the Poetic Genius adapted to the weaknesses of every individual.[30]

This cannot mean that the actual imagery of expression is the same for all men at all times. If anything, the image is more dated than the concept, for it reflects more literally man's fallen restriction to a particular time and place. Nevertheless, the universal language of symbolism is the original language of the Poetic Genius which is the unity of man's existence in Eden, and it foreshadows his possible return. From the empire of Rome to his own day, Blake notices a loss of original inspiration in the arts, but he does not prescribe the revival of the rites and ceremonies of an institution or a cult. Instead, through the impact of his prophetic visions, he attempts to restore the perspective of the Golden Age when men were of one language, or more accurately, when they recognized that they were of one language. This is not a primitive nor an archaistic conception, for Blake's Eden is not a temporal state; but it is still a conception based on a theory of cyclical decline and renewal in distinction to the gospel of progress which his contemporaries were preaching. Vico, for example, applied a technique of criticism to history and supported the hopes of the new science by describing the progress of the human race from a primitive to a developed attitude of mind, from a visionary to a rational and experimental conception of knowledge. According to his theory, works of art were merely the effects of environment and circumstance. His critical opinions formed the basis of the new approach to history, and he was the predecessor of writers such as Gibbon and Hume whose point of view Blake rejected.

[30]*All Religions are One*, Keynes, pp. 148–9.

In his *Nuova Scienza*, Vico's outline of historical progress begins with the primitives whose imaginations were both vigorous and productive of works of art. These works, among various peoples, formed the basis of religion. "The first sages of the Greek world were the theological poets, who certainly flourished before the heroic poets, just as Jove was the father of Hercules."[31] The poets who were responsible for the first theologies reflected the natural inclinations of the first men who were children, as it were, of the human race, and who, "not being able to form intelligible class-concepts of things, had a natural need to create poetic characters, that is, imaginative class-concepts or universals, by reducing to them as to certain models or ideal portraits all the particular species which resembled them."[32] These lines recall Locke's postulate that perception is the first simple idea of reflection, for Vico was following the same pattern of thought. Placing the power of reason at the end of man's historical evolution, the philosopher traced it from "poetic wisdom" in the beginning. The poetic faculty was born with the first men, "born of their ignorance of causes, for ignorance, the mother of wonder, made everything wonderful to men who were ignorant of everything."[33] This view attributed the rise of poetry to a deficiency in human reasoning power, and in this way, disposed of the matchless wisdom of the ancients. For the human race had outgrown poetry with its credible fantasies by progressing through three stages. The first was the poetic or creative, also called the divine; the second was the heroic; and the third was the human "recognizing for laws conscience, reason and duty."[34]

Vico's approach was followed by Montesquieu in his *Esprit des lois*, and the purely natural and rational criticism of history was firmly launched on the sea of eighteenth-century thought. This view of human history eliminated spiritual agency from the course of events in much the same way that the mechanistic cosmology had eliminated all but the divine clock-maker. The search for causes was transferred to the material of history and became an integral part of historiography.

[31]Giambattista Vico, *The New Science*, trans. T. G. Bergin and M. H. Fisch (Ithaca, N.Y., 1948), p. 65.

[32]*Ibid.*, pp. 66–7.

[33]*Ibid.*, p. 104.

[34]*Ibid.*, p. 302.

The reasoning historian, turner and twister of causes and consequences, such as Hume, Gibbon, and Voltaire, cannot with all their artifice turn or twist one fact or disarrange self evident action and reality. Reasons and opinions concerning acts are not history. Acts themselves alone are history, and these are neither the exclusive property of Hume, Gibbon, nor Voltaire, Echard, Rapin, Plutarch, nor Herodotus. Tell me the Acts, O historian, and leave me to reason upon them as I please; away with your reasoning and your rubbish! All that is not action is not worth reading. Tell me the What; I do not want you to tell me the Why, and the How; I can find that out myself, as well as you can, and I will not be fooled by you into opinions, that you please to impose, to disbelieve what you think improbable or impossible. His opinions, who does not see spiritual agency, is not worth any man's reading; he who rejects a fact because it is improbable, must reject all History and retain doubts only.[35]

Blake does not believe that reasons have anything to do with acts, and he therefore disagrees with the method of presenting history which Gibbon and Hume employed. An individual acts either from his Selfhood which is his natural self-will or from his genius which is the "spiritual agency" of imagination. He may give reasons for acting in a certain way, but the reasons are not the real causes of his actions. The discovery of reasonable causes appears to Blake, with his eye on the old chronicles, as an elaborate and unconvincing rationalization of the historian's own opinions. Gibbon might disbelieve the legend of Arthur, because he did not think it plausible, but what is plausible to one man may be absurd to another, and what is considered possible by one age may appear impossible to another. The reasoner is in no position to say what is possible or has been possible.[36] In short, the historian who rejects a fact, because it is improbable to him or to the opinion of his time, is biased by an incredulity which can lead him at least as far into error as its opposite. Rational historiography is either propaganda or the arrogant guesswork of a writer who seeks to impose his own limitations and convictions on the "Evidence."

[35]*A Descriptive Catalogue &c.*, Keynes, p. 610.

[36]Gibbon expressed the spirit of the enlightened historian with his rational modesty which concealed pride and his pride which concealed contempt. After stating that "every nation embraced and adorned the popular romance of Arthur," he remarked: "At length the light of science and reason was rekindled; the talisman was broken; the visionary fabric melted into air; and by the natural, though unjust, reverse of the public opinion, the severity of the present age is inclined to question the existence of Arthur." *The Decline and Fall of the Roman Empire* (3 vols., Random House ed.), II, chap. XXXVIII, pp. 429–30.

Such an outlook gives a wide berth to the rational conception of true history based on the reasonable assumption of the uniformity of nature and the theory of probability. An action may be true when it is related by the actor; otherwise, it is either a reconstruction of what someone has thought probable or it is the recreation of events by the imagination in a work of art which should bear the insight of inspired genius. So-called biblical history falls into the latter category according to Blake.

> Of what consequence is it whether Moses wrote the Pentateuch or no? . . . If it is True, Moses & none but he could write it, unless we allow it to be Poetry & that poetry inspired.
>
> If historical facts can be written by inspiration, Milton's Paradise Lost is as true as Genesis or Exodus; but the Evidence is nothing, for how can he who writes what he has neither seen nor heard be an Evidence of The Truth of his history?[37]

The narration of events can either be a chronicle of facts without the historian's interpretation, or it can be a recreation of the events by the genius of the writer. Between these two contraries—which Blake does not find mutually exclusive—lie the negations and assumptions of the reasoning historian with which Blake will have nothing to do. Being an artist, he gives the term "art" a meaning which includes all determinate acts and thoughts. From his vocation of artist come his opinions on history, science and religion. Genius is the imagination of the artist; religion is his point of view, science the extent of his perception, and history the pattern of his perspective, or, simply, the vision of his place in space and time. He transforms the artist into the universal bard and prophet who is the living synthesis of the arts and sciences in his perception of the field of experience and his expression through the word of communication. The ancient and modern arts are "the extent of the human mind."[38] They are also the work of genius and imagination which is character in the individual and culture in the state of society; they are not to be confused with the effects of the probable causes of the reasoner.

This use of the term "imagination" is not so very unusual, and much of what Blake says about it may be found—to quote Johnson—somewhat "faintly" expressed in the pages of the *Spectator*. But

[37] *Annotations to Watson's "Apology for the Bible,"* pp. 15–16.

[38] *A Descriptive Catalogue &c.*, Keynes, p. 610.

Addison's imagination is placed midway between sense and understanding, and Blake's includes both. For Addison, the imagination increases the awareness of the perceiver, so that he may surpass nature itself, but perception is still utterly conditioned by nature, and can see nothing beyond what sense can naturally discover.

We cannot indeed have a single Image in the Fancy that did not make its first Entrance through the Sight; but we have the power of retaining, altering and compounding those Images, which we have once received, into all the Varieties of Picture and Vision that are most agreeable to the Imagination; for by this Faculty a man in a dungeon is capable of entertaining himself with Scenes & Landskips more beautiful than any that can be found in the whole Compass of Nature.[39]

Addison identifies the imagination with the imagery of sense-perception, but Blake makes it include sensation, feeling and reason—that is, he identifies it with perception itself. Addison's imagination reconstructs imagery in the memory by a combination of fancy and judgment to produce the work of art. He interprets his notion of imagination in the poet as an extension of the rational understanding of the philosopher, and places the imagination where Blake asserts it was placed by the Greeks—in the memory. The active effort to surpass nature is no more than an effort to embellish and ornament and perfect what is received from the appearances of sense. But by his own statement, Addison admits that it is possible for a "man in a dungeon" to stand apart from the accidents of his immediate natural environment, not merely by remembering scenes in the past, but also by being "capable of entertaining himself with Scenes & Landskips more beautiful than any that can be found in the whole Compass of Nature." In this very possibility lies the crux of Blake's contention: that man's perception and his powers of recreation extend beyond "the whole Compass of Nature." He is, in fact, not limited to the reception of sense-data nor to the mere memory of it. Coming nearer to Blake's point of view, Addison goes on to say that the mind of man requires something more perfect in nature than what he finds there. Turning from the mind of man, however, to the mending and perfecting of nature, he emphasizes his belief in the natural, rather than the human, source of excellence: "In a word, he has the modelling of nature in his own hands, and he may give her what charms he pleases, provided

[39]Joseph Addison, *Spectator*, nos. 411 ff.

he does not reform her too much, and run into absurdities, by endeavouring to excel."[40] Addison's source of excellence is ultimately the natural existence; Blake's is the human existence.

Finally then, if the terms are to be distinguished, the mnemonic fancy, or what Addison calls imagination, is concerned with temporal existence, but visionary fancy, or Blake's imagination, reveals the "Existent Images" which contain the forms of nature, which is man's eternal existence. The former is passively metamorphic and changing; the latter is anthropomorphic and organized. Thus Blake distinguishes between allegory and fable, which are mnemonic, and vision, which is imaginative. But he does more than this; he enlarges the distinctively human basis of perception to include the entire scope of what he believes is the eternal origin of human existence. Dispensing with the prevailing notion that the rational is the distinctively human faculty, and therefore the highest, he deals with the faculty which gathers up the whole of experience, and calls it imagination. Including the unawakened and unrealized root of perception in the term imagination, he disposes of Locke's theory of the association of ideas as superficial and totally inadequate. Instead, he speaks of his own theory of images existing in man's original being or in the depths of the universal Poetic Genius.

> The Nature of Visionary Fancy, or Imagination, is very little known, & the Eternal nature & permanence of its ever Existent Images is consider'd as less permanent than the things of Vegetative & Generative Nature; yet the Oak dies as well as the Lettuce, but Its Eternal Image & Individuality never dies, but renews by its seed; just so the Imaginative Image returns by the seed of Contemplative Thought; the Writings of the Prophets illustrate these conceptions of the Visionary Fancy by their various sublime & Divine Images as seen in the Worlds of Vision.[41]

Strictly speaking, the imagination is not merely a faculty of man; it is his existence which is the ground of his appearance in "Vegetative & Generative Nature." Using the analogy of the artistic process throughout, Blake asserts that this "Eternal nature" consists of "Worlds of Vision," and that these are creations *like* the work of art. The process of creation is re-enacted in the activity of contemplative thought. A work of art is a prophetic illustration of the inner perspective of the seer.

[40] *Ibid.*, no. 418.
[41] *Vision of the Last Judgment*, pp. 68–9.

To identify art with this inner perspective is to create and perceive by inspiration. The artist-seer uses the "things of Vegetative & Generative Nature" as illustrative material and not as the ultimate data of knowledge. As illustrative material, an object of perception such as Blake's "tyger" becomes the "Existent Image" of being a tiger, and is not limited to being an example of any tiger. For it is not a datum of general reference in a scheme of classification but a particular point of view in the artist's vision. In this way, the prophetic visionary creates his work of art which expresses his particular vision of eternal existence illustrated by a natural image and suited to his imaginative eye.[42]

One remove from him is the artist of fable or allegory whose work is an interpretation and imitation of the work of the seer—work which the allegorical artist frequently accepts as definitive revelation. As for the natural material which is used by the original seer, Blake evidently claims that he knows it in a degree and after a manner which Thomas Aquinas attributes to the angels, that is, "by his essence and by innate species."[43] In other words, he perceives directly what rational definition and systematic generalization seek indirectly to establish. But the artist of fable and allegory finds that his material reflects the changing forms of natural appearances rather than the intact identity of original vision:

> In Eternity one Thing never Changes into another Thing. Each Identity is Eternal: consequently Apuleius's Golden Ass & Ovid's Metamorphosis & others of the like kind are Fable; yet they contain Vision in a sublime degree, being derived from real Vision in More ancient Writings . . . . A Man can never become Ass nor Horse; some are born with shapes of Men, who may be both, but Eternal Identity is one thing & Corporeal Vegetation is another thing.[44]

Imagination sees "Eternal Identity" in "Corporeal Vegetation"; fable sees only the forms of the latter and makes them into an allegory of the unseen. Such is the nature of fable or allegory; but the extreme remove from the visionary is the artist who imitates nature—Blake's "portrait and landscape painters." These are the prototypes of the indeterminate line both in art and in the conduct of life. Self-realization or genius is the source of art, and how can the artist find himself and

[42] *Ibid.*, pp. 69–70.
[43] Thomas Aquinas, *Summa Theologica*, I, Q, 57. Art. 5 (trans. Pegis).
[44] *Vision of the Last Judgment*, p. 79.

his identity, if he is looking only at nature and at his own reflection in nature?

Narcissus was neither a prophet nor a seer, and one who expresses the entangled fragments of his Selfhood and calls the blot or blur art is no artist. The identity is what stands apart from changing conditions, and while the natural ego or Selfhood consists of nothing but these, the identity is the real man—his existence. This existence or genius is the original source of human life. The active form of life is character or the expression of its genius which speaks through the art of the seer; this speech is its illustration. Such illustration will be definite and determinate, for its source is not cultured opinion nor education nor learning nor technical excellence.

> The Man who asserts that there is no such Thing as Softness in Art, & that every thing in Art is Definite & Determinate, has not been told this by Practise, but by Inspiration & Vision, because Vision is Determinate & Perfect, & he Copies That without Fatigue, Every thing being Definite & determinate.[45]

In his annotations to the *Discourses* of Sir Joshua Reynolds, Blake distinguishes between imitative art where the forms are copied from the appearances of nature and visionary art where the forms which comprise the language of art are "copied" from the original archetypes. "All Forms are Perfect in the Poet's Mind, but these are not Abstracted nor compounded from Nature, but are from Imagination."[46] These forms are also the "Innate Ideas" of the individual, which are born with him and are "truly himself." Genius is this true self unseparated from its individual field of perception which consists of the innate ideas. In a very concrete sense, Blake regards what he calls the body of imagination as the individual field of experience. If the individual acts from his genius, he will express an identical consistency throughout his work.

The consistency of the true prophet, however, is derived from an inner realization of what is "truly himself" and not from any outer conformity to the reasonable and the conventional. Conformity implies passive reception, rather than active perception, of the field of experience, and then the individual becomes identified with the conditions of his state. The binding of Orc by Urizen in the seventh

[45]*Annotations to Reynolds's "Discourses,"* pp. 46, 48.
[46]*Ibid.*, p. 60.

night of *The Four Zoas* expresses Blake's vision of the consolidation of this ultimate error—an error which leads to the loss of individual identity. Loss of identity is loss of genius and entrance into the states of sleep leading towards non-entity. As the expression of imagination, genius cannot be trained or modified, it can only be expressed or rejected, for it is not an aberration to be put right but an aspect of Eternal Existence and the underlying source of all actual order. "Genius cannot be Bound; it may be Render'd Indignant & Outrageous."[47] Blake's own indignation finds its earliest expression in the role of the revolutionary and its later fulfilment in the mantle of the prophetic Reprobate. His earlier manifestoes and his later prophecies are themselves directed towards awakening the essential principle in man which he calls "Imagination" and the alchemists called *Homo Maximus*. Considered as a principle, this is the "Energetic Genius" in the individual, and its original derivation is the "Poetic Genius." Considered as the archetypal form of human existence, *Homo Maximus* becomes the "Giant Albion" within the scope of the later prophetic books.

[47]*Ibid.*, p. 180.

9. The Prelude to Prophecy

THE "WORK" OF ART, as Blake understood the term, was living according to individual genius, and such a life would be illustrated by the products of art which were printed in books and hung in galleries. These products were given their form by the imagination which united the other faculties and acted as their basis of operation. In a very literal sense, imagination was the beginning and end of all human activity as distinct from the life of nature, and this was what Blake called art. Conscious of the struggle between art and nature, he resisted any attempt to soften the rigour of the conflict by compromise. To become satisfied with anything less than this conflict was to fall from the state of Generation into that of Ulro, or what his contemporaries called the state of nature. When it became painfully clear to him that the revolutionaries were not revolting in the name of humanity but in their own, and that they were not transforming the political state but appropriating it, the subject of his verse became less revolutionary and more prophetic. Politically, he hated priests and kings to the end of his life, but these were not the priests and kings of the political arena but their originals in the substance of human life and thought. Urizen became his "primeval Priest" and Tiriel his royal tyrant.

These subjects of his minor prophecies formed a prelude to the more extensive works of later years, and taken as a whole, they represented parts of an inevitable development. Blake called the biblical record "the Great Code of Art" not because it outlined the rules of composition, but because it presented a collection of literary forms inspired by the Hebrew genius who was Jehovah in the Old Testament and Jesus in the New. It had an inevitable pattern undistorted and unrestricted by the accidental events of the narrative. The outline of scripture remained unobscured by the story which was sometimes edifying and sometimes boring, but clearly emerged as a vision of history from creation to redemption seen by the prophets. His own prophecies concentrated on the same universal theme.

In *The First Book of Urizen*, Blake began an account of creation which he later incorporated in *The Four Zoas*, and he stated his subject to be the "assumed power" of the "primeval Priest." Urizen separates himself from the Eternals by an assumption of spiritual authority and is committed to the void which he has himself created by his act of isolation. Nevertheless, he is also exiled from the communion of Eternity as a way of indicating that what he does in himself is also done to him. The chaotic void is the beginning of the isolated conditions of the fallen world of which Urizen is the self-appointed creator. He moves from the eternal south or zenith to the northern region of Los, the regent of vision, and the axis of his entire field of experience is utterly reversed. The active intellect of his eternal wisdom which knows by direct perception becomes the reasoning negative of the first dogmatist who establishes his "religion" by the denial of every contrary truth. Assertion by means of denial, the discovery of truth by means of error, and the establishing of certainty through doubt are the outcome of Urizen's fall from intellectual insight to the indirect logic of trial and error. In the tragic effort to regain his lost certainty, he imposes the arbitrary rule of law.

"One command, one joy, one desire,
One curse, one weight, one measure,
One King, one God, one Law."[1]

The victim of his own desire for absolute authority, he becomes the creator of the closed order of nature and the prototype of the fallen mentality which demands a definitive answer to every problem of experience.

Urizen is the active intellect of unfallen man, and it is in his search for a secure certainty beyond the constant "torment" of experience that he creates a world of necessary conditions—a "circle of destiny." In this search, he descends from the zenith or brain of the Eternal Man into the nadir or feet which is the region of the visionary imagination. He falls from being the fountain of intellectual wisdom into being the "reasoning negative," the polar opposite of his original state. Los, the prophetic visionary, saves him from utter annihilation

[1]*The First Book of Urizen*, II, 8, 46–8. The name "Urizen" is evidently derived from the Greek οὐρίζειν, an Ionic form of the Attic ὁρίζειν, meaning to divide or separate, to mark out by boundaries, to limit, determine, appoint. See F. E. Pierce, "Etymology as Explanation in Blake," *Philological Quarterly* (1931), 395–6.

by maintaining the former contact with Eternal Existence and forestalling the fall of Urizen into non-entity, although he cannot prevent the separation of him and his world from Eternity. Like an alchemist at his forge, Los supervises the changes of Urizen whose sleep has reduced him to a "clod of clay." From the intellectual pride which exchanges the paradoxical unity of the contraries, the basis of eternal experience, for an exclusive and definitive certainty, a dead world which is finite and limited is created in the mind of the Demiurgic Urizen. The original fountain of his brain is enclosed by the cavern of the skull, and the intricate labyrinth of this cave symbolizes that natural curiosity which, in fallen man, takes the place of devotion and direct perception. What happens in the mind of Urizen also happens to the world of his experience; his fall, his creation in the fallen state and the creation of his world are aspects of one event in the imagination of Blake. This is the fundamental event of man's conscious life, and at birth, everyone as a perceiving subject falls into Generation and creates the world afresh.

Before the fall begins, however, there is a description of the preceding chaos in the brooding mind of Urizen. Out of this chaos has not yet emerged the universe of nature. Chaos arises as a "shadow of horror," and its contradiction of the eternal knowledge which is both creative and prolific is associated with that solitude which is arrogant and unprolific. Urizen begins by creating the chaos of self-contemplation which Blake calls the Selfhood and ends by providing the inner and outer conditions of man's natural existence which will contain it and give it form and substance. Once those conditions are consolidated, Urizen pursues the aim of his quest within the world to which that quest has led him. He has left Eternity with the reason for his departure on his lips: he is seeking a fixed retreat from too much living. Like the eighteenth-century philosopher, he seeks the utopian dreamland of limited perfection, virtuous complacency and progress within the state of nature.

"From the depths of dark solitude, From
The eternal abode in my holiness,
Hidden, set apart, in my stern counsels,
Reserv'd for the days of futurity,
I have sought for a joy without pain,
For a solid without fluctuation."[2]

[2] *Ibid.*, II, 4, 15–22.

Like Epicurus whom Blake compares with Bacon, Urizen is looking for the complete isolation of pleasure from pain as the final basis for natural virtue. The irony of the term "eternal abode" is heightened by the association with a solitary, self-righteous holiness which is derived from the conception of a benevolent "Deus" who has created the fixed and predictable motions of the stars. The pattern of mechanism is the rule of virtue, and the theory of atomism provides the fixed scale of perfection.

Urizen's fall, however, occurs not merely because of his pride, but also because of a failure in conscious awareness. He is stupefied by his isolation and frightened by his own uncertainty. Out of his resistance to the unknown and the uncertain, he seeks to perpetuate the known "in books form'd of metals." " 'Why will you die, O Eternals?' " he asks, for his retreat is also a defence against the life of Eternity which dies to each experience and is born to a new one.[3] From his defence against eternal life, he turns inward to the establishment of the Selfhood or ego, and attempts to encompass the non-ego, nature. By means of the Selfhood, he recognizes the need for a moral order, the need for an inner necessity to conform to the outer necessity of the natural order. The two orders of eighteenth-century rationalism are given their beginning, and Urizen has divided himself from the active vision of Eternity in the person of Los, for he has turned away from being into the perpetuation of his fallen state. "Forgetfulness, dumbness, necessity"[4] describe the conditions of the fallen mentality; Urizen sinks from eternal existence into that fixed and necessary ordering of experience which his search for an exclusive security entails. These fallen conditions of the mind are hammered into their corporeal form by Los who rescues him from falling into non-entity by the creation of the natural body. Even the vision which Los represents is reduced to the physical organs of perception:

All the myriads of Eternity,
All the wisdom & joy of life
Roll like a sea around him,
Except what his little orbs
Of sight by degrees unfold.[5]

[3] *Ibid.*, II, 6, 33; 4, 21.
[4] *Ibid.*, IV(b), 4, 24.
[5] *Ibid.*, V, 2, 9–13.

The "degrees" of sight are the moments of perception which reduce the entire vision of eternity to the partial vision of temporal succession. Urizen enters the fallen "Abyss" of his conceptions through the labyrinth of temporal process, and the seven ages through which he passes are the changes which Los binds with "rivets of iron and brass."

The separation between Los and Urizen is the separation between man's original powers of perception and conception so that the latter become wholly dependent upon the "deadly sleep" into which he has fallen. The sleeping intellect can neither control the dream nor awaken from it, and it is only through the active intervention of Los that the mind is kept from falling away from existence completely. As the power of perception, Los is affected by the condition of Urizen, and he forms out of his own "dark visions" the "globe of life blood."[6] The red globule of blood suggests the process of life in Generation: birth and death in the physical life of man, the incarnation of conscious perception, the divided selves whose field of observation rests in the "endless Abyss of space." The globe of blood is the essential image of man's field of experience in the state of nature: the flow of time in his veins, the urge to procreate, the fight to survive on a thousand battlefields, the symbol of race and family and the final gift of life to the earth. To gain and possess, to conquer and keep the phantom of natural existence is the tragic pity of man's incarnate existence. The vital response to the futile challenge of the conquest of the natural void and the no less futile relapse into self-contemplation is the division of Los and Enitharmon—the separation into male and female. Out of this separation the living aim of natural existence is provided, and man is partly rescued from the ultimate pursuit of a futile goal.

Wonder, awe, fear, astonishment
Petrify the eternal myriads
At the first female form now separate.
They call'd her Pity, and fled.[7]

[6]*Ibid.*, V, 7, 52–3.

[7]*Ibid.*, V, 10, 66–9. The name Los could have been derived from either the Greek λόγος or the Latin *sol*. At the end of *Jerusalem*, when Jesus as the Lord and the Universal Humanity appears standing beside the awakened Albion in "the likeness and similitude of Los," we may assume that, as Christ is the divine Word or Logos, the name of Los is merely a shortened form of the Greek word. Blake may, however, have been thinking of the Divine Sun, the focal point of eternal life—a conception of which Swedenborg made much. Enitharmon has been derived from ἐναρίθμιος, "numbered," or ἀνάριθμος, "numberless," since the Queen of Heaven or

Blake also makes use of a sexual symbolism to express the sympathetic attachment between man as a perceiving subject and the spatial world of objects which he must desire or hate, win or lose, covet or despise. The union of the heartbeat which is the hammer of Los with the senses of sight and touch which provide man with his contact with the forms of space complete his experience of generative existence. Space and time become Enitharmon and Los, and out of these conditions the immortals are represented as weaving that structure of apprehensible reality which forms the basis of all natural knowledge or "Science."[8]

Los and Enitharmon are the vital limitations of man's natural existence, and from them the redemptive force is born in the person of Orc. The limiting conditions themselves are made the means for realizing man's possibilities and even for pointing the way to redemption. But Blake's Promethean hero is also the demonic force of revolution introduced into the circle of time to provide movement and growth in the forms of nature. He is conceived a worm, and through the evolution of natural forms reaches the stature of humanity.

> Many sorrows and dismal throes,
> Many forms of fish, bird & beast
> Brought forth an Infant form
> Where was a worm before.[9]

The birth of Orc is also the "birth of the Human shadow," for he represents the energy of desire, and desire gives the natural man the form and direction of his life. He is that spirit of life which is born from the Abyss and can still lead the fallen man back to Eternity. To Los, however, who no longer "beheld Eternity," Orc is Orcus or hell, a demon and not a hero, an alien force which is distrusted and must be reduced to submission.[10] Like Prometheus, he is therefore chained

---

Space becomes the basis of the commensurable structure of natural reality. Cf. Northrop Frye, *Fearful Symmetry* (Princeton, 1947), chap. v, n. 29. D. V. Erdman (*Blake: Prophet against Empire* (Princeton, 1954), p. viii) simply, and perhaps rightly, points to Blake's "choice of the name Los (loss) for his visionary prophet (profit) in a world of Paradise *Lost*." Frye, in *The Divine Vision*, ed. de Sola Pinto, 1957, 100–1, suggests the *los* or *loos* which is a synonym for fame in Chaucer's *House of Fame*.

[8]*Ibid.*, V, 12, 77.

[9]*Ibid.*, VI, 6, 24–7.

[10]In *America*, Orc is the spirit of revolution. His name is taken from the Latin *Orcus* denoting the infernal regions, sometimes used to refer to Pluto, the god of Hades. The term first emerged in Old English in the word *orcneas* which means "evil spirits" or "monsters" (*Beowulf*, 111–14).

to the top of a mountain by the iron restrictions on desire which the "Chain of Jealousy" represents. Henceforth, the restricted vision of Los and the rational programme of Urizen isolate and enslave the energy of Orc. Urizen invents weight and measure, and Los as the spirit of time begets on Enitharmon the "enormous race" of the star-worlds.

Urizen's subsequent exploration of what Blake calls his "dens" suggests the earthbound mentality seeking out the extent of its scope. He finds merely the disorganized, macabre shreds of living forms, and the only race which he can bring forth are his four sons, born of the elements, and his daughters, from vegetation and creatures of the earth. Like Tiriel, whose story forms one of the other minor prophecies, Urizen curses his race for not realizing his hopes, but he is forced to see that his programme of laws cannot be kept. Like Thel, whose story is also another of the minor prophecies, he becomes aware of the mortal conflict between life and death. With a frustrated perversity which Blake always associates with religious dogma, he finally forms a "Web" from his own disillusionment and contradictory designs, called the "Net of Religion."

From the chaining of Orc and the triumph of Urizen originate all that Blake connects with rule, law and reason in human civilization. Cultural forms, religious myths and the entire social manner of living begin with Los and end with Urizen who applies the rule and the compass to the original vision of the possibilities. The cities of this world are the cities of Urizen, and they can only exist in relative security by chaining Orc. But this constant triumph of reason over energy continues to obscure the power of vision, until the possibility of any life but this one is forgotten. Thus, Blake's cycle of fall and creation up to the founding of Egypt—that epitome of intellectual, moral and political slavery—is completed.

And their children wept, & built
Tombs in the desolate places,
And form'd laws of prudence, and call'd them
The eternal laws of God.[11]

Out of the final triumph of Urizen's power and out of the "thirty cities" corresponding to the thirty sons of Tiriel, the paternal tyrant, his remaining children escape under the leadership of Fuzon. Fuzon,

[11] *Ibid.*, IX, 5, 29–32.

an incarnation of the fiery energy of Orc, seems literally to represent the "fusion" of the energetic and rational aspects of life which move in the direction of human redemption through the planned revolt of the exodus. He is the spirit of Orc acting through reason, and therefore, the prophetic part of the Mosaic dispensation.

With this interpretation of the exodus, Blake brought his own Genesis, in its first draft, to a close. The nine chapters were later expanded into the nine "nights" of *The Four Zoas* where the cycle was completed up to the coming of Christ and redemption. As he became less involved with the visionary form of his creation, he saw more of it in perspective, like a painter standing back from his canvas. The minor prophecies were separate explorations into the various aspects of his vision.

The Book of Ahania (1795) is in this respect a continuation of *The First Book of Urizen*, and its subject is an examination of the Mosaic dispensation. Ahania herself closes the book with a lament, but is otherwise scarcely mentioned. In *The Four Zoas*, however, her rejection by Urizen breaks the "bounds of Destiny"[12] and separates intellect from the guidance and inspiration of faith; faith becomes confused with hope and despair. Blake barely suggests this in the earlier work when he associates her with the moon as the "mother of Pestilence" and lunacy. Once separated from Urizen, Ahania becomes Blake's Pallas Athene (as her name implies), and Urizen his Zeus. The bright, armoured goddess of abstract values who executes the commands of her father reflects the Greek reliance on the rule of reason. For Blake, however, the wraith-like Ahania, mysterious, formless and well-nigh indiscernible, expresses his dislike of abstraction as rational knowledge divorced from the active intelligence, with its iron-clad laws and its impersonal formulations of experience. Such knowledge is a means to rationalize and implement man's hopes rather than to animate and inspire his thoughts. In her closing lament, Ahania contrasts her present state with her former happiness as the unfallen Sophia or Wisdom, the bride of intellect; while Urizen broods alone she weeps "on the verge / Of Non-entity."[13]

[12]*The Four Zoas*, III, 129–32. The origin of Ahania, in *The Book of Ahania*, I, 7–8; II, 1, "read like a travesty of the birth of Minerva" (H. M. Margoliouth, *William Blake's "Vala"* (Oxford 1956), xxii).

[13]*The Book of Ahania*, V, 2, 9–10.

The main part of the work is devoted to a description of the struggle between Fuzon and Urizen, between the active and the passive intellect. Urizen concentrates on overwhelming the prophetic energy of his rebel son whose "Globe of wrath" is the immediate cause of the separation between him and Ahania, "his parted soul." To the fallen mentality the energy of Fuzon has become merely a force; his consort merely an object of lust and a possession to be jealously concealed. In addition to this apt description of the supreme intellectual, Blake emphasizes the anarchy of energy divided from the guidance of the mind. Fuzon's globe of wrath, like the red globe of blood, is the vital subterfuge of life to outwit the living death of Urizen's rule; but it misses its mark. Confident that he has slain his adversary, Fuzon is overcome by a rock poisoned by the "Serpent"—the last of those perverse forms of energy which Urizen's isolation calls forth. The rock itself becomes "Mount Sinai in Arabia" representing the tables of the law—the most deadly aspect of the Mosaic dispensation, for the "reasoning negative" can hardly sink below the point where it confuses a code of prohibition with the revelation of divine order. The crucifixion of Fuzon on the Tree of Mystery[14] is the climax of Urizen's victory—the subjection of man's life to a dying "corse" impaled on the sacrificial tree of moral conditions.

Neither the abortive intellectual revolution of Fuzon nor the emotional and instinctive rebellion of Orc provides a sufficient response to the challenge of redemption. Los himself, who is the power of perception and the basis of existence, does not provide the means to redeem man's fallen condition, although it is through him that redemption is later to come. Meanwhile, Blake continues to explore error and reveal the state of fallen man, "the son of perdition,"[15] as a prelude to the later prophecies with their completed cycle of fall, consolidation in the fallen state and redemption. Since Blake's devil or "man of sin" is to be found in man's existence as a dependent creature of nature limited to an inner and an outer set of conditions, the process of redemption must begin with the gradual recognition of this state of affairs. The minor prophecies examine all that is destructive

[14]In *Jerusalem*, 28: 15–16, this Tree is called "Moral Virtue and the Law / Of God who dwells in Chaos hidden from the human sight."

[15]Cf. II Thess. ii: 3–4: "Let no man deceive you by any means: for that day shall not come, except there come a falling away first, and that man of sin be revealed, the son of perdition. . . ."

and negative, so that the false may be isolated and thereby destroyed, for it has no independent existence. The greatest error, and the root of all the others in Blake's opinion, is the inability to see truth except through error. Out of this basic slavery to the "cloven fiction" of the fallen reason and its logic comes man's judgment of right and wrong, true and false, good and evil. Blake tries to move beyond this kind of judgment towards what he calls the "Last Judgment" which culminates in a final isolation of error, and therefore, its destruction. If one can muster the stamina to outstare the devil he will disintegrate. The difficulty is that he has come to affect the way one stares: Urizen has dragged Los down with him. Nevertheless, the world of Los remains the world one can see, while the world of Urizen is the world one thinks one knows—an invisible world of concepts and measurements, much larger, cold, dark and void of feeling and sensation. The conflict between these two worlds and the tendency of Urizen's "horrid vacuity" to swallow up the perceptual world of Los forms the subject-matter of *The Book of Los* (1795).

At the beginning of *The Book of Los*, Blake wrote an antediluvian Genesis, a lament by the "aged Mother" of temporal existence for the "Times remote"—a reference to the entrance of man into the state of Generation. Going back into the womb of temporal generation, the book opens with this speech of Eno, the maternal aspect of time as it gives birth to succeeding moments, events and lives. She is therefore represented as guiding "the chariot of Leutha,"[16] the union of the natural urge to procreate with the eternal power of affection. Eno is a daughter of Beulah, the state of existence beyond Generation, where the contraries are "married" and the moment of perception raised to the intensity of vision opens into Eden.[17] She is thus a Muse of Vision and a "daughter of Inspiration" distinguished from the Classical Muses whom Blake called "daughters of Memory." She is also the mother of time or of that aspect of time in the natural man which can too

[16] *The Book of Los*, I, 1; 2. The name "Leutha" suggests a combination of Luvah, man's eternal power of love or affection, and Lilith, to whom, according to Hebrew legend, Adam turned after the loss of Eden. In *The Song of Los* she helps provide Mohammed with a "loose Bible" (The Koran has nothing of the Bible's epic narrative structure), and in *Milton* she becomes the "emanation" of Satan, corresponding to Milton's Sin.

[17] Eden opens into Eternity, and is Eternity viewed from the perspective of time; but Beulah is the repose of Eden and the state immediately below it and above Generation. Blake obviously derived the term from the prophet Isaiah (lxii: 4). It is the realm of sexual delight, and the beginning of visionary inspiration.

easily degenerate into a sense of panic, as he reflects upon the drum-beat of the heart leading him from the womb to the tomb. Restricted to this natural perspective, he feels compelled to find survival in procreation and in continuing himself through his descendants. Like Adam in the Hebrew myth, he turns from Eve to Lilith, his animal nature, and begets upon her the titanic or "giant race."[18] Such is the measure of his fall from Generation to Ulro, from the sexual delight which is an act of affection to the natural "Wantonness" which is an act of possession. The desire to perpetuate himself through his children is symbolized by "the chariot of Leutha" in whom the struggle between affection and possession is contained.

In Eno's lament, this mixture of affection and possession brings about the fall of desire—a theme expanded and treated at length in the second night of *The Four Zoas* where desire is called Luvah. The same theme is also worked out in the earlier *Visions of the Daughters of Albion* (1793), but *The Book of Los* is mainly concerned with the initial effect which the fall of desire produces on the conflict between Los and Urizen. The living fire of divided and restricted desires is represented as subjecting the world of perception to that of conception, so that the vast, solid, commensurable world distracts and fascinates the Eternal Prophet who is bound in a chain and "Compell'd to watch Urizen's shadow."[19] The "doors of perception" are locked shut, and Los is confined like a dead Pharaoh within the impenetrable "marble of Egypt." Called a "Solid without fluctuation," the fallen world is given both its opacity and its solidity by the weakness of organic perception which sees as definite and determinate what is to the eye of vision the indefinite rim of chaos. Blake associates this weakness and slowness of perception with the reduction of energy or desire to a fire which has fallen away from its true light and heat—from its eternal wisdom and love.[20] The imagery of darkness and night suggests the opaque appearance of natural objects perceived by the reduced

[18]*Book of Los*, I, 5; 24–5.

[19]*Ibid.*, I, 6, 32.

[20]The "flames of desire" run through heaven and earth, bringing destruction and plagues (*ibid.*, I, 6, 27–30). Los, however, is shut out from both the *light* and the *heat* of these fires (I, 9, 49–50), that is, according to Swedenborg, from understanding and will, love and wisdom, for these are the correspondences of light and heat. Swedenborg also states that all perfections are perfections of love and wisdom (*Divine Love and Wisdom*, secs. 200–1 and *passim*). Separation from this union of love and wisdom produces "destruction & plagues."

power of vision. But Los finally rescues the effects of light and heat, and out of them he fashions the counterpart of the eternal sun of love and wisdom—the "immense Orb of fire" which "flowed down into night" and is the living sun behind the dead sun of natural appearances.[21]

Depth and night are the two recurrent images expressing the fall into the generative matrix of time and space which the ancients called the "light-hating world."[22] The form of this world is basically circular, and Los is represented as circling around Urizen, as he beats out the orb of fire—the external pulse of the universe corresponding to the red globe of blood, the internal pulse of man.[23] Man's sense of time stretches all the way from the momentary pulsation of the artery to the cyclical revolutions of the stars, from the perception of his own moments of experience to the conception of cosmic cycles. History is the temporal extension of man's individual experience, and it foreshadows within the universal round of nature the eternal background of his source and of his destiny. The cosmic and the historical cycles bring the two worlds of Urizen and Los into one vision of the entire state of Generation. Blake sees this vision as the dream of one man, the Giant Albion, and in *The Four Zoas* he makes use of Los as the living spirit of time which keeps the Giant's pulse beating and provides the possibility of his awakening. Los becomes the genius of man's sense of

[21]*Ibid.*, IV, 9, 45–6. The Orb becomes the Sun to the eye of fallen perception, but Los remains the *being* of this appearance. Blake refers to Los as "a terrible flaming Sun" (*Milton*, 20: 6). Cf. Letter to Thomas Butts. Nov. 22, 1802:

> Then Los appear'd in all his power:
> In the Sun he appear's, descending before
> My face in fierce flames; in my double sight
> 'Twas outward a Sun, inward Los in his might.

[22]Proclus, *In Platonis Timaeum Commentaria* (*Timaeus*, 43A), lib. v, 339B: "And the light-hating world, and the winding streams, under which many are drawn down." Thomas Taylor (*Collectanea*, London, 1806, p. 99 n.) attaches an explanation to this passage, which is taken from the *Chaldean Oracles*. "The winding streams signify the human body, and the whole of generation, externally placed about us." Compare this statement with Blake's description of Urizen at the end of *The Book of Los* (IV, 9, 43–8):

> Till his Brain in a rock & his Heart
> In a fleshy slough formed four rivers
> Obscuring the immense Orb of fire
> Flowing down into night: till a Form
> Was completed, a Human Illusion
> In darkness and deep clouds involv'd.

[23]*Book of Los*, IV, 3, 15–17.

time; and Orc, who was born of Los and Enitharmon, the revolutionary force, the red blood which pulses through the cyclical movement of history. This cyclical vision of time is regulated by Los and transformed by the energy of Orc who awakens in each individual the hope of redemption, and, in each historical culture, the revolutionary drive toward a communal and ordered life. However, Orc is invariably crucified before the paternal and priestly image of Urizen as the original cultural vigour becomes moribund and freezes into the fixed forms of the social mores. Los or the quickened sense of purposeful time likewise degenerates into the cyclical round of mere duration. The history of the great cultures like the history of man himself takes the form of fall, consolidation in the fallen state and an attempted redemption which can become the exodus of the chosen few from the decaying civilization to a new land.

The First Book of Urizen ends when Fuzon leads the "remaining children of Urizen"[24] out of the state of nature towards redemption. The earth is called "Egypt," and the exodus of Israel from a decadent, priest-ridden culture is used to suggest the union of historical revolution with prophetic redemption. The cyclical rise and fall of civilizations is the repeated expression of man's attempt to resolve once again the ambiguity of his position, as he stands midway between the eternal source and the natural conditions of his life. The vision of the prophetic Reprobate always attempts to rescue the creative life within the great cultures from the authority of the Elect, and the followers of the prophetic revolutionary are the Redeemed. In Blake's terms the phenomena of the great cultures are works of art undertaken in the spirit of the highest adventure, and they are inspired by the hope of restoring what he calls the Golden Age. His Golden Age is, however, a state of realization—the Alpha and Omega of historical process—which redeems man from the circle of destiny and returns him to Eden.

This cyclical pattern begins to take definite form within the minor prophecies, and, as suggested earlier, it gave Blake his central theme and his life's work its purpose. By the end of *Jerusalem*, he had brought together the world of Los which was that of Chaucer, Shakespeare and Milton and the world of Urizen which was that of Bacon, Newton

[24]IX, 8, 44–7.

and Locke into one vision.[25] The orbit of space and time was redeemed from its fixed condition, and he saw it as a creation of the human imagination—as a part of Eternity. But in the minor prophecies, he still struggled within the cyclical pattern of history which keeps the perception of time bound to the world of Urizen and divides vision from apparent reality. This very division holds man subject to nature and makes him distrust that power of imagination in himself which can give the true perspective. Nevertheless, the meaning of history emerges as a path toward freedom, and references to previous civilizations of Africa, Asia, and Europe lead on to America, the hope of liberty. In *The Song of Los*, Blake indicates that the attempts represented by the earlier cultures were doomed by the laws of Urizen which consolidated and reduced the living message of the prophets, the "children of Los."

> Adam stood in the garden of Eden
> And Noah on the mountains of Ararat;
> They saw Urizen give his Laws to the Nations
> By the hands of the children of Los.[26]

The prophets themselves become more restricted in their perceptions, until the leaders of thought turn out to be a Newton and a Locke

> Thus the terrible race of Los & Enitharmon gave
> Laws & Religions to the sons of Har, binding them more
> And more to Earth, closing and restraining,
> Till a Philosophy of Five Senses was complete.
> Urizen wept & gave it into the hands of Newton & Locke.[27]

The "terrible race" of the prophets become lawgivers and culture-heroes to the "sons of Har" whose energies have no other expression than through the natural or corporeal Selfhood. Har himself is that Selfhood separated from the quickening spirit of life which Blake calls the imagination. Imagination is the essentially human nature of man which liberates him through creative activity from the mere reaction to the natural environment and the preoccupation with corporeal needs. Har and Heva flee from the possible misuse of energy into the

[25] *Jerusalem*, 98: 9.
[26] *Song of Los*, "Africa," 6–9.
[27] *Ibid.*, 44–8.

denial of it, and with the decay of vigour comes the decay of consciousness which is the visionary imagination. The triumph of reason and nature is complete.

Blake probably appropriated the term "Selfhood" from Swedenborg, for the latter had written: "Man's selfhood is in the will; this selfhood is evil by his first birth, but becomes good by the second birth. The first birth is from parents, the second from the Lord."[28] There is in this outlook a fundamental agreement with Blake's own doctrine of redemption from that natural self which is acquired and fostered by the family, the tribe, the clan and the race. The "New Selfhood" is born from the Lord who is the human imagination or the true man—realized as the goal of individual existence. The primary obstacle to this goal is rooted in the "first birth" from parents, consisting of fears, demands, worries and frustrations—of all the nonsense educated into childhood in the name of experience. Blake's *Songs of Innocence and Experience* present an earlier prelude to his minor prophecies by confronting the innocence of immediate vision (Los) with the experience of calculated opinion (Urizen) and presenting both as the dialectic of the "first birth." Out of this opposition within the field of history comes his interest in revolution and the attempt to resolve the dilemma by recurrent bursts of energy (Orc). In *Thel, Tiriel* and *Visions of the Daughters of Albion*, he first explores the failure of innocence, then of experience, and in the last work, of both, when they fail to become the basis of the "second birth from the Lord." But this "second birth," or what Blake calls redemption by individual "Genius," is restricted and even prevented by a tyranny masquerading under the plausible cloak of moral virtue and duty to one's own kind. The paternal and the maternal solicitude represents that paralysis of continued growth which afflicts the tribal life of the primitive, and is also the outstanding symptom of the decline of individual and social life within the great culture. Tyranny and suicide are the two results of this failure, and tyranny becomes most obvious in the ruler who can give full expression to it when he has reached the stage of old age and its paralyzing effect is fully apparent. Blake uses the figure of the senile Tiriel, the "king of the west"[29]—and the west is the region of the body—to clarify his vision of such an existence.

[28] *True Christian Religion*, chap. XI, sec. 658.
[29] *Tiriel*, 3, 19.

In *Tiriel* (1789) he illustrates the biblical maxim that "whosoever will save his life shall lose it."[30] The aged monarch has made the mistake of hoarding that wealth which is the experience of life, and confusing life with the memory of experience—a trick which natural existence plays on the aging. The miser of life is more especially a tragic figure when the vitality which he has sought to keep and use only for himself has begun to wane, and the powers which have never transcended the natural self become impotent with the approach of death. By his sons, Tiriel is told, but does not recognize, that the benevolence of the selfish heart is at last accursed. With the death of his powers in the person of Myratana, he is confronted with the approaching end of spent mortality and the frustration of all the hopes which he has attempted to realize through the Selfhood. In his dismay, he searches through the wasteland of natural experience for the only paradise which he is capable of conceiving—and finds it in the realm of indefinitely protracted infancy. The inhabitants of this realm, Har and Heva, represent the life of the "child of nature" without the re-creating power of the imagination. It is a condition of peace without honour, of nature without art and science—an existence which relies solely on the natural wisdom of memory, symbolized by the aged Mnetha whose name suggests the combination of the Greek word *μνήμη* and Athena. Tiriel attempts to return to this state, if state it may be called, for he has given up the human adventure in favour of the dream of natural survival.

It has been said that without memory man is a perpetual infant. To Blake, however, man is even less than an infant if he possesses only memory, for memory without vision is only habit. Har and Heva are like children, but no real child would have anything to do with them. They embody the merest physical attributes of a plant inseparable from the common earthly mother, having the negative "innocence" of impotent dependence. They think of Tiriel only as someone in a state of physical decay, and they are frightened. Their fears are allayed by the harmlessness and the extreme mildness of the tyrannical hypocrite and dissembler. His humility is a cloak for his pride, and from the depths of his self-dramatization he assumes the role of the tragic actor.

[30]Luke ix: 24. According to Cornelius Agrippa (*De Occulta Philosophia* (1531), lib. II, cap. XXII, p. 148) "Tiriel" was the Intelligence of Mercury, and in Blake's work represents the fallen understanding operating through the spirit of life.

> Then Tiriel rose up from the seat & said: "God bless these tents!
> My Journey is o'er rocks & mountains, not in pleasant vales:
> I must not sleep nor rest, because of madness & dismay."[31]

He leaves the vegetative paradise of Har—Blake's satirical picture of the eighteenth-century "state of nature"—and encounters the real savagery which emerges from the primitivist dream in the person of Ijim.[32] By remaining shut up in the confines of the Selfhood, and by failing to realize his full humanity, Tiriel has exhausted his energies by dominating the lives of others. His mode of domination has not been that of a Borgia who frankly follows the impulses of an aggressive nature, but that of a paternal despot who identifies virtue with his own will, and morality with the means of achieving his aims. To Blake, this kind of morality conceals an actual slavery to the fear of death, and finally culminates in the mere struggle for survival. Tiriel, when he meets the counterpart in nature of his own degenerate will, is overawed, and simply begs to survive.[33]

Since he is represented as the progenitor of a race of men, Tiriel is not merely typical of an aged individual but also of an aging culture. Blake is never tired of pointing out the fallacy of a moral science which ignores the spiritual needs of man and relies upon expedient generalizations. To direct the vital springs of action according to the principle of self-interest, however enlightened, will sooner or later reveal the natural savagery of Ijim and the tyranny of the political heirs of Tiriel. The typical tyrant usually invokes "nature," "fate" or "destiny" whenever he feels obliged to account for his conduct or renew his prerogative. Did not Robespierre attempt to establish the rule of reason and "nature," and was it not Napoleon who called himself the child of "destiny"? Tiriel who has masqueraded as the instrument of Providence recognizes in the words of Ijim "the voice of Fate,"[34] for he has really

[31] *Tiriel*, 3, 24–6.

[32] The Hebrew word "Ijim" is translated in the English Authorized Version of the Bible as "satyrs," and the satyr in Greek mythology was a demonic inhabitant of woods and forests, often depicted with the tail and ears of a horse, symbolizing a lascivious and savage nature. Cf. Frye, *Fearful Symmetry*, pp. 242–3.

[33] Similarly, Lear is overcome by the vision of his own acquisitive beast-qualities as mirrored in his daughters (*King Lear*, IV, ii, 42–4):

> Wisdom and goodness to the vile seem vile;
> Filths savour but themselves. What have you done?
> Tigers, not daughters, what have you perform'd?

[34] *Tiriel*, 4, 26.

submitted to nature, and is under fate. The tragedy of physical mortality is its tendency to reduce life to its own terms which are the opposite of man's larger possibilities. Returning on the shoulders of Ijim to his desolate palace, Tiriel hopes to subjugate his unruly children by the savagery of elemental nature, but Ijim refuses to recognize, much less revive, the household of age and decline, and he turns back to the forest. Tiriel himself, after cursing his race, wanders back to the land of Har, and the book ends with his lament on the hopelessness of correcting the effects of self-will by the natural experience which is derived from it. Why is man's life reduced to a condition which leads only to death? Why does the course of destiny turn out to be a trick for humbling "the immortal spirit" and turning man from the path of life? Blake provides no immediate answer but implies that anyone who takes that long to ask the question will likewise perish.

This failure to achieve humanity at the stage of maturity has its complement in the failure to begin natural existence at the stage of infancy. In *The Book of Thel* (1789), the prototype of the will to live, in the person of Thel, is prevented from entering into the experience of the natural world by inquiring too deeply into the ends and ultimate values of such a life. She represents the wilful rather than the willing spirit, and there is a concealed petulance in this denizen of the realm of the unborn, with her desire to know all the answers before she will take the step which leads into earthly existence. Tiriel's failure is a failure of the fallen understanding based on the collection of experience and the assertion of the will. Thel fails initially in her response to the will to live.[35] She does enter the northern gate, however, which is the gate of Los or visionary perception, and takes a look at Urizen's world of experience.[36] The perversity of the incarnate will and the contentious use of the avenues of knowledge frighten her, so that she

[35]The name "Thel" may come from Greek θέλω, the shortened form of ἐθέλω, meaning "will" or "wish." [Cf. the "Wille" of Chaucer's *Parliament of Fowls*, 214-N.F.]. Or, as G. M. Harper suggests ("Thomas Taylor and Blake's Drama of Persephone," *Philological Quarterly*, XXXIV, no. 4 (Oct. 1955), p. 386), "Thel" as an anagram of "Lethe" symbolizes that river of forgetfulness which encloses the whole of Generation. The latter sense emphasizes the wider implications of *Thel* as a failure in consciousness.

[36]Cf. *ibid.*, p. 382. The reference to Taylor's account of Porphyry's explanation (*De Antro Nympharum*) of the two gates in the thirteenth book of Homer's *Odyssey* should not obscure the original development of Blake's own symbolism. As pointed out earlier, the region of the north becomes in *The First Book of Urizen* the field of conflict between Los and Urizen, and out of this conflict, the creation and fall—which is the birth of the natural man—occurs.

flees back into the "vales of Har." Thel is represented as a woman because she succumbs to mortality in a feminine way—that is to say, passively—by a retreat into wish-fulfilling fantasy. Tiriel is represented as a man because he succumbs in a masculine way, and actively pursues the lure of tyrannical power, only to find that it ends in the impotence of old age and death. Both lose themselves—Tiriel by the path of tyranny, and Thel by the way of suicide. She gives way to that indolence which refuses to desire a human life, and he gives way to that aggression which fails to understand and realize it.

The possibility of hypocrisy is what really frightens Thel and drives her back to the protected vales of Har:

> "Why cannot the Ear be closed to its own destruction?
> Or the glist'ning Eye to the poison of a smile?"[37]

The division between acts, thoughts and affections made possible by the covering carapace of the Selfhood terrify her, but her fear leads her back to the very realm which finally receives the arch-hypocrite Tiriel. The way of retreat implies the same concentration on one's own safety and the same lack of faith which distinguishes both the coward and the tyrant. Both seek the false security of the Selfhood, and in so doing, create the protective mask which encloses a disintegrating life. This fundamental chastity is repugnant to Blake, and in *Thel* and *Tiriel* he is writing a commentary on the failure to unite the two contrary states of the soul which he has described in the *Songs of Innocence and Experience*. Thel is unable to take the state of innocence into that of experience; Tiriel has submerged the state of innocence in experience, and has become imprisoned in the natural self terrified of the expansion of life to which innocence is the key. Both make the mistake of regarding the two states of innocence and experience as mutually exclusive.

The problem of the insufficient will which Thel by her very name symbolizes is translated by Blake into the problem of unorganized desire. For, strictly speaking, man in the state of Generation does not possess will, only desire. To attempt to enforce desire for the expression of the Selfhood is to descend into the tyrannical self-will of a Tiriel, for fallen man does not possess that union of understanding and

[37] *The Book of Thel*, IV, 11–12. Hypocrisy is the natural basis of earthly existence, for it is the root of the Selfhood's defensive isolation (19–20):

> "Why a tender curb upon the youthful burning boy?
> Why a little curtain of flesh on the bed of our desire?

Inhibition and deceit are the necessary conditions of the restricted enjoyment of the senses and the inevitable results which follow.

will, of heart and eye, which can redeem activity. As pointed out in the aphorism at the beginning of the *Visions of the Daughters of Albion* (1793): "The Eye sees more than the Heart knows"; and this condition persists in the state of nature where desire for fulfilment continues to suffer from a separation between what is seen or desired and what is experienced or known. In Blake's terms, the organization of desire can only mean the union of the innocence of desire with the experience of its fulfilment, the marriage of the unrealized hell with the realized heaven. Innocence precedes experience and makes it possible, but this kind of freedom renders the activity of desire unpredictable, uncertain and forever new. Free love is beyond the scope of the fallen understanding of Urizen, and is therefore not only unreasonable but also unnatural. Blake explores the failure of the fallen understanding to cope with the organization of desire in his *Visions of the Daughters of Albion* where Oothoon's union of innocence and experience in the free act of love is made to confront the regulation of desire by Theotormon and Bromion. Theotormon is the social conscience of the moral code, and Bromion is its basis with his conviction that it somehow conforms to a mysterious necessity underlying the order of nature.

Theotormon interprets commonsense after the manner of the Enlightenment, as a system of generalizations on conduct, while Bromion[38] is the titanic basis of law and the lawgiver. As such, he shows up the moral code for what Blake thinks it is—a form of tyranny. The law is originally an attempt to control energy, but in effect, it tends to degenerate into a despotic restriction of liberty. The organization of energy is the only real way to control desire, short of destroying it altogether, but Blake sees that destruction is usually promoted in the name of control.

> Those who restrain desire, do so because theirs is weak enough to be restrained; and the restrainer or reason usurps its place & governs the unwilling.
>
> And being restrain'd, it by degrees becomes passive, till it is only the shadow of desire.[39]

[38]Bromion suggests "Bromios"—a title of Dionysus or Bacchus, as Damon, Pierce and Harper have pointed out. Harper ("Thomas Taylor and Blake's Drama of Persephone") connects Oothoon with Persephone or Proserpina in Taylor's *Eleusinian and Bacchic Mysteries* (ed. A. Wilder, New York, 1891) in which the following passage occurs (p. 163): "Nor is it without reason that Iacchus, or Bacchus, is celebrated by Orpheus as the companion of her search: for Bacchus is the evident symbol of the imperfect energies of intellect, and its scattering into the obscure and lamentable dominions of sense." See Ovid, *Metamorphoses*, iv, 10.

[39]*Marriage of Heaven and Hell*, Keynes, p. 182.

Since energy is the "only life," the price of staying alive is a choice between deception and restraint. Bromion is fully aware of this, and he is also aware of the necessity for some kind of enforced order to take the place of actual organization. This kind of order finds its theoretical expression in the moral law and its practical application in a display of force. Enforced order produces the illusion of unity within the individual and the community—a unity founded on general rules applied indiscriminately to every type of character. The result is to prevent the kind of individual development which leads on to eternal life, and to reduce the individual to a phantom, by restricting him to his spectral or natural condition. Bromion describes the frustration of the individual and the society which remain imprisoned within the conception of enforced conformity.

> "And is there not one law for both the lion and the ox?
> And is there not eternal fire and eternal chains
> To bind the phantoms of existence from eternal life?"[40]

All collective law leads to this denial of man's spiritual birthright, according to Blake, and when it becomes social custom, and finally, the absolute law of God, God has been turned into the devil.

Such is the way of nature, and as a son of Los, Bromion proves to be the prophetic initiator of Oothoon into the actual implications of her natural state. She is described as "the soft soul of America"[41] or as desire seeking liberty, but the liberty which she seeks is not to be found within the limitations of the state of nature. It is also beyond the scope of any society which is based on a moral order derived from that state, and this is the problem which Theotormon's rational view of life proves incapable of solving. He knows Oothoon's desire is more human than the taboos which she has ignored, but he cannot ignore his own fear of the apparently unreasonable and unconventional. She is not, however, merely an emancipated female, like the daughters of Albion in *The Four Zoas*[42] who assert their individuality as female wills in the fallen world of war and domination, but she is rather the sum of man's affections seeking eternal freedom through the wisdom of the heart. These affections form Blake's original vision of the daughters of man's titanic prototype—the Giant Albion. Oothoon's desire is "organized" in his sense of the term, because its innocence has not

[40] *Visions of the Daughters of Albion*, 108–10.
[41] *Ibid.*, 3.
[42] II, 61–2 [271–2].

become mixed with the contradictory experience of self-interest but has united with the immediate experience of its fulfilment to form one vision. At the same time, this organized desire of hers has clarified the vision of unorganized desire in a world divided between the innocent "Eye" of sense and affection and that subjection to reason and common-sense which conventional experience seems to teach. But although she catches this glimpse of visionary, free love, she is still surrounded by the world which, because of its basic separation of self-interest, called experience, from the innocence of desire, cannot afford to agree with her. Theotormon's relation to her is like that of a bishop to a prostitute: he has committed himself to a theoretical view of society which somehow outlaws her way of existing without actually permitting him to deny it. Blake rejects all pseudo-mystical denials of sex; he calls the sexual the repose of the human, not because it is "impure," but because it is less than eternal. It is impossible to circumvent the temporal by going around time, however, because there is no "around."

The significance of Blake's treatment of this theme lies in the emphasis he places on the impossibility of completely reconciling innocence and experience on the level of natural existence. Natural existence is itself the condition of their separation—a separation which he later expands in *The Four Zoas* into the division between instinct (Tharmas) and desire (Luvah), and between vision (Los) and reason (Urizen). The earlier prophecies fall into a fragmentary pattern of preparation for the later ones, and *The Four Zoas* makes the transition by bringing into focus all that has gone before it. At each stage of completing his scriptural canon, Blake penetrates deeper into the roots of what he is expressing, and for that very reason, it becomes more difficult to follow him. He moves closer and closer to the source of his inspiration or the basis of his creative activity. What he has to say in the *Songs of Innocence and Experience* is carried still farther in this direction in *Thel*, *Tiriel* and *Visions of the Daughters of Albion*, and these works along with the ones dealing with the struggles of Los and Urizen are absorbed into the nine nights of *The Four Zoas*. Taken in their entirety, the minor prophecies provide Blake with the structural framework of his epic theme, and with some dismay, the reader who perseveres discovers that the scaffolding has been removed. Events are treated as the mental realities of his inner experience, and are not accommodated to any supporting narrative which might be called a story.

In the minor prophecies, Blake begins to write solely from what he calls the "Imagination" or inspiration. Somewhat abruptly, but definitely, he ceases to make any use of the mirror of nature. The reflections in "this Vegetable Glass of Nature" no longer provide him with his basic mode of communication, and he utterly abandons any reference to the natural experience of events. As he says in his *Vision of the Last Judgment* (pp. 71–2) there is a "Mighty difference between Allegoric Fable & Spiritual Mystery," and he gives himself up completely to the latter. Evidently, any reliance whatever on the field of temporal experience in the narrative of his visions causes "Spiritual Mystery" to be contained, and presumably obscured, by "Allegoric Fable." Blake prefers to express his vision without this pattern of applied illustration.

> Fable is allegory, but what Critics call The Fable, is Vision itself. The Hebrew Bible & the Gospel of Jesus are not Allegory, but Eternal Vision or Imagination of All that Exists. Note here that Fable or Allegory is seldom without some Vision. Pilgrim's Progress is full of it, the Greek Poets the same; but Allegory & Vision ought to be known as Two Distinct Things, & so call'd for the Sake of Eternal Life.[43]

Fable or allegory is the imitation of vision, whether this vision originally existed in the memory of the writer or in the writings of others, but vision itself is the direct and immediate communication of inspiration. The story gets in the way of the immediate communication, by transferring attention from the actual vision which it exemplifies to itself. The best that can be said for the story in any work of literature is that it does exemplify original vision—either that of the author or that of his sources—the worst, that it reveals a mere portrait-painter's look at life and no actual vision at all. By Locke's association of ideas, a writer can produce a poem out of his memory, his reading and his immediate impressions, but he still fails to produce anything Blake can call poetry or art. No facility of description, technical ability, sensibility or subject-matter makes the poet. "One Power alone makes a Poet: Imagination, The Divine Vision."[44] And according to Blake's own practice, one theme alone makes the poet: the expression of this "Vision" as the immediate experience of his own existence within his perspective of the history of human life and thought.

[43] *Vision of the Last Judgment*, p. 68.
[44] *Annotations to Wordsworth's "Poems,"* I, p. viii.

10. Human Existence: The Epic Theme

IN OUTLINE, the earlier works of Blake which have already been discussed converge on his vision of the origin and possibilities of human existence. Man's possibilities can only be understood in terms of his origin, just as the possibilities of an acorn can only be understood in terms of its origin in the parent oak. By his natural birth, man's possibilities are limited to the scope of natural process which ends in death. And in this perspective the fullest expression of human existence is to acquire, retain and pass on to descendants as many natural goods as the field of this kind of experience affords. Wealth, progeny and power are the sum of human greatness, and in Blake's opinion, the Homeric epics seem to concentrate on this view of the possibilities. They even extend these possibilities for the hero, who is said to gain fame among his contemporaries, the favour of the gods, a memorable name and the descent of power to his successors and retainers. What can be made of his natural existence is the measure of the hero's fortune and is also the measure of his possible achievement. The Homeric gods and the hero's own virtue are, after all, merely aids to gain the most from fortune and keep it, within these limitations. Blake calls this kind of heroism "a Miser" and objects to Dante's praise of Fortuna as an instrument of Providence in the sphere of nature: "The Goddess Fortune is the devil's servant, ready to Kiss any one's Arse."[1]

Emphatically opposed to any view which seemed to give ground to naturalism, he attacks those works which can be made to promote and abet it. He also takes every precaution that his own work shall never be used in the same way. The usual accommodation to natural

[1] *Notes on the Illustrations to Dante*, Design no. 16. Dante might well have considered this a petulant comment. The fact that he not only made use of the Hellenic conception of Fortuna like Boethius and Albertus Magnus, but also raised her to an angelic intelligence (*Inferno*, vii, 94–6) is what infuriates Blake.

incident is eliminated, and the epic story becomes the narrative of his own visionary perspective. Dante took the trouble to explain that the *Commedia* contained an inner meaning which was his visionary perspective, but his work can still be read without reference to it. Blake's prophecies are evidently written so that they cannot be read in this way. They must be read from what Dante called the "anagogic" point of view or they cannot be understood at all.

The rejection of any concession to naturalism makes it necessary for Blake to discard occasional subjects such as the siege of Troy and the founding of Rome—subjects which suggest an ideal of heroism which he despises. The image of the Greek and Roman hero is merely a projection of man's natural Selfhood in all its supposed grandeur and its apparent magnificence. The Homeric hero holds fast to duty, power and wealth, and as Blake remarks, the ultimate ideal of this "Heroism" appears to be no more than that of a glorified "Miser."[2] He can still say that in his work he undertakes to portray "The Hero."[3] His hero cannot be mistaken for the magnified image of man's natural self but is his vision of the possibilities of human existence in terms of its origin in what he calls the "Ancient Man"—Albion. This kind of hero is difficult to accommodate to the epic form, for the scope of the epic has to be enlarged to include within the mind of the reader the whole of Jacob's ladder and not just the earth on which he slept. The twelve trials of Hercules were represented as natural events ending in the hero's apotheosis and final participation in the immortal life of the gods. The travels of Ulysses were brought to a close with his return home, but the events recorded could be interpreted as the reader saw fit. These narratives took place with the hero in the foreground of the surrounding world of nature. Blake's epic narratives take place within the background of the hero's human existence, and the foreground includes the perspective of natural experience. This is evidently not an extended expression of self-contemplation; inner and outer, self and non-self are included within the possibilities of the hero's existence.

Blake combines the individual human observer with the field of his observation, and places both within the dream of a Giant Man who is the universal expression of experience as Blake sees it. In other

[2]*The Laocoön Group.*

[3]*Annotations to Reynolds's "Discourses,"* p. 106.

words, he sees the world as history and not as nature, as a process of perception in living minds and not as a reality apart from human experience. Underlying the world as history or process, and indeed containing it, is that unity of perception and creation which is called the "Poetic Genius"—the basis of human experience. The Poetic Genius is the power or faculty of experiencing, and this power to experience, perceive and create is what gives man the world which he can know directly, apart from inference and abstraction. This is the state of Generation into which he is born, and in which history takes place. To search for the underlying existence of the world is to search for the basis of experience in man, for the mind of man creates the world of human experience out of the state of Generation, and can therefore be said to be its existence. "Where," asks Blake, "is the Existence Out of Mind or Thought? Where is it but in the Mind of a Fool?"[4] The "Existence" of which he speaks, however, cannot be the organ subject to sense, for what appears and disappears as the effect of forces other than itself cannot be said to have an original existence at all. An "Existence" is what gave unity to experience and contains its own beginning and end in time, its own cause and effect, its own origin and possibilities.

Blake's vision of what constitutes "Human Existence" involves a distinction between the "natural organ subject to Sense," which he also calls the "Selfhood" or "Spectre," and "the faculty which experiences," which he also calls the "Poetic Genius" or "the true Man."[5] The Selfhood is the rational product of memory and sensation, forming the basis of the individual's reasonable view of experience, for it is the "Ratio" of experience, and it tends to obscure the faculty which experiences. It becomes the identification of the individual with his habits and his tastes, his opinions and beliefs, his name and reputation, and most of all, with his environment and conditions—or the natural state of existence itself. It is the known as opposed to the unknown. "As none by traveling over known lands can find out the unknown, So from already acquired knowledge Man could not acquire more: therefore an universal Poetic Genius exists."[6]

If man has any possibilities beyond those already realized, he must

[4]*Vision of the Last Judgment*, Keynes, p. 651.
[5]*All Religions are One.*
[6]*Ibid.*

also have the ability to move from the known to the unknown. Rational inference and the knowledge acquired from the memory of previous experience can provide nothing ultimately new. Original invention can only be the activity of the faculty which experiences—that faculty by which the individual participates in the universal source of his human existence. Invention is this inspired vision, and it sets in order the knowledge already acquired. Blake's own prophetic works are an expression of what he means by this kind of ordering and this kind of original knowledge. Restricted, however, to the logic of inference and the use of memory, the individual knows as a Selfhood, and divides knowledge from being, until both become more and more limited, like the knowledge of the expert specialist and the being of the absent-minded professor. Such an individual lives in the world of the shrinking ratio of experience, and his knowledge is contained and limited, like a commodity, by his own reasons for acquiring it. Blake is careful to distinguish this kind of knowing from what he means by inspiration where the seer's knowledge is one with his existence by participation in the "faculty which experiences."

As an effect of temporal process in the state of Generation, man's natural self is caught between two terminal points: birth and death, a beginning and an ending in time. As the one who experiences through the medium of time, the "true Man" contains the beginning and the ending as an aspect of his own being, or to use Blake's term, as a particular state of his existence. States of existence are permanent in the universal Poetic Genius, and the "true Man" passes through them.

> As the Pilgrim passes, while the Country permanent remains,
> So Men pass on, but States remain permanent for ever.[7]

But the individual may fall asleep in one of them, become identified with the conditions of his growth rather than with the growth itself, forgetting the possibilities of the "faculty which experiences." This faculty gives him his outward form and the field of his possibilities which are the limits of his particular state. This is the faculty of vision by which he perceives himself and the forms of others in the same state of existence. The description of his own perspective of experience includes that of the others whose company he keeps and whose existence he shares; the description becomes the biography of a giant hero whose

[7] *Jerusalem*, 73: 42–3.

"lineaments" are the cosmology and the history of his race. Cosmology is Urizen constructing the mental image out of the materials of sensation (Tharmas), while history is Los giving that mental image its contact with experience by means of the affections (Luvah). Since experience as the act of perception is far more important to Blake than any construct derived from it, Los and Luvah become the main instruments of redemption and the final apocalyptic awakening of "The Hero." They are that imagination and affection which awaken him from the dream of Nature constructed out of reason and the senses. Prophetic vision conquers systematic abstraction and restores innocence to experience.

The restoration of innocence to experience in the free act of perception implies an original fall, and this fall must have been a failure in perception—or a falling asleep. The main feature of sleep is the helplessness of the dreamer before the conditions of his dream—his lack of existence, his inability to come to himself. Blake does not suggest that the state of Generation into which man is born is itself a dream, but that man is a dreamer in it, and he makes a dream out of it. The art is to recreate, find, and at the same time, discover the unity of the individual in the organization of the faculties. In *The Four Zoas*, the means is centred in the emotions; the power of affection brings the vision into focus.

The original title of this work was *Vala*, the consort of Luvah who is the faculty of desire, of feeling and emotion. Finally, however, Blake concentrated on the drive towards a union of all the faculties in the person of the Giant Albion whose emanation is Jerusalem. The later work brings together the four faculties into the author's visionary commentary on human existence and completes his definition of being as the discovery of the "true Man." In this discovery, which is also a revelation, the environment of experience is transformed. For the "organ subject to sense," the environment is a set of conditions, but for the "faculty which experiences," it becomes the degree of being in relation to what is called "Eternal Existence."

To see the field of experience as a progression through degrees of being or states of existence, it is necessary to awaken the "Humanity" by reaching the "faculty which experiences," thereby becoming free of the Spectre or Selfhood which is the "organ subject to sense." The Selfhood is not sensation but the identification of the individual with the limitations of the senses, and it produces a gradual deprivation of the individual's power to exist. More than that, however, it is the tyranny of the mental background of temporal experience which isolates the individual from the free insight of an eternal innocence. The creature of habit and rule becomes the spectre of himself, searching for an established community of lawful interests and necessary conditions, avoiding the spirit of adventure which can lead him to the real community of human experience. This kind of community is the actual goal of Blake's epic adventure, and it brings into one perspective the individual, the race of which he is a part and the Eternal Existence which makes such a community of experience possible. For Eternal Existence is the origin and the goal of experience to Blake, as it was also to the visionary who wrote the book called Revelation and who united in his apocalyptic vision of Christ the biblical record of his people and himself: "I am Alpha and Omega, the beginning and the ending, saith the Lord, which is, and which was, and which is to come, the Almighty."[8]

Blake's own vision of Eternal Existence includes the Christ of Revelation and the historical Jesus of the gospels, for Christ was God as only man could know him, and Jesus was man as only God could create him. In his humanity, man is a member of the eternal "Brotherhood of Eden" whose unity is the universal humanity which Christ embodied: "we are his Members."[9] In the temporal cycle of history, he is an individual moment in the generation of a whole race of men whose unity is their titanic, racial progenitor, Albion. The dream of Albion in *The Four Zoas* is itself the description of the state of Generation seen outwardly or cosmologically as the natural world, and inwardly or historically as the circle of destiny. To realize or perceive his human existence, the individual makes use of one of the "Seven Eyes of God,"[10] one of the seers who give each of the seven revelations within the completed cycle of time. The last of these is the revelation of Jesus and the dispensation represented by Christianity.

In the dream of Albion Blake brings together the four aspects of the work of imagination in the form of his visionary epics. Dante called these four aspects levels of meaning, and interpreted them as

[8] Rev. i: 8.

[9] *The Laocoön Group*. Cf. *The Four Zoas*, I, 4–6; *Jerusalem*, 96: 3–7.

[10] *The Four Zoas*, I, 242–5; VIII, 387–95; *Jerusalem*, 55: 31–2.

critical categories, but Blake introduces them as points of view established in the four faculties of man's human existence. Dante gave his universal vision a particular perspective, and he himself was the hero. In this he did not follow his Classical model, the *Aeneid*, for Virgil used the progenitor of the Roman people as his hero, and he was concerned explicitly with the vision of natural justice from the standpoint of the literal, allegorical or historical and moral levels only. Like the author of the *Iliad*, he concentrated on the historical and moral aspects of his story, using the literal level of character, plot and incident to illustrate the other two. Dante, however, gave his attention to the literal, the biographical details of his own spiritual pilgrimage, and brought his experience with its historical and moral levels into the anagogic vision of eternal existence. Blake still sees Dante's vision as hag-ridden by the Classical inheritance of the search for a doctrine of moral virtue to rationalize and explain the effects of outrageous fortune. Both Virgil and Dante were apologists for history, and were therefore committed to showing that it was morally justifiable. Virgil showed that the trials of Aeneas led to the founding of Rome, and Dante, that his own trials led to the vision of divine justice. Blake leaves the moral allegory behind when he makes his hero contain history as a state of existence and shows that good and evil, fortune and misfortune, are all due to a failure to see individual and universal history in this way.

Any state of existence implies an ultimate context which Blake calls "Eternal Existence," the final community of individuals, the "Brotherhood of Eden" from which the descent into states takes place. In a particular state of existence, conditions are limited to the relationship between it and the individual pilgrim in it. In eternity, the organization of existence is itself infinite, and only the conditions of possible states of existence are finite, for the perceiver is infinite with respect to any fields of perception. The abiding condition of such existence can only be described as an infinite love of life expressed through the creation of states which makes a more abundant life forever possible. An amoebic proliferation of the "Universal Humanity" is seen to be the supreme activity of Eternal Existence in the form of Christ—an activity in which his "Members" pass through the cycle of states to establish their existence as creators of Eternity. One of these "Members" is Albion, the progenitor of our own human race.

"Albion goes to Eternal Death. In Me all Eternity
Must pass thro' condemnation and awake beyond the Grave . . .
Albion hath enter'd the State Satan! Be permanent, O State!
And be thou for ever accursed! that Albion may arise again.
And be thou created into a State! I go forth to Create
States, to deliver Individuals evermore! Amen."[11]

Satan is Albion's spectre, the limit of his fall into dismemberment, a permanent condition created "to deliver Individuals evermore!"

The present human race whose original existence Blake describes as that of "Angels of the Divine Presence" is given a field of finite experience by Albion's fall, and a human form in the image of Christ's "Divine Humanity."[12] The realization of this human form is the work of art in eternity, and as far as Blake is concerned, it is the basis of all real art. But the activity of realization can be subverted by the very conditions created to make it possible, and the Selfhood composed of the conditions of experience can be mistaken for the human existence in man.

"Judge then of thy Own Self: thy Eternal Lineaments explore,
What is Eternal & what Changeable, & what Annihilable.
The Imagination is not a State: it is the Human Existence itself.
Affection or Love becomes a State when divided from Imagination.
The Memory is a State always, & the Reason is a State
Created to be Annihilated & a new Ratio Created."[13]

Identification with the conditions of a state can be annihilated; the attitude of mind can be changed, while the source of existence itself is discovered to be eternal. There is still an apparent contradiction in the added statement: "Whatever can be Created can be Annihilated." How can this be reconciled with the doctrine that states are both created and permanent? A state of mind, however, can be annihilated for the individual, and yet the state of existence which contains the possibility of such an attitude of mind cannot, but remains a part of the permanent architecture of eternity.

In *Jerusalem* the permanent architecture of eternity is called "Los's

[11]*Jerusalem*, 35: 9–10, 13–16. Albion is the human race as an English poet sees it. In his *Eisagoge*, Porphyry remarked that, by sharing the same species, many men are one man.

[12]*Milton*, 35: 10–23.

[13]*Ibid.*, 35: 30–5 and *passim*.

Halls" which provide the archetypal pattern of all activity, the substantial forms underlying every possible attitude of mind.

> All things acted on Earth are seen in the bright Sculptures of
> Los's Halls, & every Age renews its powers from these Works
> With every pathetic story possible to happen from Hate or
> Wayward Love; & every sorrow & distress is carved here,
> Every Affinity of Parents, Marriages & Friendships are here
> In all their various combinations wrought with wondrous Art,
> All that can happen to Man in his pilgrimage of seventy years.
> Such is the Divine Written Law of Horeb & Sinai,
> And such the Holy Gospel of Mount Olivet & Calvary.[14]

These "Halls" provide the calendar of occasions for the thoughts and acts of "every Age." As formal limitations within the field of experience, they are the sum total of the divine law originally written by the finger of God, for Blake considers the legal prohibitions of the Mosaic code a travesty on the prophet's actual vision. As creations of Eternal Existence, they are also the means of redemption and the gospel of salvation which ecclesiastical Christianity has turned into exclusive systems of doctrine and belief. But the "Sculptures" themselves are the work of Los who creates them in Eternity to make possible the experience of time, and in time, to make possible the vision of Eternity. Blake uses his description of this structure in the first chapter of *Jerusalem* as an introduction to his doctrine of states in the following chapters. He is careful to point out that the temporal environment of human existence is no mere accident or illusion but is an appearance based on an abiding reality. He therefore shows the counties of the British Isles opening out into the limits of the Mundane Shell and reflecting the halls of Los. "States" are this substantial basis of every field of experience as seen by the imagination. The natural man or spectre cannot see his state because he is a product of it. Seeing it as a whole entails seeing through the personal accidents of individual life to the universal structure of human existence. To express this notion, Blake creates his hero in the "Giant Form" of Albion who includes Blake's own life and opinions, his environment of England and his historical perspective within the context of an epic myth.

The myth of Albion is an inheritance from the pre-Christian past in which man is understood not as a disjointed section or part of the

[14] *Jerusalem*, 16: 61–9.

universe but as an individual embodiment of the whole of it in the image of a giant progenitor or "ancestor." And the "ancestor" himself takes the form not of a creator merely but of existence uniting any particular being to the ultimate possibilities of its source. "Therefore God becomes as we are, that we may be as he is."[15] This notion that the unity underlying any and all classes of existences is an original existence itself is often repeated in the cosmogonic myths of the ancients who apparently believed in the living reality of universals. Among so-called primitives, even the beaver finds its source in the "great beaver," and the horse in the "great horse." Blake gives no indication of knowing anything about the law of the totem and the belief in tribal descent from non-human progenitors, but if he did, he would probably consider it the natural man's degenerate interpretation of the original vision expressed in ancient Jewish tradition: "You have a tradition, that Man anciently contain'd in his mighty limbs all things in Heaven & Earth: this you received from the Druids."[16] The Cabbalistic Adam Kadmon whose powers became the forces of nature and the vital functions of organic life undoubtedly formed a part of this tradition. But Genesis provides an expression of the same myth, for Jacob is the progenitor of the Israelites, Adam of all races, and Jehovah of humanity itself and the entire world of human experience. The accounts given of the names of the most outstanding races of antiquity along with the family names of the ruling houses also support the claim to a descent from an original patriarch, progenitor or tutelary deity.[17]

Blake's "Patriarch of the Atlantic" whom he calls Albion grows into his final stature from those heroes, titans or gods seen by the writers of cosmogonies when they looked back towards the horizon of time when heaven and earth were one. Since Greek mythology produced from the union of heaven and earth Saturn or Cronus, the ruler of the golden age, it is not surprising that Holinshed, the Eliza-

[15] *There is no Natural Religion*, II.

[16] *Jerusalem*, 27, Preface.

[17] In the biblical narrative, the ancestor of the Hebrews is represented as attaining the patriarchal power of sovereignty and the title "Contender with God" or "Israel." As progenitor, he is declared the father of "a company of nations" (Gen. xxxii: 25 ff.; xxxv: 10–12). Earlier (iv: 26), men had begun to call themselves by the name of "Jehovah." Similarly, in the northern *Eddas*, Woden is represented as the progenitor not only of the *aesir* but also of most of the royal houses of the north.

bethan chronicler, placed Albion in this first period of the world. In Milton's version of the fable, he is called "Son of Neptune" and is said to have made an incursion into Gaul in aid of his brother against Hercules.[18] Holinshed, however, furnishes a story which is more in line with Blake's initial use of the myth.

This Albion (that thus changed the name of this Ile) and his company, are called giants, which signifieth none other than a tall kind of men, of that vncorrupted stature and highnesse naturallie incident to the first age (which Berosus also seemeth to allow, where he writeth, that Noah was one of the giants) and were not so called only of their monstrous greatnesse, as the common people thinke (although indeed they exceeded the vsuall stature of men in these daies) but also for that they tooke their name of the soile where they were borne: for *Gigantes* signifieth the sons of the earth: the Aborigines, or (as Cesar calleth them) Indigenae; that is, born and bred out of the earth where they inhabited.[19]

Albion is the ancestral soil of England on which Blake stood and from which he sprang. He is also the titanic forefather of Blake's own hinterland of symbolism—the original "Giant Form" composing the greater world of his inner life from which are derived the "Zoas" or living creatures who make up the *dramatis personae* of the prophetic books. Historically, Albion is the dreamer whose dream is the vision of history or the circle of destiny, and morally, or in terms of human nature, he is the field of spiritual adventure for the race. Finally, he is the description of the origin and destiny—that is, the essential existence —of humanity.

The existence of humanity is an original form which includes the world of man's immediate environment. The immediate environment of an acorn planted as the seed of an oak is the earth. But if its form is to be completely described in terms of its possible destiny, the description must include that unplanted or "unfallen" form of the original oak, appearing and disappearing within the realm of created nature.

"Whatever can be Created can be Annihilated: Forms cannot:
The Oak is cut down by the Ax, the Lamb falls by the Knife,
But their Forms Eternal Exist For-ever. Amen. Hallelujah!"[20]

[18]Milton, *History of Britain*, bk. I, chap. 1 (*Works*, New York: Columbia University Press, 1932, X, pp. 4 ff.). The reference is connected with the sons of Japhet after the flood and also with the derivation of a line of giants—which presumably included Albion—from some oceanic abode reminiscent of Atlantis. [Cf. Spenser, *The Faerie Queene*, IV, xi, 16–N.F.].

[19]Holinshed, *Chronicles* (London, 1807), I, chap. 3, p. 432.

[20]*Milton*, 35: 36–8.

The painter who attempts to paint the acorn in its plot of earth will be painting its "portrait," but if he wishes to paint it "historically"—in terms of its origin and its possible destiny—he will be obliged to paint an oak. Blake calls himself a "History Painter," and his vision of human existence is the oak tree itself, the Giant Albion, the hero of the prophetic books. He is, however, careful to distinguish his vision from the rational abstractions of a philosopher of history. Albion is not merely the general concept of humanity: "A History Painter Paints The Hero, & not Man in General, but most minutely in Particular."[21] As the hero of this kind of history, Albion includes within himself all that man has been and can be, for he is the particular exemplar of man's origin and his possible destiny. In his fallen condition, he is, however, separated from the complete realization of his powers, represented by his "emanation" whose name is the name of a Christian's vision of the eternal city—Jerusalem.

Like Dante's Beatrice, Jerusalem partakes of this world and the next, and she is that part of Albion which remains separate only in his wandering away from eternal existence. Their reunion, therefore, is part of Albion's recognition that she is herself united to the "Divine Image" as illustrated by the engraving at the end of the epic, *Jerusalem*. By this use of Albion and Jerusalem, Blake shows the change which has taken place in the relationship between the macrocosm, or the great world of nature, and the microcosm, or the little world of man. In this change of outlook, unfallen human existence becomes the macrocosm, and the natural field of experience the microcosm. If this is man's possible goal, it must be latent in his origin. Blake's expression of such an origin and its fulfilment takes the form of a movement from the original innocence of a Garden of Eden to the final experience of a New Jerusalem. The entire theme is foreshadowed in his *Songs of Innocence and Experience*, satirically corrected and sharpened in *The Marriage of Heaven and Hell*, symbolically tried and proved in the minor prophecies, outlined in *The Four Zoas*, and completed in *Milton* and *Jerusalem*. Using his interpretation of the Bible from Genesis to Revelation as a model, he looks back to man's origin

[21]*Annotations to Reynolds's "Discourses,'* p. 106. This vision goes beyond the appearances of nature and cannot be derived from them. Cf. Letter to Thomas Butts, Nov. 22, 1802: "If you have not Nature before you for Every Touch, you cannot Paint Portrait; & if you have Nature before you at all, you cannot Paint History; it was Michael Angelo's opinion & is Mine."

as to a garden newly planted and sown, and forward to his consummation as to a city "prepared as a bride adorned for her husband."[22] According to the fourfold method of interpreting scripture, Jerusalem is literally the earthly city, allegorically the body of the faithful, morally the believer, and anagogically the heavenly city of the Redeemed. As the bride or "emanation" of the Giant Albion, Jerusalem is Blake's way of uniting the Christian tradition of an Englishman to the English inheritance of a Christian.

Since the "emanation" is the power of direct or intuitive perception resulting in the creation of the data of experience, it is usually symbolized as a woman.[23] The separation between man and his emanation had originally been part of his fall from the possession of direct perception into the condition of a reasoning "Spectre" who could only know by inference and generalization. Direct perception and creative activity, however, can still be enjoyed by fallen man through inspiration, and Blake calls Jerusalem the sum of all men's emanations or the aggregate of "the daughters of Inspiration."[24] The source of inspiration is, after all, also the source of the individual's intuition of life and his grasp of existence. Each man's emanation is what he can directly understand and express; this is Jerusalem in every man, and she is the real basis of communication. But after the fall, she is separated from Albion, and her place is taken by a process of justification which man's Spectre uses to defend itself against its lack of understanding and its lack of

[22]Rev. xxi: 2.

[23]*Jerusalem*, 88: 3–15; 53: 24–9. As noted by D. J. Sloss and J. P. R. Wallis (*The Prophetic Writings of William Blake*, Oxford, 1926, II, 153), the term "Emanation" occurs first in added passages in *The Four Zoas* (e.g. VII(a), 327). Only twice does Blake mention masculine emanations (*Jerusalem*, 49: 47; 88: 11), presumably because, as a man, he sees the vision and value of experience as feminine. As "Man," however, the regenerate inhabitant of Eden, he also sees the separation of male (creator) and female (creature) in Beulah as objective projections or "emanation" of an original integrity. They eventually become "Time" and "Space" for the fallen "Spectre" in the state of Generation (*Jerusalem*, 85: 7–9):

for in Beulah the Feminine
Emanations Create Space, the Masculine Create Time & plant
The seeds of beauty in the space. . .

[24]*Vision of the Last Judgment*, p. 68: "Fable or Allegory is Form'd by the daughters of Memory. Imagination is surrounded by the daughters of Inspiration, who in the aggregate are call'd Jerusalem." In opposition to the "daughters of Inspiration" are the "Daughters of Albion"—Albion's female will—who, in the aggregate, are *Vala or Rahab* (*Jerusalem*, 64: 6). The Daughters of Albion are called the "Emanations of the Dead" (*Jerusalem*, 17: 13), and are also associated with Babylon. In time, Vala's name is Rahab (*ibid.*, 70: 31), a name meaning "violence" and connected with Babylon in Ps. lxxxvii: 4. Cf. Isa. li: 9.

communication with others. The root of this process, this self-deception, is Rahab, who confirms fallen man's false sense of integrity through his settled convictions, his self-respect and the reasons he gives for his actions. Blake calls her "Religion hid in War," dogmatic belief which produces misunderstanding, "Moral Virtue" and the "Reasoning Power." She is "Babylon the Great," the false integrity of the Spectre set up against Jerusalem, the original integrity of the unfallen Albion. Rahab is the epiphany of error at the end of each epicycle of history, and more especially, at the end of the entire historical cycle, the point where the attempt to make the fashionable culture of accepted opinion a substitute for actual, inspired understanding is finally revealed.

> And Rahab, Babylon the Great, hath destroyed Jerusalem.
> Bath stood upon the Severn with Merlin & Bladud & Arthur,
> The Cup of Rahab in his hand, her Poisons Twenty-seven-fold.[25]

The poisons which kill the great historical cultures are distilled from the fruit of the forbidden tree, the origin of the search for a natural standard of good and evil to confirm and strengthen the root of fallen existence. The attempt to make out of the mortal state a basis for anything but movement beyond it has been the sustaining condition of Albion's slumber and his separation from Jerusalem.

Once separated from Jerusalem, Albion loses direct knowledge of the "Forms" of existence, and henceforth is limited to what he can make of their temporal effects by means of reason and the senses. He has, in other words, entered into the power of his reasoning spectre who cast him out of the brotherhood of Eden.

> In Great Eternity every particular Form gives forth or Emanates
> Its own peculiar Light, & the Form is the Divine Vision
> And the Light is his Garment. This is Jerusalem in every Man,
> A Tent & Tabernacle of Mutual Forgiveness, Male & Female Clothings.
> And Jerusalem is called Liberty among the Children of Albion.
>
> But Albion fell down, a Rocky fragment from Eternity hurl'd
> By his own Spectre, who is the Reasoning Power in every Man,
> Into his own Chaos, which is the Memory between Man & Man.[26]

[25] *Jerusalem*, 75: 1–3. Bath, who is called both the "physician and the poisoner" (37: 1–2) is here given the latter or spectral form. Merlin, the "Immortal Imagination" (32: 23–4), has become Reuben (32: 40–1), the "Vegetative Man." The two legendary kings of Britain, Bladud and Arthur, are mentioned earlier (73: 31–40) along with Satan and Cain as states of existence which are the uninspired counterparts of the "Twenty-seven Heavens & their Churches."

[26] *Ibid.*, 54: 1–8.

As a result of this fall, he suffers a decline from the eternal law of liberty to the temporal law of moral virtue which establishes precedent and rule founded on past experience and the "Chaos" of memory. But only the exercise of original vision can really unite Albion's members (that is, mankind), and without this vision man fails to perceive unity outwardly as well as within himself. In fact he ceases to be "Man" at all, for he has lost his integrity which is the "Divine Vision" and the "Light" which is his true sense of values. Philosophically, Jerusalem is Albion's theory of value, and her separation from him makes him seek a substitute in Rahab, in nature and in generalizations on natural effects. It is in the very nature of man's fallen state that Rahab who is "Babylon the Great" should obscure Jerusalem, and that rational generalization of the fading images of memory should supplant with a chaotic confusion of tongues the awakened participation in a larger and ordered life. Lack of participation in turn implies failure to communicate completely between one man and another, as well as loss of that individual integrity which is the balance of man's powers of perception and expression.

This first epic, *The Four Zoas*, in which Blake endeavoured to complete his vision of man's fallen state, is itself a collection of much of what he had written before. It is a tormented and restless work, a product of Energy in conflict with Reason, the "Bible of Hell" to which he had referred in his *Marriage of Heaven and Hell.*[27] The two dominant themes are love and death, and they are both included in the second and accepted title. The first of these themes is most fully expressed in *Vala*, the first title he used. Vala's temporal name is Rahab, and she later becomes the emanation of the living being [*Zoa*] of affection in man, whose name is Luvah.[28] Luvah's fallen condition is represented by Orc, and the separated Vala or Rahab becomes the symbol of all that happens to man's affections in the state of Generation. Unaffected and innocent love leads to death, but when the moral issue is introduced, jealousy becomes the counterpart of love, and some kind of judgment the counterpart of death. The morality of experience takes over from the original vision of innocence, for it is in this presumption that he can judge what is finally valuable that man falls from Eden. The second and accepted form of the title was *The Four Zoas*, and under it: *The Torments of Love &*

[27]Keynes, p. 191.
[28]*Jerusalem*, 70: 31.

Jealousy in the Death and Judgement of Albion the Ancient Man. The two themes are united in terms of the four aspects of man's existence.[29] In the first title, the term of reference is Vala, and the emphasis is placed on the symbol of love and jealousy, the conflict between desire and reason. It is the theme of innocence in conflict with experience, and it is the description of everyone's youth. Blake, however, was no longer a youth, and *The Four Zoas* does not satisfactorily express the integration of these two themes.

At the end of the fifth Night of *The Four Zoas*, Urizen states the basis of the conflict between himself and Luvah: "When Thought is clos'd in Caves Then love shall shew its root in deepest Hell."[30] The "Caves" are evidently those of the fallen intellect, and long before this, the Daughters of Beulah have declared that love is changed to "deadly Hate."[31] Affection has turned into its contrary because thought has separated from visionary perception. The disintegration of fallen existence has created the notion of possession and separated interests. Luvah becomes Orc or "Dionysus," and after his birth into time, he is bound with the "chain of Jealousy."[32] Frustration and desperation take the place of faith and hope which are the positive basis and the eternal associates of the joys of love. The discovery that the kind of love which is mixed with jealousy leads inevitably to death, and can only be redeemed by a Last Judgment—a transformation and inner change of being—is the final theme of *The Four Zoas*. Wordsworth's pursuit of this transformation through the ministry of "Nature" puts Vala in the place of Jerusalem as the object of aspiration.[33] The pursuit

[29]The term "Zoa" is literally derived from the Greek word ζῷον meaning "a living being." In Revelation (iv: 6–8), the phrase τέσσερα ζῷα is translated in the Vulgate *quatuor animalia*, and in the Authorized Version of 1611, *four beasts*. The secondary meaning of the Greek word which, in this instance, is usually found in the plural is "figure" or "image"—as in painting or sculpture. In the poetry of his prophetic books, Blake used the plural form "Zoa" (ζῷα) to denote the image of one of the four original aspects of man's Eternal Existence. From this he made the English plural "Zoas."

[30]V, 241.

[31]*Ibid.*, I, 103.

[32]*Ibid.*, V, 95.

[33]Cf. *Annotations to Wordsworth's "Poems,"* p. 1. In his letter to Allsop (Aug. 8, 1820), Coleridge condemned Wordsworth's poetry for its "vague, misty, rather than mystic, confusion of God with the world, and the accompanying nature-worship." Blake also rejected Byron's attempt to make love to the world in the erotic longings of a Don Juan and the romantic travels of a Childe Harold—a *tour de force* which amounted to an escape from prophetic vision through a mystic worldliness. See the introductory note to *The Ghost of Abel*.

of Vala ends in the pursuit of death, that natural doom which takes the place of the transforming Last Judgment because the movement from the birth of generation to the rebirth of regeneration remains unfulfilled. This is a tragic vision of fallen existence, and although Blake saw through its pathos to the redemption of the Last Judgment, he evidently did not find the tragic effect acceptable.[34] *The Four Zoas* remains more of an epitaph on the fall of man than the gospel of redemption which he had in mind as his epic theme.

From the standpoint of his own development, its author was in that phase in which a poet of genius and vision frequently writes works of a tragic nature. That pathos which arose from the conflict between thought and feeling was now seen against the background of the earlier discovery of sorrow in the child's world of joy. He had moved on from this early struggle to youthful assurance and then to a sterner sense of duty and a search for deeper conviction in the face of life's apparent futility. This stage is illustrated in the development of those poets whom he often used to represent the prophetic tradition he inherited—Chaucer, Shakespeare and Milton. Chaucer wrote *Troilus and Criseyde* in which the theme of love and jealousy is united to that of death and judgment in the manner of Blake's *Four Zoas.*[35] Shakespeare wrote his great tragedies which sometimes find unmistakable echoes in the characteristics and activities of the Zoas themselves. The preoccupation of Los with the value of existence and his effort to see through the tragic implications of birth and death remind one of Hamlet. Urizen's obsession with what had been partly expressed through Tiriel recalls Lear's madness and his attempt to create a world out of chaos. His ambition to usurp supreme power, while succumbing to the "Shadowy Female," suggests the tragedy of Macbeth.[36] The

[34]Cf. Northrop Frye, *Fearful Symmetry* (Princeton, 1947), p. 269: "*The Four Zoas* remains the greatest abortive masterpiece in English literature." Bernard Blackstone (*English Blake* (Cambridge, 1949), p. 121) remarks: "There was too much William Blake in it, and not enough of Eternity."

[35]After his death Troilus is caught up to the eighth sphere (V, 1811–13) where, "with full avysement," he gains the vision of the celestial harmony. At the end of *Jerusalem* (98: 9), the three poets, Chaucer, Shakespeare and Milton, are united to the contrary tradition of Bacon, Newton and Locke in the final vision.

[36]As pointed out earlier, Blake's conception of "character" involved the whole while it referred to the part. All of these Shakespearean "characters" are considered to be, like the Zoas, aspects of human nature, and at the same time, human beings. Cf. *A Descriptive Catalogue, &c.*, no. III. Joseph Wicksteed (*William Blake's "Jerusalem,"* London, 1953, pp. 12–14), suggests a comparison of Hamlet with both Albion and Los.

fallen Tharmas who represents the betrayal of man's instincts is comparable to the degenerating Othello whose "spectre," in Blake's eyes, would be Iago, and his "emanation" Desdemona. Luvah and Vala, both in their tragedy and in the redeeming force of the love which they incarnate, suggest Antony and Cleopatra. In the divorce tracts and the political pamphlets, Milton deliberated on the conflict between reason and desire, between public duty and personal conviction. His doctrine of Christian liberty was his Last Judgment in the world of the pamphleteer. Like Chaucer and Shakespeare, however, it was in his poetry that he gave fullest expression to the tragic vision. If, therefore, *Paradise Lost* be taken as the counterpart of *The Four Zoas*, then *Paradise Regained* and *Samson Agonistes* parallel the perfected fulfilment of Blake's *Milton* and *Jerusalem.*

The final stage of reconciliation and understanding is reached by Chaucer through his vision of the universal journey from the terrestrial tavern to the celestial shrine in *The Canterbury Tales*. The same stage is expressed in Shakespeare's later comedies, especially *The Tempest.* Each of these later works was the culmination of its author's development. The previous stage which concentrated on a final examination of the tragic vision had something of a cathartic about it, and even suggested the process of regeneration and rebirth. But Blake never did agree with the traditional Aristotelian opinion that tragedy possesses curative powers. The vision of tragic suffering does its best work when it implies the spectator to go beyond it, not when it purges his emotions through pity and terror. For pity divides the pitier from the pitied, and terror is produced by disclosing the source of the victim's suffering. What takes place in the spectator is the self-justification of a moral judgment rather than the rebirth of a Last Judgement,

> as at a trajic scene
> The soul drinks murder & revenge & applauds its own holiness.[37]

The basis of Blake's conception of tragedy is to be found in the account of the fall of Luvah in the second night of *The Four Zoas*,

[37]*Jerusalem*, 41: 29–30. Cf. Aristotle, *Poetics*, cap. VI, 1449B. See also *Book of Urizen*, chap. V, 7. Thomas Taylor (*Works of Aristotle* (London, 1812), II, chap. VI, p. 241 n.) considers that pity and terror are simply the means for purging the spectator of other passions. "For it must by no means be said that the meaning of Aristotle is, that tragedy through terror and pity purifies the spectator from terror and pity. . . . " Limited to the sphere of the moral judgment, love mixed with jealousy becomes destructive—the tragic passion represented by Vala. Cf. *Jerusalem*, 64: 24: "Without Forgiveness of Sin, Love is Itself Eternal Death."

which results in the separation of lover and beloved. In this division and separation of affection from its unfallen unity with the visionary imagination lies the root of pity and the association of love with possession. Tragedy arises from the further division between the pathetic victim and the inviolate beholder where pity triumphs over sympathy, and moral virtue over conscience.

In *The Four Zoas* Blake evidently intended to write a work which would develop the conflict between reason and the passions within the field of the natural environment. The field is twofold in its extent, and it includes the immediate environment, the "Body of Man" or the fallen Tharmas, and external nature represented by Enion, the Earth-Mother. The regenerating force of the passions in the person of Orc is to seek redemption through the prophetic vision of Los. But as the actual history of this epic struggle discloses more and more clearly the sacrifice of the passions to religious mysteries and moral virtues up to the time of Christ and the relegation of reason to the fallen world of nature, the Last Judgment, which is added as the revelation of Jesus Christ, takes on more pity and terror than the end of a divine comedy should have. According to his own statement, Blake wrote *The Four Zoas* during a period of emotional and intellectual turmoil which apparently ended around 1804 when he had already begun *Milton* and *Jerusalem*. In a letter to William Hayley (October 23, 1804) he wrote:

> Dear Sir, excuse my enthusiasm or rather madness, for I am really drunk with intellectual vision whenever I take a pencil or graver into my hand, even as I used to be in my youth, and as I have not been for twenty dark, but very profitable, years. . . . In short, I am now satisfied and proud of my work, which I have not been for the above long period.

Unfinished or not, *The Four Zoas* remains Blake's *Purgatorio* in which the matter and aim of his later work becomes clarified.

The aim does not change, and the original theme is the same: the fall, regeneration and final resurrection of the Giant Albion—

> His fall into Division & his Resurrection to Unity:
> His fall into the Generation of decay & death, & his
> Regeneration by the Resurrection from the dead.[38]

What does change is his expression of the way to redemption. While writing *The Four Zoas* Blake started to describe how passion and

[38] *The Four Zoas*, I, 18–20.

instinct remain unredeemed under the tyranny of reason and law until the passion of Christ, who is Urizen's greatest victim, and whose gospel of brotherhood triumphs over the accuser at last. He concentrated the fallen power of the passions in Vala, who becomes the "aggregate" of the daughters of Albion. As the central figure of the earlier draft, she represents the driving force of that natural love which leads to the torments of jealousy and the consequent distraction from the search for redemption. She is the mysterious "veiled" goddess of natural religion who is redeemed only by the death of Luvah, a type ot Christ, and finally regenerated in the Last Judgment. As first conceived, *Vala* is the "Song of the Aged Mother" who, like the ancient Sibyl, recounts the fall of man, the creation of the world and human history.[39] The revisions indicate Blake's loss of interest in this particular treatment of his theme and a desire to develop the activities of the Zoas themselves. Interest in Vala, who represents the tragedy of *eros*, man's natural fate, gives way to a growing preoccupation with Jerusalem, the providential ideal of brotherhood. The crucifixion of man's energies in the character of Orc also gives way to the redemption of his faculties, the Zoas, through Los, the faculty of vision.

The redemption of the faculties is the final subject of *The Four Zoas*, and the marginal references to scripture at the beginning reflect Blake's enthusiastic study of the Greek Testament as well as the revised context of the subject itself.[40] He is going to represent the process of redemption as an "Intellectual Battle" which takes place within the giant brain of the Hero, and includes an entire historical cycle. The principal combatants are the Zoas, and the narrative begins within the unfallen life of Albion, while he is still a part of the "Brotherhood of Eden," before his sleep in Beulah, his fall into Generation and his "Death and Judgement" in Ulro. In the unfallen state of Eden which is Eternity seen from the fallen state of Generation, Albion is a creator, and his creatures are his own four immortal senses—the Zoas. The source of

[39] *Ibid.*, I, 1. Frye's suggestion (*Fearful Symmetry*, p. 270) is that the name "Vala" came from Mallet (*Northern Antiquities* (1770), II, p. 202) where "Vola" is the wise woman whose prophetic song is the *Voluspa*. H. M. Margoliouth (*William Blake's "Vala"* (Oxford, 1956), p. xviii) disagrees and points to Blake's phrase "the veil of Vala" (Cf. *Jerusalem*, 23: 5; 42: 81) as the source. For the early development of Jerusalem, see *The Four Zoas*, VIII, 181–6, 251–4; IX, 1–3, 204–23.

[40] Blake was no Greek scholar, and his quotations in Greek omit breathings and accents. He refers to his study of Greek, Latin and Hebrew in a letter to his brother (Jan. 30, 1803).

his life is the total life which is called the vision of Jesus. Participation in this life brings one into the "Universal Brotherhood of Eden" which is also the "Council of Eternals" or "Members" of Christ. In the possession of his fully awakened human existence, Albion is fourfold, and since his existence is itself perception or vision, his four immortal senses are the four ways he can perceive. What he perceives is a field of experience from which he is not cut off by the fallen senses—a field to which he is not related self-consciously, but somewhat like the dreamer to his dream. However, his dream, unlike the dreamer's, is vision, and is known for what it is: the creation of conscious existence. He contains his field of experience through Urthona, the unfallen Los. After the fall, this capacity is either lost to the passive fantasies of the dream-world or is actively used for the creation of works of art. The immortal Urthona becomes Los, whose struggles to regain for fallen man the lost harmony of Eden identify him with both the artist and the visionary.[41]

Urthona is the basic unity of the "Eternal Body of Man" which Blake also calls the "Imagination," the form of man's existence as a creator. Within this body the other three Zoas operate as the head, heart and loins—the regions of the unfallen faculties which correspond to thought, emotion and instinct in fallen man. A definitive system of correspondences is always avoided by Blake, for the relationships vary within the individual from one state to another, and between one individual and another. He also avoids the false precision of a neat and tidy allegory which would abstract his Zoas from the living forms of actual life. Urizen has both feelings and instincts, and he is frequently possessed by his own kind of vision. He is, however, essentially the man of reason and thought, just as Luvah is the man of feeling and emotion, and Tharmas of instinct and sensation.[42] Their female

[41]The name "Urthona" may be an anagram of the Greek θρόνου which occurs in Revelation (iv: 6) along with the description of the four living creatures. Cf. Proclus, *Theology of Plato*, trans. Thos. Taylor (London, 1816), II, p. 84: "For a throne is the vehicle and receptacle of those that are seated on it." The unfallen "body" is the "Divine Body" which manifests itself in "Works of Art" (*The Laocoön Group*). The name also suggests the eternal "earth" or field of experience which Blake calls Eden (*The Four Zoas*, I, 13) and the possession of it as knower of the field or "earth-owner" (cf. S. Foster Damon, *William Blake: His Philosophy and Symbols* (Boston and New York, 1924), p. 326).

[42]Tharmas has been associated with *Tama* (*tamas*), the third *guna* of the *Bhagavadgita* (*The Bhagvat-Geeta, or Dialogues of Kreeshna and Arjoon*, trans. Sir Charles Wilkins, London, 1785, p. 108), the one involving the most instinctive kind of activity prevailing in sleep and indolence

consorts or "emanations," are their fields of experience. Like Albion's Jerusalem, who is the archetypal "emanation" of them all, they are the means of expression and creation connected with each of man's immortal senses. Urizen is man's sense of order and disorder, Luvah his sense of beauty, and Tharmas his sense of strength and power which, in Eternity, can alter the conditions of experience.

Albion's fall, as stated by Los at the beginning of *The Four Zoas*, is a turning away from the divine vision.

> "Refusing to behold the Divine Image which all behold
> And live thereby, he is sunk down into a deadly sleep."[43]

Like the typical dreamer, he becomes passive to the operations of his faculties, loses the unity of his existence, and falls from Eden. Eden is that state of unity where the creator and the means of creation are one. In Beulah, the repose of this state, each of the Zoas in turn falls from union with his emanation and begins to war with the others within the field of the universal man's slumbering existence. Tharmas, the original faculty of altering the data of experience, becomes the fixed data of fallen experience—the body of man and the instincts and habits which regulate its functions. Enion, his emanation, becomes the forces of nature as the field of organic life and growth. Having turned away from the true source of the unity of his affections, Albion becomes involved with self-love and infatuation as Luvah falls under the sway of Urizen. Separated from Jerusalem, he turns to Vala, or rather Rahab, and begins to confuse love with possession in a divided allegiance to the persons and objects of his dream. The Zoa of intellect, Urizen,

---

(cf. Damon, *William Blake*, p. 167). The name may also have some connection with Tammuz or Thammuz, the Syrian name for Adonis (Ezek. viii: 13–14). Sloss and Wallis (*Prophetic Writings of William Blake*, I, p. 140), refer to Tharmas as "a symbol of obscure and uncertain reference." But Blake's "fall" is a fall in perception, or a fall in the relationship of the observer and the observed. This is, initially, the fall of Tharmas, who becomes the consolidation of fallen man's relationship to the immediate data of experience, that is, his instincts and sensations. Tharmas and Enion are said to be the parents of Enitharmon or "space," since the instinctive functions reveal space, and Tharmas is specifically associated with the tongue (taste and touch). Their names were formed from ENI-tharm-ON. Cf. Margoliouth, *William Blake's "Vala,"* p. 159. See also Paul Miner, "William Blake: Two Notes on Sources," *Bulletin of the New York Public Library* (1958), 206–7. [Tharmas may be derived from the *guna* Tamas, from Tammuz, from the Hesiodic sea-god Thaumas, from the Thames, from the disciple Thomas (he is associated with both touch and doubt), from (Thomas) Paine, from the Greek words thermos and thymos, or from anything else that looks remotely possible.—N.F.]

[43]I, 283–4.

separates from Ahania, loses the power of creative thought and begins his attempts to dominate instinct and emotion by restriction and limitation alone. His activity becomes completely negative, so that the only ideas are those derived from sense and feeling.

The state of Generation is the revolving circle of destiny, the wheel of necessity which consolidates what has been begun in Beulah. All life becomes derivative and exists through the cyclical and automatic process of birth, growth, decline and death. Unless some kind of inspiration from the state of Beulah is maintained, the individual in Generation is cut off entirely from Eden and descends into Ulro, the state of nature. The only kind of unity in Ulro is an enforced adjustment to natural conditions, and the only kind of communal life is that based on uniformity of behaviour. Albion divides into countries and races, and comes under the sway of his reasoning "Spectre" which can only compare and relate according to probability what is perceived by the senses. This is the final state of the natural organ subject to sense which has no will of its own but merely reacts to the "Female will" of mother-nature. In *Milton*, Albion's Spectre, representing fallen humanity, is identified with the builders of the tower of Babel,[44] the first utopians who try to pursue communal happiness apart from eternal life. The world of the utopian dreamer is one of measured uniformity and predictable behaviour in the image of Newton's stellar universe resting in the space Blake calls Ulro.[45] Ulro is the tyrannical rule of the circle of destiny as it revolves in the void of non-entity into which Albion has finally fallen.

Blake carefully avoids describing the fall of Albion in terms of the accepted conceptions of moral virtue. Albion does not fall from the presence of an outraged deity into a state of punishment for some positive act of revolt against the eternal order. He falls asleep and turns away from the activity of eternal life, so that his faculties become his own enemies and the enemies of one another. The traditional "war in heaven" takes place during the fall and not before. It is the immediate result and not the cause of man's fallen condition, and it can be turned to his ultimate advantage and become the means of his

[44] *Milton*, 6: 23. Gen. xi: 1–9.

[45] *The Four Zoas*, I, 93–4. The name "Ulro" may be derived from "ruler" or simply "rule"—the rule of that "Mathematic Form" which is "Eternal in the Reasoning Memory" (*On Homer's Poetry & on Virgil*). Wicksteed (*William Blake's "Jerusalem,"* pp. 116, 218) connects it with "the rolling-on of Time without ultimate end or apparent purpose."

redemption. What little is left of Albion's life is in the wars of the Zoas, and the submission to his present state—which each of the Zoas in turn suggests for their own ends—can only lead to the disunity and chaos of eternal death. His real hope lies in continued struggle and not in resignation. Milton attributed the fall of man to the titanism of Satan, and Hesiod's fallen titans were justly beaten in their war against the Olympian gods. Blake, however, describes "the Gods of the Heathen" as the Zoas themselves who try to subdue and devour the energies of the Titan Albion.[46] But man ought to subdue his gods and not be subdued by them, for his task is to awaken Albion and restore him to the full possession of his faculties.

The dream of the Titan is the dream of universal humanity acting and reacting, like a giant somnambulist, to the pressure of inner and outer conditions. The signs of his sleep are the recurrent patterns which emerge in religious myths, in the monuments of artistic achievement, in the development of thought and in the histories of civilizations. His sleep contains not only the cyclical movement of history but also the cycle of each individual life, for his fall is that of Everyman. It signifies both an outer dispersal of his powers which is his subjection to the world of nature and an inner reduction of his fourfold being to the panorama of scattered sensations. This fourfold being is the key to his redemption and restoration to Eden.

In *The Four Zoas*, Blake gives an account of the fourfold character of Albion through the characters of the Zoas, and in the tradition of the epic bard, he speaks of it as containing "the ancient history of Britain." But the greater history of the death and judgment of Albion, who is Blake's original Arthur, takes precedence over any narrative of historical events, just as the books of Urizen, Ahania and Los have already superseded the political prophecies of *The French Revolution*, *America* and *Europe*. The history of Albion becomes concentrated entirely in the activities of the fallen Zoas, for these are the activities—in the individual and the race—which make history what it is. The Zoas are described as the strong man or Tharmas, the beautiful man or Luvah, the ugly man or Urizen and the divine image or Los, and each corresponds respectively to the three classes of men: the Reprobate, the Redeemed, the Elect and the human existence itself.

[46] *The Four Zoas*, I, 16. The conflicts resulting from the attempt of each of the Zoas to become all-powerful reach a climax in the fourth night, just before the creation of fallen man (IV, 34-156).

The Strong Man represents the human sublime. The Beautiful Man represents the human pathetic, which was in the wars of Eden divided into male and female. The Ugly Man represents the human reason. They were originally one man, who was fourfold; he was self-divided, and his real humanity slain on the stems of generation, and the form of the fourth was like the Son of God. How he became divided is a subject of great sublimity and pathos. The Artist has written it under inspiration, and will, if God please, publish it; it is voluminous, and contains the ancient history of Britain, and the world of Satan and of Adam.[47]

Albion's fall into division is the process of limiting the powers represented by the Zoas to the natural field of experience which Blake calls "the world of Satan and Adam."

Satan is the first result of the fall and is called the "limit of opacity," the ultimate extent of sense-perception which shuts out the translucent perception of original vision. Adam is the second result and is called the "limit of contraction." Just as Satan represents the loss of the visionary power to see beyond the immediate effects of nature, Adam is the complement of this loss. Perception becomes limited to proximity in space and time, so that the observer sees a field of wheat at a distance, and the individual stalks only after he approaches. Synthesis and analysis are confined to the fixed ratio of the organs of sense. Corresponding to these limits of the individual observer's ability to perceive are the limits of the world he does perceive: the "Mundane Egg" (Adam) extending to the "Mundane Shell" (Satan) which contains fallen man's possibilities, or his circle of destiny.

> Thus were the stars of heaven created like a golden chain
> To bind the Body of Man to heaven from falling into the Abyss.[48]

The extent of the "Body of Man" is the universal extent of what Blake calls creation. Creation is the organization of life perceived by the five senses. It includes all forms or bodies from stars to minerals, for it is the total life of Albion adapted to his sleep in the state of Generation. From the isolated point of view of the individual dependent on it,

[47] *A Descriptive Catalogue &c.*, Keynes, p. 609. For the description of the fallen world of Satan and Adam, see *The Four Zoas*, IV, 269–73. It will be noted that Tharmas or the "Strong Man" is rarely mentioned in *Milton* and *Jerusalem*, and then only with reference to the tongue uniting touch and taste—the senses most dependent on the natural environment. In Eternity, however, he is the "Parent power" (*The Four Zoas*, I, 18), who organizes the relationship between the observer and the field of experience. The "Ugly Man" is the deformed or fallen intellect or reason which is the "incapability of intellect," as Blake puts it.

[48] *The Four Zoas*, II, 474–5.

it is a machinery of natural law which keeps the creature from falling into the "Abyss" of non-entity.

Dependence on the natural creature or Selfhood is a dependence on the world of nature as perceived by it—on the non-human or what is not at the root of human existence. Into such a dependence man is born, and his attempts to escape from it by natural means are doomed to failure. His attempts to do this are the basis of the distinction he makes between soul and body. As a body, man sees himself as an effect of natural law, but as a soul, he sees himself capable of independent action. Blake tries to eliminate this distinction by describing body as a section of soul perceived by the bodily senses which are the limitations of the state of existence as a creature. "Man has no Body distinct from his Soul; for that call'd Body is a portion of Soul discern'd by the five Senses, the chief inlets of Soul in this age."[49] This "age" refers to the particular stage or degree of participation in existence according to the dial of the circle of destiny. Animals too, however, and even vegetables and minerals represent different stages or "ages" in the process of creation described by Blake as the process of redemption which is his epic theme. From the point of view of man's humanity, the whole of creation forms an image of his own inner possibilities. By a dependence on his human existence, he can awaken the Titan Albion.

[49] *Marriage of Heaven and Hell*, Keynes, p. 182.

11. Natural Existence: The Selfhood

THE EFFORT of the Enlightenment to emancipate man from religious and metaphysical delusions of grandeur aroused Blake's ire only to the extent that such emancipation implied a passive acceptance of man as limited to the state of nature. The movement which could be discerned in the rise of empiricism and the search for an inductive logic of facts underlying the deductive logic of mathematics was so far in harmony with his own outlook that he attacked Plato and made fun of the doctrinaire Swedenborg. But he had no intention of leaving man "a natural organ subject to sense." Although he could have accepted La Mettrie's contention that the natural man who believed that he had free choice was labouring under a dangerous delusion, he asserted that the natural man was only a section of human existence, and that freedom was characteristic of that existence. He could have accepted Diderot's statement that the power of the soul came from the harmonious balance of the passions and not their destruction, but he would most certainly have disagreed with him on how this harmonious balance was to be achieved. Yet the contemporary interest in the problem of knowledge and sensation formed a point of departure in Blake's own attack on traditional rationalism. The psychological insight of Hume, who had stated that reason had usurped the rule which sensation in fact exercised in the formation of ideas, reduced the earlier rationalistic unities of experience—soul and substance—to speculative assumptions with no foundation in the nature of things. Dominated by a renewed search for some inner connection which would unite one sense with another, eighteenth-century epistemology and psychology followed a course which was, so to speak, the natural parallel of Blake's own visionary development of the concept of imagination.

The similarity between the outlines of the two different points of view is striking. In his *Optics*,[1] Molyneux had discussed the possibility of arriving at a sufficient basis for linking one field of sense-perception with that of another. Berkeley had been occupied with the same problem before writing his *New Theory of Vision*. In that work he had arrived at the conclusion that "objects of sight and touch make, if I may say so, two sets of ideas which are widely different from each other."[2] The question was whether the senses alone could be made to account for the intuition of the natural world put together from the data of the radically diverse fields of the different senses by some common root of sensation in human consciousness. Berkeley solved the problem to his own satisfaction by introducing the unity of the creative and moving principle in the form of his Eternal Perceiver which accounted for the total act of perception in the individual observer. Later philosophers of the eighteenth century found it difficult to determine whether this consistency attributed to perception was indeed by analogy with man and man's psychological nature, as implied by the system of Berkeley, or by analogy with the universe of nature as Bacon had declared. Bacon, however, had failed to emphasize the problem contained in his "Idols of the Tribe." The observer of nature must consistently interpret reality from the standpoint of man (*ex analogia hominis*), and the problem was whether such knowledge of the world could possess the desired objective validity. On the ground of argument Blake appeared to be on the side of Berkeley, for he wrote: "Mental Things are alone Real; what is call'd Corporeal, Nobody Knows of its Dwelling Place: it is in Fallacy, & its Existence an Imposture. Where is the Existence Out of Mind or Thought? Where is it but in the Mind of a Fool?"[3] But he still made a definite distinction between his own outlook and that of Berkeley.

The distinction rested on the different basis which he chose as a means of expression. The prophet's vision was intended to disclose a way of life, and the philosopher's discourse sounded too much like generalizations of experience by a complacent spectator. The immaterialism of Berkeley was developed empirically, but instead of

[1]Cf. Ernst Cassirer, *The Philosophy of the Enlightenment*, trans. F. C. A. Koelln and J. P. Pettegrove (New Haven, 1951), pp. 108 ff.

[2]Sec. 111.

[3]*Vision of the Last Judgment*, Keynes, p. 651.

using, as Mill later did, the concept of the uniformity of nature to give coherence to the act of reason, Berkeley made use of the theologian's disembodied, creative Spirit. But "body" is a synonym of organized existence in Blake, and the disembodied is unorganized chaos, not the Uncreate. He therefore annotated the philosopher's Platonizing descriptions of "pure mind" and "perfect spirit" by reiterating the bodily form of imagination which was man's "Divine Body" or the functioning reality of his human existence. Reality was not to be conceived as the idea of spirit, nor as pure subjectivity, but as *vision* of which spirit was an abstraction, and the subject-object relationship, a degree. In the *Annotations to Berkeley's "Siris,"* he called this unity of perception the "Imagination or the Human Eternal Body in Every Man."[4] This "Body" was the integrity of the unfallen powers or faculties which were "The Four Senses . . . the Four Faces of Man & the Four Rivers of the Water of Life." Blake was not an immaterialist in Berkeley's terms at all. He did not seek to undermine the concept of substance as an answer to the "materialists," but regarded the whole mind-matter problem as a dilemma created by the rationalists themselves. Far from adopting speculative idealism, he endeavoured to bring back a concrete and embodied individuality into the vacuum created by idealistic concepts of "self-consciousness" and "spirit," and to eliminate the religious error that "spirit" was life and "body" of no account. Blake's rejection of "what is call'd Corporeal" was a rejection of a closed system of nature.

The vegetable body, as Blake calls it, is the source of whatever power man has to transform his existence. The soul without a physical body dwells in a limbo,

[4]Keynes, p. 818. Attention has already been drawn to Blake's impatience with the Platonic snobbery of Berkeley. Although an empiricist in his philosophical method, Berkeley's ethical opinions and his social idealism proved irritating to one who, as Reprobate, suspected a tyrannical undercurrent to any caste-conscious intellectualism. The precipitate of such a view could only be the closed society. K. R. Popper's description of the initial impact of Christianity expresses the point of view of Blake: "In its beginning, Christianity, like the Cynic movement, was opposed to the highbrow Platonizing Idealism and intellectualism of the 'scribes,' the learned men" (*The Open Society and Its Enemies*, London, 1945, II, p. 21). According to Blake, "Jesus supposes every Thing to be Evident to the Child & to the Poor & Unlearned. Such is the Gospel." *Annotations to Berkeley's "Siris,"* Keynes, p. 819. The "Poor & Unlearned" had not accepted the intellectual deceit of the idealist and remained fallow ground for the prophet and his gospel of vision. As for the Cynics, Blake indicated that he regarded Diogenes as the Greek counterpart of Ezekiel and Isaiah (*Marriage of Heaven and Hell*, Keynes, p. 186).

> Where Souls incessant wail, being piteous Passions & Desires
> With neither lineament nor form, but like to wat'ry clouds
> The Passions & Desires descend upon the hungry winds,
> For such alone Sleepers remain, meer passion & appetite.[5]

The spiritual aim of man is not to become a disembodied spirit but to become embodied.[6]

Blake's rejection included the contemporary natural philosopher's limitation of knowledge to what could be perceived with the five senses united by the reasonable concept of the uniformity of nature. After finding that each sense disclosed a different kind of world, the thinkers of the Enlightenment declared all knowledge relative and chose the inductive method of probability corrected by statistical norms and a universal logic of mathematics. Voltaire even improved on Plato's eternal geometer, and called the Demiurgus the eternal machinist whose machine turned under the influence of the natural forces in the world and the passions in man.[7] The divergent sense-fields were ultimately united by a kinetic law of association on the analogy of the natural law of gravitation. Although Blake admitted these different worlds of sensation, he asserted that they grew out of faculties underlying each, and that each faculty corresponded to a given organ of perception. Comparison and relation characterized man's organ of sight which corresponded to his faculty of reason; this was the fallen Urizen. Contact with a world of particulars characterized taste and touch which were united in the tongue—corresponding to Tharmas who symbolized the identity of "vegetable" man's instinctive nature in the form of the physical body. The corresponding faculty to the sense of smell was more obvious in the beast of prey than in man, and there it was clearly the expression of desire which was represented by Luvah. Until these faculties were awakened into a distinct unity by Los, the underlying faculty of vision, man had no unified existence as a knower of himself, let alone of the world.

[5]*Milton*, 28: 26–9. With Blake's description of limbo compare the descent of Aeneas into the infernal regions (*Aeneid*, vi, 237–8):

> Spelunca alta fuit, vastoque immanis hiatu,
> Scrupea, tuta lacu nigro, nemorumque tenebris.

[6]Blake's view here marks his divergence from the Platonic "soul" descending to the body and his adherence to the Hebraic and Christian distinction between a spiritual and a physical body. Cf. Phil. iii: 21.

[7]*Traité de métaphysique* (1734), chap. VIII.

The senses, however, were not synonymous with the faculties, but were the reduction of these: they were *sub specie naturae* what the faculties were *sub specie aeternitatis*. By means of the senses, the spectre or natural man began to awaken into the use of the faculties. By touch and taste the individual discovered the possibility of a power over the data of experience through the medium of juxtaposition and assimilation. These senses were the reductions of the faculty which Tharmas represented. By means of smell (which comprises most of what we usually attribute to taste), the individual discovered the faculty of emotion and desire, and thereby began to perceive the world of Luvah. By sight he commenced to know, and the discrimination of outline initiated him into the world of reason or Urizen whose unfallen condition as an eternal "Sense" was the direct perception of the intellect. By sound he began to participate in the faculty of imagination which corresponded to the art of music—the least naturalistic of the arts and the one farthest removed from the possibility of copying nature to gain its effects. Architecture corresponded to the faculty of intellect and was the counterpart of its systematic and structural activity. The art of painting was associated with Luvah, and poetry, or the art of re-making and re-creating experience, corresponded to the faculty represented by Tharmas. It is significant that Blake did not limit the faculties to the definitive characteristics outlined. Each participated in the activities of the other three, and their worlds intersected within the consciousness of the awakened man. The conditioned and limited senses and their fields presaged the unconditioned and limited faculties and their worlds: "If the doors of perception were cleansed every thing would appear to man as it is, infinite. For man has closed himself up, till he sees all things thro' narrow chinks of his cavern."[8] Cleansing the doors of perception was to be undertaken by "corrosives" —the "infernal method" which was to melt "apparent surfaces away." "This will come to pass by an improvement of sensual enjoyment," Blake says in the same passage. The improvement of sensation included the restoration of the faculties and their powers.

The discipline involved in this kind of improvement was what Blake called "Art," and it began with the cultivation of the faculty which he considered least fallen, that is, least dependent upon, and passive towards, the fixed data of nature. This faculty was imagination,

[8]*Marriage of Heaven and Hell*, Keynes, p. 187.

symbolized by Los—not to be confused with fantasy, the perversion of imagination, leading to madness, the parody of vision. Los was Urthona in Eden, the "throne" or vehicular body of human existence; the underlying basis, the last of the faculties, he became the first or foremost as the perspective of the individual was converted from the headlong fall into Generation to the return to Eden. His four sons, the aspects of the other three Zoas contained in him, became the types of the redemptive force which he represented. In the developed pattern of *The Four Zoas*, the first to fall was Tharmas, the faculty of power over experience, who became the bodily instincts of man, completely passive to the natural forces within and without him. The fall of Tharmas continued beyond Generation, the state of limited equilibrium between man and nature, into Ulro or the state of complete automatic dependence upon nature, for the instincts could not be directed toward any other end than the satisfaction of natural needs. Less dependent were the emotions and desires, and Luvah was the second to fall. The cultivation of desire redeemed man from Ulro, and made it possible for him to live in the state of Generation. His thoughts also, symbolized by Urizen, might be directed towards the building of the City of Art or civilized life, but both thought and desire were inescapably and deceptively dependent on the instinctive nature, unless the faculty of imagination was directed toward the Eternal City. Blake emphatically insisted that no amount of culture or knowledge of nature could redeem man from his servitude to a spectral, and at bottom, automatic existence within the circle of destiny and the state of nature. Only by the analogies and the conceits of the prophets could he be led to undertake the adventure of the return.

In the shorter epic, *Milton*, the four universes or fields of the Zoas are depicted as intersecting globes which are empty of conscious content, for the organized perceptive functions were restricted to the organs of sensation after the fall; and there remained

> the Egg form'd World of Los
> In midst, stretching from Zenith to Nadir in midst of Chaos.[9]

"Chaos" was the disorganization or disorientation of perception which was characteristic of our fallen or unawakened consciousness. In this state we were supported and organized in our perceptions by the

[9]*Milton*, 38: 33–4.

Universe of Los which was the integrity of temporal succession and spatial juxtaposition. It was this world of Generation, both in its psychological and its cosmic aspects, which prevented the complete triumph of chaos. The rule of chaos was directly modified by the limitations placed on perception by "the Egg form'd World of Los" which was the world of Satan and Adam—the "Nadir" and the "Zenith"—where vision was limited to a sense-perception of a fixed degree of opacity and translucence. The shell of this mundane egg must be broken, and it could only be broken by the unity of perception in the knower which the gestating fire of an awakening vision alone could give. Into this egg or womb of time and space man was planted by his first birth—hence, his corporeal nature was referred to as "vegetable." Out of it he must be awakened by a new birth in the full possession and integrity of his faculties. Blake considered the faculties or Zoas to be the real senses of man; the corporeal senses were merely the "narrow chinks of his cavern" out of which he made bold to declare that he could know the world. But if awakened vision were denied or remained undeveloped, the interior integrity of man was utterly lost, and he could only rely on the fixed forms of eternal nature. He therefore passed from the state of Generation which was the preparatory stage for his awakening into Eden and descended into the state of Ulro where the necessary conditions of an external world were alone real, and man was an automatic "Reactor"[10] to these conditions. The natural man without internal integrity or unity was considered dead and was called a "spectre."

The Philosopher of the Enlightenment assumed that, by nature, man already had an existence or being which was capable of real knowledge, the kind of knowledge which had objective validity. Blake asserted that man as a spectre or natural self could *know* nothing, because he was nothing but a mass of impressions received through unrelated sense-fields. He might make his way through his own interior chaos by a reliance upon a reasonable organization of his

[10]In *Jerusalem* (29: 13–15), Albion's "Reactor" or the ability to relate action to prevailing conditions, has become passive and obedient to necessity:

"he admits of no Reply
From Albion, but hath founded his Reaction into a Law
Of Action, for Obedience to destroy the Contraries of Men."

This passage is a direct comment on Swedenborg's notion of man as a "Recipient of Life" (see Blake's *Annotations to Swedenborg's "Divine Love and Divine Wisdom,"* p. 56).

impressions of nature—that is, by the "divided compasses" of Urizen—but he was deceiving himself if he thought that the exercise of one separate faculty could give him that unity as an observer which would lead to the eventual conquest of nature and the perfecting of his humanity. The very world which he perceived was given its unity by the unrecognized faculty of vision or imagination. This was the *communis sensus* of the philosopher's search, not a transcendental unity of apperception but "The Eternal Body of Man" which gave unity to the faculties underlying the senses and to the senses themselves. "The Eternal Body of Man is The Imagination, that is, God himself,"[11] the humanized Eternal Perceiver of Berkeley, understood in the concrete and immediate activity of the creative and moving principle. In this way Blake solved the problem of the senses and their unity, a problem which had become dominant in the philosophy of the eighteenth century.

The iconography of the Zoas or faculties of the soul gave Blake a psychological method for exploring the condition of man implied by his solution to the problem of sensation. This method required, and was apparently intended to induce, not the hypothetical comprehension of the philosopher but the complete insight of the seer. For such complete insight all the faculties must act in unison, for it is clear that in their chaotic or fallen state vision is considered to be impossible. Knowledge of this kind was directly related to, and proceeded on a level with, the seer's inner development or state of existence. Even within a given state of existence or world of particulars there were definite gradations. Blake was emphatic on this point: "I see Every thing I paint In This World, but Every body does not see alike."[12] Knowledge which could be isolated and dealt with apart from the integration or lack of it in the individual possessor, he valued little. Generalizations derived from the experimental sciences and imitations of nature in the arts fell into this category, one which he usually

[11]*The Laocoön Group*, Keynes, p. 580. Terms like the "Divine Humanity" are not to be confused with the humanitarianism of the age nor with the later Hegelian social absolute which transferred Christ's union of the divine and human from a unique historical exemplar to the whole human race (cf. Strauss, *Glaubenslehre*, Thuringer, 1840). "Divine" and "Humanity" are both synonyms for the origin of existence in Blake. They do not indicate any "synthesis" of the natural and the divine.

[12]Letter to Trusler, Aug. 23, 1799, Keynes, p. 835. Cf. "As a man is, so he sees. As the Eye is formed, such are its Powers."

associated with the words "reason" and "memory." Experimentalists and "Portrait Painters" were technicians of nature, not architects of eternity. In this mood he wrote: "Science is the Tree of Death,"[23] for the knowledge of the perishable and the perishing was lost. His method prescribed an ambivalent degree of conscious attainment to correspond with the state of existence or field of knowledge of the individual seer. Visionary knowledge was knowledge based on senses which surpassed our senses—the "enlarged & numerous senses" of the ancient poets referred to in *The Marriage of Heaven and Hell*—and an intellect which surpassed our ratio of the things of memory. Visionary knowledge among the ancients took the form of myths which represented direct knowledge. The so-called myth-making consciousness was not the primitive gift of unlearned masses, but the inspired gift of the few seers who had attained a higher degree of vision.

The individual was said to remain within a given degree of vision as long as his vision was identified with it—as long as he saw his particular "state" as the inevitable field of knowledge. To see the world as an inevitable field of knowledge was to see it as Nature. To see it as a world of effects, the causes of which were characteristics of an Eternal State made actual in time, was to see it as Creation. And finally, to see the world as a degree of visionary experience was to see it as Generation. To see the world as Nature was wrong, and confined the perceiver to the closed world of "Ulro," which included the bounds of the physical body. Blake called the natural body of man a "Shadow," for it was the shadow cast by the limitation of the spiritual body. The natural existence Blake called a "Spectre" or "Selfhood," whose roots were in an inner chaos of impression and not in an inner integrity of real existence. The philosopher of nature could only look for a sub-human origin of his present condition in the chaos and ancient night out of which the Selfhood came and into which it disappeared. As the eye of the observer was conditioned, so was his conception of the world. Creation considered as "an act of Mercy" could become Nature considered as an accident of chaos, if the individual's perspective or "Eye" remained fixed by his corporeal and vegetative existence.

The "Eye" thus conceived was vision itself, and when it became

[13]*The Laocoön Group*, Keynes, p. 582. The other half of the statement, "Art is the Tree of Life," marks Blake's departure from the self-expressive conception of art.

fixed by the "limit of Contraction," the present human body symbolized by Adam, the natural man was "created." Creation took place to prevent Albion from falling through chaos into non-entity, and was, in this sense, an "act of Mercy" or providential. In his three prophetic epics, Blake used the term "Seven Eyes of God"[24] to indicate seven successive ways of breaking the hypnotic fixation of the "Eye" of man whose universal existence was symbolized by Albion. Each of these "Eyes" was given a name which signified a particular religion in its final form; the seventh was called Jesus. The process of awakening, which forms the central theme of the prophetic writings, is a consistent struggle *against* nature and against the natural form of the individual, or the Selfhood. This struggle presupposed a difference of perspective respecting the world. Seen as "Nature," the world did not contribute to the individual's awakening at all, but on the contrary, deepened his sleep. However, as Swedenborg had written, "the Image of Creation is Spiritual,"[15] and when seen as such an image, Nature itself became a "World of Imagination & Vision."[16] Within the visionary dialectic of these contrary perspectives, Blake wrote his three epic prophecies.

In the first of these long prophecies, *The Four Zoas*, he determined the form of expression which he would give to the theme of his works. The theme, however, was consistently adumbrated much earlier. The form of expression went through certain phases of development. To use an analogy from music, each of these phases constituted a prelude or overture and a main body of work. The *Poetical Sketches* (1769–78) formed a "Preludium" (Blake's term) to the *Songs of Innocence and of Experience* (1789–94). The minor prophecies formed a "Preludium" to *The Four Zoas* (1795–1804). The struggle to organize his material in this way is significantly illustrated in *The First Book of Urizen* (1794) which, in expanded form, might easily have taken the place of *The Four Zoas*. In this work, the "Preludium" defined the theme and invoked the source of inspiration. Correction, definition and the presentation of subject-matter distinguished the "Preludium" which was the author "finding" his theme, and at the same time,

[14]*The Four Zoas*, VIII, Keynes, p. 341; *Milton*, 14: 15 ff.; *Jerusalem*, 55: 30 ff. Cf. Zech. iii: 9; Rev. iv: 5.

[15]*Divine Love and Wisdom* (London, 1788), p. 285. Swedenborg, like Paracelsus and Blake, seems to have used the term "image" in the sense of "prototype."

[16]Letter to Trusler, Aug. 23, 1799, Keynes, p. 835. In the same letter Blake says, "But to the Eyes of the Man of Imagination, Nature is Imagination itself."

presenting it. Within the canon of his own works, correction and definition took the form of a development and extension of his mythology along with the gradual maturing of his individual point of view. But Blake did not consider himself an isolated phenomenon in the history of the literature of his country. Like the Hebrew prophets, he was the heir of a prophetic tradition, and as a successor to Chaucer, Shakespeare and Milton, he was responsible for completing the prophetic message of his predecessors. Milton, especially, was his immediate original, and the work which bore the name of that poet recreated the Miltonic theodicy in the light of Blake's perspective. It also became an extended "Preludium" to *Jerusalem*.

If *The Four Zoas* was the *Purgatorio* of Blake, clarifying and gathering together the tragic vision of man's fallen condition, *Milton* introduced his *Paradiso*, or final vision of redemption, in *Jerusalem*. Written ostensibly "To Justify the Ways of God to Men," *Milton* was Blake's personal theodicy. By writing a work which used the name and theme of the earlier poet, he was freeing himself from the effects of Hayley's patronage and the Neo-Classical burden of approved taste which had gone with it.[17] He was also purging himself of the urge to justify his view of life as a compensation for personal disappointment. In this spirit he became the reincarnation of Milton's search for prophetic or poetic justice, a justice to which mercy was united as a contrary. For without mercy, which was freedom, the law of justice became the despotic "ratio" of conduct, the basis for self-justification which was the inner tyranny of the Selfhood. If mercy or freedom existed without justice, it became self-indulgence, the inner weakness of the Selfhood. As contraries, however, their complementary nature was understood, and their ultimate union was realized through the redemptive principle of the forgiveness of sins. Through the mediation of this principle, the original sin against Eternal Existence was cast out. The original error was the attempt to know good and evil apart from inspiration and apart from direct communion with the universal humanity which spoke through the prophet as his individual Genius. In Milton himself, Blake discerned the conflict between the Selfhood seeking justification

[17]Blake met Hayley in 1800, and went to live at Felpham under his patronage in the fall of that year. The gradual estrangement which took place between them was partly reflected in the struggle between Palamabron (Blake) and Satan (Hayley), near the beginning of *Milton* and in the eighth night of *The Four Zoas*.

and Genius seeking Christian liberty. Milton's desire for self-justification was the expression of his Selfhood which had to be cast out before his Genius could redeem his creative work, called his emanation, from appearing to be the isolated apology for his natural existence instead of the complete expression of his human existence. The redemption of his emanation took the form of a clarification of the background of Milton's theme. He was represented as moved by a "Bard's prophetic Song"[18] to return and complete his work. His "Sixfold Emanation," on earth the three wives and three daughters who were the immediate victims of his Selfhood, was called Ololon, a name probably derived from a Greek word (ὀλολύζειν) which signified the crying of women to the gods. Hitherto the scapegoat of his failure to realize the union of justice and mercy, of duty and freedom, she became the "Garment"[19] of his final vision of the integrity of his human existence. The sexual garment which had appeared during his life as a threat to his integrity and as a distraction from duty was finally cleansed of a chaste separation from awakened existence and was shown to be an integral part of it. Ololon was for Milton what Jerusalem was for Albion, and *Milton* was the particular individual prelude to a universal human vision.

As one who had chosen to be the spokesman for the Puritan Elect, Milton had first to annihilate in himself the addiction to being right. This would have been done for him by his own experience, if experience could teach anything. But experience teaches nothing; it only illustrates what the individual can learn by other means. Were this not so, the seer would be the normal result of old age, not the exception at any age. "But there is a spirit in man: and the inspiration of the Almighty giveth them understanding. Great men are not always wise: neither do the aged understand judgment."[20] Like Job, Milton had experienced disillusionment, and just as Job had been awakened from the sleep of self-justification by the words of Elihu, Milton was

[18]*Milton*, 2: 22.

[19]*Ibid.*, 49: 15. The outward "Garment" is "A Garment of War," a struggle involved with necessary atonement, but the inner reconciliation between Milton and his affections is the vision of free redemption. Crabb Robinson reported (Dec. 17, 1825) Blake's statement that he was "told" by Milton to beware of being misled by his *Paradise Lost*. "In particular he wished me to shew the falsehood of his doctrine that the pleasures of sex arose from the fall. The fall could not produce any pleasure." Crabb Robinson, *Diary, Reminiscences and Correspondence*, ed. T. Sadler (Boston, 1869).

[20]Job, xxxii: 8–9.

represented as moved by the prophetic bard to reorient his vision of the field of experience. His descent into the world of Generation for this purpose formed the plot of Blake's epic, which was divided into two books. The first book took the form of a rediscovery of what was usually called justice—an analogy based on natural law—and this was set over against Blake's conception of creation as an act of mercy. In the second book, this vision of creation triumphed over that of nature and law, while mercy was seen to be the complement of true justice.

The first book began by emphasizing what Milton had not admitted: that the creation of Adam as a natural man was also his fall into error. The first part of the bard's song recounted the seven ages of creation, where "Age" and "State" were given the significant relation of organ and object of perception; for as the organs of perception or the faculties of knowledge became limited, the world which could be perceived by their means was consolidated. The presiding faculty or Demiurge of creation was the fallen Zoa of intellect, Urizen, whose separate search for a fixed justice isolated from injustice and a consistent order isolated from chaos caused him to turn from "Definite Form" to "the Abstract Horror" which arrested him within the confines of a given datum of existence and produced from the state of nature the world of nature. Natural knowledge was possible only through trial and error, but on sacrifice alone could be raised the central repository of wisdom, "Great Golgonooza"[21]—the city built on the impermanent marsh of corporeal nature out of what had been understood within the inspired vision of the individual and the race. The building of it was a sacrificial act, and its site included the formless lake of reflected and obscured perception and the dark forests of error and the uncertain way. Opposed to the wisdom of vision was natural knowledge represented by Satan, the spectral Urizen, who, as "Miller of Eternity" and "Prince of the Starry Wheels," was the regent of the field of

[21]In one of his most celebrated pamphlets, Milton had tentatively assumed that "this is that doom which Adam fell into of knowing good and evil; that is to say of knowing good by evil" (*Areopagitica*). Blake rejected naturalistic demonstration by means of trial and error, as a means which would essentially reduce all acts to a dead level of imitation and comparison of the effects of action. All acts which sprang from individual existence formed the architectural basis of a city which was continually built by the sacrifice of error to the positive vision of truth, and not by any negative process of elimination. Golgonooza, as its name implies, was a Golgotha of sacrifice, but what was sacrificed was ultimately man's natural suffering while building it.

nature. But beyond this field of regulated order, the natural principle of regulation was contained by that of redemption, Palamabron's "Harrow of the Almighty," and that of apocalyptic renewal or the "Plow of Rintrah" the prophetic Reprobate. Both of the last two effected transformation, while the former, based on the analogy of natural process, was limited to regulation within the state of nature. For Satan, the informing scheme of redemption lay outside his field of vision and beyond his understanding.

> "Art thou not Newton's Pantocrator, weaving the Woof of Locke?
> To Mortals thy Mills seem every thing, & the Harrow of Shaddai
> A Scheme of Human conduct invisible & incomprehensible."[22]

And yet it was Satan who sought to take over the "Harrow of Shaddai" from Palamabron and impose the regulative order of his "Mills" on the life of Generation. The disaster which overtook this action was illustrated by an episode. . . .

[22]*Milton*, 4: 11–13.

[The author's MS ends at this point.—Ed.]

INDEX

www.ingramcontent.com/pod-product-compliance
Ingram Content Group UK Ltd.
Pitfield, Milton Keynes, MK11 3LW, UK
UKHW032118310125
454513UK00001B/67

9 781487 598563